The Seven Sacraments

ANSELM GRÜN

The Seven Sacraments

Translated by

JOHN CUMMING

continuum
NEW YORK · LONDON

Continuum

The Tower Building, 11 York Road, London SE1 7NX

370 Lexington Avenue, New York, NY 10017-6503

www.continuumbooks.com

First published in English 2003

British Library Cataloguing in Publication Data

A catalogue record for this book is available from the British Library

ISBN 0 8264 6703 2 (hardback)

ISBN 0 8264 6704 0 (paperback)

Typeset by BookEns Ltd, Royston, Herts

Printed and bound in Great Britain by Bookcraft (Bath) Ltd, Midsomer Norton, Somerset

Contents

Introduction

'Yes, but what does it do for me?' Variations on this question are asked or have to be answered by so many Christians today, particularly in respect of the sacraments.

This book is not a theological treatise on the sacraments. It is addressed to all those who actually receive and administer the sacraments in today's world, whether the ordinary Christians for whom they are intended, or parents, young people, priests, ministers, parish workers, teachers, carers, counsellors and others with a more specific interest in some of them or certain aspects of all seven sacraments.

In other words, I have written these pages for all those concerned with the major themes and events of birth, death, health and sickness, growing up, responsibility and guilt, and mission, and how the Church acts with regard to them.

I have included a certain amount of history, when it seemed relevant, but I have concentrated more on the living meaning of the sacraments as expressed in their often ancient symbolism, imagery and language. I wanted to bring out the positive, life-giving and life-enhancing function of the sacraments. Therefore, whenever possible, I have made practical suggestions drawn from my own experience of people's difficulties with the sacraments in the present-day world, from successful celebrations, and from many years of conversations, talks, preparatory courses and constant thought about and meditation on the sacraments as expressions of God's love for us.

I ask how baptism can shape our everyday existence, how the mystery of the eucharist can transform both individual and community, how confirmation can be experienced as initiation into the art of living effectively, how reconciliation can help to make

1

awareness of guilt an opportunity for renewal, how marriage can prove a daily blessing for a couple learning to live together, how priests can nurture the sacred fire of God's love and guide others to true self-fulfilment, and how the anointing of the sick can offer not only comfort but healing, and help us to understand the meaning of illness.

I hope that this book will help to banish many mistaken and, indeed, harmful notions of the sacraments that have led so many Christians to avoid them, and that it will renew people's confidence and joy in them as channels of authentic life. In that sense, I trust, reading this book may prove a celebration in itself.

Anselm Grün, OSB

1

Baptism: celebrating life

INTRODUCTION

A new identity

The rite of baptism in the early Church left a deep impression on the candidates and on the congregation. It took several years to prepare for reception of the sacrament, which introduced the newly baptized to the mystery of Christian life. The early Church was clearly able to fill people with enthusiasm for living with and by the power of Jesus Christ. This new life offered them an alternative to the empty, godless striving that was characteristic of late antiquity. Baptism allowed Christians to break with their life-histories up to that point. The life they chose instead would be guided by what Jesus had said and draw its strength from a new, divine source. The newly baptized felt that their lives were starting all over again. They were sure that only now, through baptism, were they alive in any real sense. Everything to date was, as the First Letter of Peter puts it, *mataios* (a Greek word signifiying futile and meaningless), quite illusory, only half a life. In baptism they surrendered their old identity and discovered a new one in Jesus Christ.

Life in the ancient world at the end of its tether stressed the importance of *panem et circenses*, bread and circuses or, as we might say, just having a good time. It was a decadent world that seemed to have forgotten the real meaning of life. Everything centred on novelty and thrills, on pleasure and entertainment.

Candidates for baptism broke free of this activity to seek a new identity in Christ. Their night-time baptism was an unforgettable ceremony that symbolized casting off the old personality. They entered the font naked and water was poured over them three times. They

3

renounced evil and the futility of a life lived far from the presence of God and chose to die to this world. They promised that they would seek their identity in Christ, abandoning all attempts to define themselves in terms of success and achievement, pleasure and excess.

A new birth

They experienced their baptism as a new birth, for they had received the gift of a new existence in Christ. This new life was marked by the feeling that they were undergoing an immense liberation. These baptized Christians thought of themselves as defined by God, for now they were free people. They were no longer subject to any emperor and no longer compelled to do what other people wanted. They were truly free men and women and could take the road that led to real life. Baptism enabled them to experience a new closeness to God and an assurance of his unconditional love. Baptism for them meant initiation into the mystery of redeemed and liberated life, and into the mystery of a God who received them into a vital system fed by his divine love. When the candidates emerged naked from the font to be anointed with fragrant oil (men by the bishop, women by another woman), they knew they were truly new people, for now they were wholly enclosed in God's love. At the same time they experienced the fellowship of new brothers and sisters in the Church. This was a community where they were accepted without prejudice, but also one that required them to lead a meaningful and fulfilled life.

Sharing in God

There can be no doubt that many people nowadays, too, long for fulfilment in life and to be freed from the claims and demands of this world. But many also wonder what this longing has to do with Jesus Christ, and why fellowship with Christ rather than anything else should make them free and enable them to lead a full life. Surely, they say, it's sufficient to commit yourself spiritually in one way or another, and you can do that quite satisfactorily without including Jesus in the formula.

4

I could certainly devote an entire book to the part Jesus plays in the process by which we become truly human. The early Christians found their encounter with Jesus so fascinating that they gladly risked persecution in order to experience personally the new quality of life that he could give them. But what exactly was it about Jesus that so captivated people that they were willing to stake their lives on devotion to him?

The Second Letter of Peter applied Jesus's message to the conditions of the Hellenistic spiritual world, and explained that Jesus's appeal was based on his gift to us of everything positive we need for ourselves and for our life. The glorious goodness of God shines forth in Jesus: 'It is through him that God's greatest and most precious promises have become available to human beings, making it possible for you to escape the inevitable disintegration that lust produces in the world and to share in God's essential nature' (2 Pet. 1.4). Baptism liberates us from any compulsion to follow the way that leads to nothing of any value but only to corruption. It enables us to become partakers of the divine nature. To share in the nature of God himself was surely the supreme goal of the questing and inquiring spirits of the ancient world. People in the last years of antiquity were convinced that a person could become truly human only if he or she shared in the divine nature.

The Jesuit priest Alfred Delp learned how true this was of his own life not long before he was hanged from a meat hook. He was executed because he followed his Christian faith and staked everything on opposition to the Nazi dictatorship. Facing death in his Gestapo cell, he wrote: 'A human being is only truly human when he or she lives in unity with God.' The Nazi ideology treated humanity with contempt. For Delp this showed clearly that if they are honest, people will recognize the fact that they can do nothing on their own: 'Left to themselves they are incomplete, not quite human. God is part of the definition of a human being; inner unity with God is the primary condition for a fulfilled and successful life.' Through baptism we share in the life of God.

Today the Church is faced with the task of celebrating baptism in

5

the right way: in other words, so that it helps people to understand something of the mystery of their life's real meaning, and enables them to find out who they truly are.

Meaning of baptism

As infant baptism became increasingly the norm, much of baptism's effect on how an individual sees and lives his or her life was nullified. Down to the present day there has been a certain vagueness and uneasiness about the exact significance of the way in which we baptize infants. The child himself or herself, to be sure, gets nothing out of it. In the past, of course, various explanations were offered that actually made infant baptism less, not more, comprehensible.

It was said, for instance, that the child was wiped free of original sin, and that a pagan child became a child of God, or that baptism made him or her a member of the Church. The first of these interpretations is sheer superstition and also sounds a pessimistic note, because it suggests that an unbaptized child isn't a child of God and can't go to heaven.

Then, if we follow the second explanation and represent baptism from a one-sided point of view as acceptance into the Church, the sacrament becomes a kind of formal incorporation into an organization. Accordingly, the Church is seen as something like a club or association that is anxious to get its members onto the register as quickly as possible.

The real questions to ask are: 'How are we to understand baptism nowadays?'; and: 'How can we celebrate the sacrament so that people are profoundly moved by the mystery of life and can rejoice over God's gift to them of this child?'

Of course baptism remains an authentically Christian act. It has its own special quality and purpose, in spite of all its similarities to Jewish ablutions of the kind practised in the Qumran community. On the other hand, all religions have rites associated with the birth of a child. All peoples and cultures manifest a need for rites to symbolize the mystery of birth and the divine gift of a child. These ceremonies often revolve round the theme of water and washing. The intention is to cleanse the child of everything that conceals his or her essential nature, and to bring him or her into contact with the true source of life.

The purpose of the following pages is not to delineate a complete theology of baptism. Instead, like the Fathers of the Church, I shall use graphic and figurative language to show what baptism (and infant baptism too) can mean for us, how we can celebrate it, and how baptism as a meaningful reality can enable us to live as free people who are loved unconditionally.

I. THE SACRAMENT OF BAPTISM

Baptism is a sacrament, a term that many people today find unhelpful. A sacrament has been defined as a 'sacred act in which a person is bound by oath.' The original *sacramentum* was a Roman soldier's oath of enlistment. In the sacrament of baptism the candidate makes a declaration of loyalty binding him or her to Christ, and states an intention to shape his or her life in unity with Christ. But 'sacrament' means something else too. It is an English translation of the Greek *musterion* and the Latin *mysterium*, which are also rendered as 'mystery', signifying the believer's initiation into the mystery of life, and into the mystery of the death and Resurrection of Jesus Christ. But do these two terms, 'sacrament' and 'mystery', help us to understand infant baptism?

Mystery of the child

In baptism we celebrate the mystery of the child. What is his or her essential nature? Who is this child in the truly profound reality of his or her being? By associating the child's life with the fate of Jesus Christ we should be able to see who this child really is, what life means, and how we can see it through the eyes of faith. The mystery of the child should be clarified by the light of Jesus's destiny. Then we perceive the child as having not only an earthly but a divine life; as one already sharing in Jesus's Resurrection; and therefore as one over whom death no longer has any dominion.

7

But what effect is the baptismal rite intended to have on the candidate and on the people celebrating the baptism? The actual rite opens our eyes, so that we see the infant no longer as the child of these parents and of this extended family, but as a divine child in whom God opens up a new beginning, and in whom something unique and singular in this world shines forth.

But the rite does more than that. Through it Jesus Christ himself affects the child, pouring out his divine life and his unconditional love, conferring God's own protection and disclosing his beauty. We not only exchange words over the child but celebrate his or her mystery by holding this child so that he or she enters God's own mystery as we know it to be most clearly evident, in Jesus Christ. But what happens in a rite always concerns all those taking part, as well as the individual who is its focus. The effect of the rite on the infant itself must remain limited, since it is scarcely aware of what is happening to it. We also celebrate the rite for our own sake, in order to see the child in a new way, and, by following the prescribed stages of the ritual, to accustom ourselves to new patterns of behaviour and forms of relationship.

The infant is not merely its parents' child but a child of God. It has a divine dignity and value. It is free, and belongs not to its parents but to God. This child will go his or her own way, with an accompanying angel to guide him or her safely through life's dangers and through an upbringing that will leave its marks on the child, however good the parents' and educators' intentions may be. Baptism takes away part of the burden on the parents, who often overexert themselves to make sure that their child is properly raised. Errors in education could have unfortunate consequences and do the child harm in the long run. Yet baptism shows us that God stretches his hand over children to guard them, that Christ's saving power is stronger than the injurious devices of our neurotic psyches, and that every child has an angel to watch over him or her.

Water

Some symbols that occur in the ceremony help to illustrate the nature of the life we celebrate in baptism. The image of water is certainly the main symbol of baptism. It was more impressive for the early Christians who went naked into the baptismal water than for us, for all we do is pour a little water over the child's head. Water is the source of all life. All life originates in water, and most us can recall fairy tales in which the water of life heals wounds and confers immortality.

Then there is the symbol of the well or fountain of youth. Whoever drinks from it will never grow old. All cultures represent springs and wells as sacred places. They are spots where people meet, and men go in search of a bride, as Moses and Isaac did. There is also an erotic aspect to a well. It can be a place of divine revelation too. It is at a well that Hagar, the maidservant thrown out of Sarah's household by Abraham, finds the courage to go on living. Jesus meets the Samaritan woman at the well known as 'Jacob's Spring', and tells her about the water he will give her. Whoever drinks the water 'I will give him or her will never be thirsty again. For my gift will become a spring in the person himself or herself, welling up into eternal life' (John 4.14). The baptismal font is a spring of this kind from which we draw water that wells up in our very own selves. It is a spring that never dries up. The erotic dimension of springs and wells is also present in the baptismal font. Ultimately, it is the love of God which is poured over us there and becomes an inexhaustible spring within us.

More than anything, we thirst for a love that will never cease because it is fed from a spring that can never go dry. We receive this divine love in the spring water of baptism. We can always drink from it when our human love fails and runs away between our fingers.

Water of purification

All religions and cultures also portray water as having the power of cleansing and renewal. The water of baptism cleanses us from the mistakes of the past and renews us so that we can go on living as new people. This is more easily understood by an adult over whom water is poured than by a child. What should we cleanse children from? They have never sinned. Of course the medieval Church believed that a child was cleansed of original sin, but we might put that in present-day terms by saying that the child is removed from the complex of circumstances we call fate. Everything a child is subject to, from genetic factors to the psychological family situation conditioned by the childhood experiences of parents, grandparents and ancestors, is washed away in baptism. Of course this isn't a magical process, and it would be wrong to say that all psychological complications are simply cancelled by baptism. But by pouring water over a child we can see that he or she is not condemned to repeat the fate of his or her parents and grandparents, and is not merely a product of an ancestral line but can begin again in his or her own right.

We celebrate a spiritual birth in baptism. A child is not the wholly predictable outcome of the past, but is open to the new things that God wants to bring about in him or her. Dark family secrets will not shape the child. Instead the angel of God will lead the child into freedom and towards life in spite of all the entanglements of the inherited family situation. We can also see the water as washing away all the worries and afflictions with which we burden children: the grime of the preconceptions with which we cover them and which disguise and block the development of their true natures. The water of baptism will cleanse children of everything that obscures the unique images of God which are manifested in them.

Spiritual fruits

Water is also a symbol of spiritual fruitfulness. There are people who are locked into a routine life, and are no longer productive. Everything in them is dried up and rigid. Baptism is a constant reminder to us that we have a perpetually renewed spring within us. It will never let us dry up. It is the spring of the Holy Spirit on which we can always draw. This spring will always inspire new ideas in us, for it lies where we are in touch with divine creativity. Whoever operates by the power of this source will never be exhausted. Our work will flow from it, and we shall take pleasure in what we do by its inspiration. We shall also find joy in the vitality that rises from it. We are all afraid that our strength might fail us, that new ideas will cease to flow, and that we shall become dull and empty. Baptism promises us that the source within us is inexhaustible because it is divine. It will keep us perpetually fresh and vital and enliven the seed within us that longs to break through and flower and fruit.

The creative aspect of baptismal water comes to the fore in the story of the baptism of Cornelius, a deeply religious Roman centurion. Cornelius has a dream in which he is told that he should send for a man known as Peter. When Peter enters Cornelius's house he speaks to the large number of people he finds assembled there, and everyone who listens to him is filled with the Holy Spirit. They begin to speak in foreign tongues and to glorify God. The Jewish believers who have come with Peter are absolutely amazed that the gift of the Holy Spirit is being poured out on Gentiles too. But Peter says: ' "Could anyone refuse water or object to these people being baptized – people who have received the Holy Spirit just as we did ourselves?" And he gave orders for them to be baptized in the name of Jesus Christ' (Acts 10.47f.).

Baptism with water is associated with the descent of the Spirit. The early Church believed that baptismal water was filled with the sanctifying and life-giving power of the Holy Spirit. That is why the water of baptism can make us productive, and sanctify and renew us.

Burying obstacles to life

Water can also have a destructive power. People in the ancient world were especially frightened of the dangers of the sea. Nowadays, too, the lethal force of water is obvious in innumerable disasters caused by floods. In dreams flooding can mean that we are overcome by the unconscious; that we are no longer living by our own power but by the strength of certain forces welling up from the unconscious. Paul is thinking of this when he tells us that all of us who were baptized into Jesus Christ were by that very action enabled to share in his death, and how Christ was raised by God from the dead (cf. Rom. 6.3f.). In baptism we, so to speak, dip down into Christ's grave and bury everything there that is an obstacle for us in life. We bury our old identity, which was intent only on acquiring as much money, power and respect as possible, only revolved round itself, and was wrapped up and entangled in itself. We also bury our past, which has ruled us until now. We bury our injuries and insults. We no longer intend to use them in order to blame others for our present situation. We die to this world in order to live as new men and women. We no longer define ourselves in terms of success and achievement, recognition and financial rewards, but in God-given terms. That is true freedom.

The baptism of a child shows us that a change of identity is taking place. The child comes into contact with his or her true nature, freed from the ties of this world. But in baptism we others also learn to treat the child in a new way. We refuse to let this child be condemned to an existence where the only things that count are recognition and success. Now we shall try to perceive the mystery of God in him or her: the mystery of freedom and uniqueness, and the mystery of divine dignity and value.

Disarming death

If we are already dead to this world, and if it no longer has any power over us, this also means that we are already living on the far side of the spring through which we have passed, and that death can no longer grip us in its fangs. Gladness about every birth is always mixed with anxiety about how long this child might still live. In baptism we express our conviction that this child will never die. Even if physical death does seek this person out at some time, nevertheless the child's own self, the core of his or her specific being as an individual, will not disappear. This means that our relationship with this child can never be destroyed. God's love, which this child shares in and which flows through us, will keep us united even beyond death. This belief will cancel our fear that the child could be taken from us by death. And freedom from this anxiety will guard us from clinging to the child compulsively and trying to hold onto it.

Open heaven

If we look for a moment at the account of Jesus's own baptism, we shall discover other aspects of water and of baptism. This is how Mark describes Jesus's baptism: 'In those days Jesus came from Nazareth of Galilee and was baptized by John in the Jordan. And when he came up out of the water, immediately he saw the heavens opened and the Spirit descending on him like a dove; and a voice came from heaven, "You are my beloved Son; with you I am well pleased"' (Mark 1.9–11).

When Jesus enters the water, this symbolizes his penetration of the depths of the earth. In depth psychology, or psychoanalysis, water stands for the unconscious. In baptism we descend into the depths of the unconscious, into the abyss of our own soul, into the shadowy realm where everything that we have excluded from life has been repressed. Precisely because we go down into our own darkness, heaven opens up above us. This is a beautiful way of expressing the mystery of being a Christian. We have the courage to accept our own humanity, with all its ups and downs, and also with the darkness that has settled in our unconscious. Even if we do not dislodge anything down there, just being brave enough to descend into our own depths results in the heavens splitting open overhead.

The open heavens reveal the horizon where we live as Christians. This is the open horizon of God. Our souls share in the broad expanse of the sky, in the brilliance of a star-spattered sky, in the glorious colours of a summer sky, and in the soft light of a sky in autumn. We should not think of ourselves too meanly but set our sights as high as possible, for the heavens have opened over us, and our life stretches all the way into God himself.

Unconditional acceptance

God speaks to us out of heaven, saying that we are accepted unconditionally and entitled to our existence. In a book entitled *From Survival to Life*, Karl Frielingsdorf describes how many children feel that they have no more than a conditional right to life. They feel that they are accepted only if they fulfil certain specific conditions: if they are successful, if they achieve something, if they don't cause their parents any trouble, if they aren't difficult to care for, and if they fit in. When children think they are accepted only on certain conditions, they resort to survival strategies. To earn love, they continually suppress their own opinions, and repress any unhappiness and anger, trying to make sure they aren't a problem for their parents. They want to be acknowledged, and so they constantly try to achieve more and more. In fact they put everything into the attempt. But they never get the confirmation they crave. As a result, they never really live their lives to the full. Instead they are cut off from life. Frielingsdorf calls this minimal life 'survival'.

To survive, children need achievement and adaptation strategies. They can go on living only if they feel they have been given an unconditional right to existence. In baptism we hear the voice of God saying: 'You are my beloved son, you are my beloved daughter. I am very pleased with you. I like you not because you have achieved something or other, but because you are who you are. You are entirely welcome, accepted and loved as you are.' This absolute entitlement to exist which we experience in baptism is the precondition not only for our survival but for our ability to live authentic lives.

Rebirth

The baptismal water vitalized by the Holy Spirit also symbolizes the sacred womb from which people are born again. The image of rebirth stands for one of the main aspects of baptism. In John's gospel Jesus says to Nicodemus: 'Believe me, a human being cannot even see the kingdom of God without being born again' (John 3.3).

Nicodemus doesn't understand this, so Jesus explains the mystery of rebirth: 'I assure you that unless you are born from water and from spirit you cannot enter the kingdom of God. Flesh gives birth to flesh and spirit to spirit' (John 3.5ff.). Rebirth means that the newly baptized person receives a new identity. The old biological identity was determined and driven by natural compulsions.

Rebirth in the Spirit, however, is the gift of freedom. In baptism a child is born again into eternal life, and is divinized, as it were. He or she is no longer flesh, no longer susceptible and weak, but spirit: that is, he or she shares in God's immortality and eternity. The child, having been immersed in imperishable divine life, has become a new person. You cannot see this divine life but only have faith in it. But if we believe in the rebirth of a baptismal candidate in the Holy Spirit, we see the child with different eyes, and detect a divine beauty, something incorruptible and everlasting, in him or her; something that now extends into God's own eternity. Then, in the child's face here on earth we can already see heaven, and the mystery of God is disclosed to us in human form.

Anointing

Anointing is another baptismal symbol. In baptism an infant is anointed twice, once with the oil of catechumens and then with chrism. The oil of catechumens is the healing, saving oil. Anointing with this oil symbolizes the truth that the saving power radiating from Jesus Christ is stronger than the injuries the child will receive throughout life. Every child will be injured, no matter how meticulous and protective the parents' care and nurture are. We cannot avoid the hurts that life has in store for us. The decisive factor is how we deal with the wounds of our life-history.

Anointing with the oil of catechumens is a vivid way of showing us that we are not left alone to lick our wounds. The rite of anointing conveys the point that Christ's love flows into our injuries, and that our wounds feel Christ's own tender touch. Oil always stands for tenderness, love, concern and a healing touch. Christ lays his hand lovingly on the precise spot where we have been hurt. His touch can heal our wounds, just as he touched and healed the sick in his lifetime. But anointing with the oil of catechumens is also intended to show us that today Christ wishes to heal through us. We have to be like the oil of anointing for the child. We have to enclose him or her in our love so that injuries can heal in our presence. The child should see us as radiating healing. But that will be possible only if, like Jesus, we gently touch people at the points where they are most sensitive to injury and insult, support them, and encourage them to engage in the venture of their own lives.

Chrism

Chrism is the oil with which kings are anointed. In ancient Israel kings and prophets were anointed with oil to symbolize the fact that God's blessing was on them and that they had received a new authority. Chrism is an oil mixed with balsam and spices, and exudes a particularly fragrant scent. Anointing symbolizes the fact that we are royal, prophetic and priestly people; that God's blessing has come upon us; and that a special scent is emitted by our lives: a rich and life-giving fragrance, and not the stench of death to be expected from those whose selves are inwardly lacerated and torn.

Baptism makes us royal individuals who are in control of themselves and ruled by no one else; people who live in their own right instead of others ordaining how they live; people who are at peace with themselves and therefore are capable of radiating peace. We are people with an unassailable dignity and value, with a divine dignity and beauty. Prophets are those who speak openly and trustworthily; who have something to say with their entire lives: something that can be said in this world only through them. Every one of us is a prophet: that is, he or she is capable of expressing through his or her personal existence some aspect of God that can be made perceptible and can be experienced in this world only through this individual life. Every human being is unique: a unique word of God that can sound forth in this world only through the medium of this individuality.

Access to God

We are all priests, too. That is the message of the First Letter of Peter, which some scholars interpret as a baptismal sermon. 'But you are a chosen race, a royal priesthood, a holy nation, God's own people, that you may declare the wonderful deeds of him who called you out of darkness into his marvellous light' (1 Pet. 2.9).

A priest is a mediator between God and people. A priest has access to God. What does that mean for us? When we are consecrated as priests and priestesses through baptism, it means that we have direct access to God, and that we unite God and humanity in ourselves. I think of a priest above all as someone who can transform what is earthly into that which is divine, making earthly things permeable to God, and discovering the tracks of God in human reality. We are all called on to transform the matter of our lives so that divine life shines out from it. Priests have the task of being wholly permeable to God's light and glory. Accordingly, God's glory is perceptible in every human being. The First Letter of Peter tells us that a priest's work is to proclaim the great things that God has done for the individual and for the community, where and how he has brought light into their darkness, and filled them with light. A priest, therefore, also expounds and interprets human life, disclosing the divine traces of light and significance in every life.

The baptismal candle

When the priest lights the baptismal candle at the Paschal Candle and hands it to the candidate for baptism, or to a godparent, the rite expresses the idea that every human being is a beam of light for this world. We sometimes experience children only as a burden. Baptism is intended to open our eyes to the fact that with each child a new light shines out in this world. This recalls the similar idea in the ancient world that with the arrival of each person a star is born to sparkle for humanity in the night sky, so that each person can make the world a brighter and kinder place. Our most profound vocation is to make the eyes of the people round about us light up and to bring some warmth into their cold hearts.

The early Church called baptism *photismos*, which is Greek for illumination. Accordingly, baptism not only shows us that a light is born for us in each child, but that the child himself or herself is illuminated by God's everlasting light. The early Church interpreted the healing of the blind in John 9.1–12 as a baptismal narrative. Our eyes are opened and light up in baptism. Then we can see reality pure and simple, as it is. The legend of St Odilia expresses this aspect of the sacrament, for she was born blind but gained her sight through baptism. Baptism illuminates our eyes so that we see God's light in us.

The white robe

The placing of a white robe on the child (or of a white cloth representing it on the child's head) in baptism symbolizes what it means to be a Christian. The early Christians, of course, entered the font naked and then were robed in white garments. This was an enactment of Paul's statement in the Letter to the Galatians: 'For as many of you as were baptized into Christ have put on Christ as a garment' (or: 'All of you who were baptized "into" Christ have put on the family likeness of Christ'). The metaphor Paul uses here recalls the notion of a heavenly robe already lying in heaven, awaiting our arrival there. Baptism made us one with Christ, and we are now, so to speak, heavenly beings reflecting the beauty of heaven on this earth.

Putting on the robe is not merely something external but transforms the whole person, heart as well. We have become different people through baptism. We have been granted a new existence. We are filled by the Spirit of Jesus who also wishes to illuminate our bodies so that they shine forth in this world, a point repeatedly stressed by the Fathers of the Church. In putting on the white robe we perform a rite in which we are trying out new ways of behaving towards the child. My sister once said of a man we knew:

'He looks at you as if he wanted to undress you.' Instead, I should treat this child so that he or she feels clothed in a white garment and wrapped in love, and can enjoy his or her true worth. My gaze should enrich, not deprive this child of value. A rite always carries the additional meaning of learning new ways of behaving that do more justice to a person than our former clever games and behaviour-patterns.

Transformation

All the symbols and rites we have examined so far say something about the mystery of the individual. But many people who can remember details of the old baptismal theology want to know what happens in baptism now that makes it so very different from the past, and what that has to do with the Church into which an individual is still received by baptism. Baptism not only represents what a human being actually is but effects a transformation. A sacrament (as Catholic teaching put it for so long) is the means by which something invisible is made visible and communicated to us. God's grace is given to the candidate through the external rites. We are not just putting on a show, but on the other hand we are not practising magic. Instead we are representing what God actually does to this person.

The Fathers of the Church believed that through the priest's or individual Christian's hand Jesus himself touched the child and carried out the action of the sacrament on him or her. What Jesus did to people two thousand years ago he does to us now. He raises us up, touches us, heals our wounds, encourages us with his words and gives us his Spirit, who is poured out over us in his death. He takes us with him on his way, which leads through the cross to resurrection, and to true and everlasting life.

In the early Church the rite of baptism was a major experience for the candidates. They realized that something extraordinary was taking place, and that a transformation had occurred. Children now certainly feel what is happening to them only unconsciously. It is difficult to imagine that the experience of baptism could mean anything more to them. But something does happen to the congregation. They arrive at a new sense of what the mystery of the child means. This changes their attitude and relationship to the child. In its turn, this new relationship will change something in the child. Baptism creates the space in people where a child has room to develop as his or her own self.

Incorporation

Since the Second Vatican Council, the main significance of baptism has been seen as incorporation in the community of the Church. Consequently, many parishes do their best to ensure that several children are baptized together in the context of the Sunday liturgy, so that the whole community can take part in the occasion. The intention here is theologically appropriate. Nevertheless, it doesn't always fit the actual situation. We have to ask if parishes really are places where the children in question feel at home, and where young families know they can find acceptance and support.

In view of this, it is quite permissible, too, to celebrate baptism in a small family circle. A family is also the church community, a local church in fact, into which the baptized child will grow. Inclusion means more than acceptance by the parish. Christians always live in and through relationships and learn about the Christian faith through others. They experience the meaning of their lives' mystery in the community of believers. Therefore incorporation in the community of the Church is meaningful only if baptism also involves the community in some way in the celebration. The baptismal rites have to ensure that the community is brought into the mystery of the child and into the mystery of redemption and liberation by Jesus Christ. The commissioning of godparents shows that baptism extends the narrow family circle and that children are meant to grow into a wider circle of people who can offer them a healing environment and strengthen their faith.

II. THE CEREMONY

What I have to say about the actual rite of baptism is intended to help the parents themselves to prepare their child's baptismal celebration and to take a part in planning its actual form. It is not enough for the priest just to carry out the prescribed rites from cold, as it were. Rites exist to enable us to express feelings that we can't express in any other way. They can bring us together in a much deeper sense than words allow. They also open up our being together to God's intervention. Rites enable another dimension to break into our lives: the dimension of heaven as it comes into contact with our world. Rites allow the form and figure of Jesus Christ to become visible in our midst. Baptismal rites are concerned not only with the priest's feelings and beliefs but with those of everyone present, especially the parents and godparents. Therefore it is advisable to look at the ceremonies in advance, to try to work out what they mean, and to see how they might be enacted and possibly altered slightly so that they turn into an authentic joint celebration. Everyone invited to a baptism is also asked to contribute something to the occasion, including the godparents' creative imagination. I certainly think that the guests shouldn't be mere passive spectators but should enter into the rites which parents, godparents and priest have prepared and prepared for. They might even make their own suggestions about how they should be included in the ceremony.

The questions

Baptism begins with questions addressed to the parents and godparents. I think it's a good idea not to rely on the set formulas but to ask the parents personally why they want their child to be baptized, what they think baptism means, and why they have chosen this particular name for their child. I let the parents know these questions in advance, when we are preparing for the sacrament. This gives them a chance to think them over. It is something of a challenge for them and makes them ask themselves why baptism is important to them. Then they have to accept responsibility for the words they have been considering, and in which they express their own faith. One woman who was alienated from the Church broke into tears when she spoke out in front of her relatives and said why she wanted her son to be baptized. She remembered how the faith had been like another home for her, and a very close and familiar environment. She didn't want her son to develop without roots in a pluralist world that was not mutually binding. She could see how baptism opened up a space for children where they could feel rooted and supported.

The name

Sometimes parents are much more concerned about the name they have chosen for the child than about anything else. But the name itself isn't important. Sometimes, of course, the actual implications of the name can affect an individual's life. One man called 'Donatus' (a Latin word meaning 'Given by God') told me how intensely he disliked this name when he was a child, but that now he was very pleased he had been given it. He had become used to his name. Now he saw himself as 'given', as God's gift. When choosing a name it is also usual to select a patron, a saint who might be a role model. You can grow into a name. A name is much more than just a name. When I think about my patron saint by name I can discover possibilities in myself that I would totally ignore otherwise. I am called by my name and this expresses my individuality. When I think about my name I am drawn increasingly into the mystery of my own uniqueness. That can make it interesting and pleasant to be called by name, and to be identified with the name my parents gave me.

Godparents

I also ask godparents directly what being a godparent means to them. Some people say that they really want to be there for the child as he or she grows up, to support him or her, to be someone he or she can turn to and confide in at any time, and that they see the function as a task for them personally: one of growing in faith and inquiring into it once again. They want to be available to the child when the parents reach the limits of their own capabilities of care and nurture. Precisely when a child rebels against the parents (in adolescence, say), it is helpful to have a third party outside the inner family circle to turn to. Sometimes godparents bring a text to the ceremony that says something to them about the mystery of baptism.

The reading

When the parents have given their answers, a special baptismal text from the Bible is read out. In this case, too, it is a good idea for the parents to decide which passage from scripture they think best expresses the mystery of baptism. The standard form of the baptismal rite offers a wide choice of suitable biblical references. Some people choose a text that doesn't necessarily say anything directly about baptism but might contain an image or words of encouragement for their child's future life as they see it. Two parents I know selected the text about the storm at sea and planned the whole service against the background of this symbol. They turned nutshells into little candle-holders to shine out symbolically on the ocean of life. Other parents read out Psalm 139, which speaks of the hand of God enclosing us on every side. They were particularly impressed by the image of God's loving hand protecting the child. Every child is protected by more than the hands of his or her father and mother holding and touching it tenderly. Every child is accompanied by an angel stretching a loving hand out to encircle and defend him or her from danger, and to make sure that this child is aware of God's inexhaustible love should the parents' love reach the limits of their competence.

Sign of the cross

After a short address in which the priest focuses on the ideas, symbols and images that have come to the fore during the general preparation for the sacrament, the rite proper begins with the sign of the cross. Not only the priest but the parents and godparents and, if possible, the entire congregation should sign the child's forehead. By making the sign of the cross we express the fact that the child belongs not to the state, and not to any king or ruler, but to God. The child is not there to fulfil other people's expectations but to go his or her own way in freedom.

The cross is also the symbol of the union of all opposites, a reconciliation of contradictions. For St John it is the sign of the love with which Christ loved us all the way to death and beyond. Consequently, when we make the sign of the cross, we tell the child: 'It is good that you exist. Everything in you is good. You are not intended to be torn apart by contradictions. You are one person, whole and entire, because everything within you is united by the love of Christ. You are wholly accepted and loved. Nothing in you is untouched by God's love.' We also make God's approval clear when we make the sign of the cross: 'I shall be with you where you go. I am at your side. I shall take all the roads you take, even ways of pain, crossroads, wrong paths and circuitous routes.'

Litany of the saints

After the sign of the cross, the saints are invoked and intercessions made on the child's behalf. Parents and relatives can shape this part in a very personal style. One way would be for each person present to think about his or her patron saint and to express a wish for the child in accordance with that saint's life and works. A mother called Mary might hope that the child would be as ready as Mary to trust in God. Or a Monica might wish that the child would never give up, even if everything around him or her seemed hopeless. A father might wish that his son would be able to fight as valiantly as St George. The thing about St Anselm that fascinates me is that he was thought to be the kindest and most likeable person of that time. And so I would hope that the child would be given some part of Anselm's warm-heartedness. Or the parents might study the child's patron more closely before the baptism. Then, at this point in the ceremony, they can relate something of his or her life and express a wish that the child should receive qualities displayed by that saint. Children present at the baptism could draw or paint pictures beforehand in which they express their wishes for the candidate. This would be an especially good way for the child's brothers and sisters to prepare for the event. Some people delay the prayers for the child until the moment when the lighted baptismal candle is handed to the parents. Then all present are invited to light their baptismal or birthday candles at the main one and to announce their wishes for the child, whether they come to mind spontaneously or have been written down in advance.

Laying on of hands

The rite then prescribes a laying on of hands and a prayer for the child's protection. I suggest that not only the priest but the parents lay their hands on the child's head or shoulders. Then the meaning of the prayer will be made evident: that God wants to hold his loving and protective hand over children always, to preserve them from evil and defend them when danger threatens. To enforce the significance of these words about protection the child is anointed with the oil of catechumens, the oil of healing, so that Christ's healing power will transform all his or her wounds into pearls. However careful and loving the parents are, they will wound the child somehow. Anointing with the oil of healing frees the parents from fear of their own errors. It strengthens their confidence that Christ's curative power will change these injuries into something valuable, into a precious advantage that will enable the child to be open for people and for God.

Blessing of the baptismal water

Then the baptismal water is blessed. The benediction, or prayer of blessing, names all the enlivening, cleansing, refreshing and renewing effects of water, as narrated in the history of God's dealings with his people Israel and as they were recounted in the time of Jesus. The prayer recalls the primal image of baptism, the crossing of the Red

Sea by the Israelites, when all their pursuing enemies, the Egyptians, were drowned. It mentions blood and water, which flowed from the pierced side of Jesus. In baptism the love of God made human flows from Jesus's heart to remake the child. To help meditation on the mystery of the baptismal water, a source-of-life or circle dance round the font is a possibility here, to indicate our desire that this life-giving water should start to flow in us too.

Renunciation of evil

After the blessing of the water the rite calls for a rejection of evil. This was a very important rite in the early Church. Then, the candidates made a conscious decision to reject the meaningless and godless life they saw going on in the world around them. They opted instead for a life with and in Christ. The rite certainly retains its full meaning when an adult is baptized. It asks us to face up to the dangers that lie in wait for us in life. The success of any life is not self-evident. It has to expect challenges. The question is how to renounce evil nowadays in a way that fits our experience. Today, evil appears in tendencies in our society that trample on human dignity, in insensitivity and undue rigour, in unjust structures, in destructive living conditions, in force and terror. To ensure that the child is not infected by evil and his or her potential is not maimed, the parents and relatives openly reject evil. They express their readiness to oppose life-threatening trends in our society, to resist assaults on human dignity, and forces inimical to life.

Some people, however, find it difficult to utter the negative statements as laid down in the formal rite. All one woman could remember of a baptism she took part in was how frightened she was because it seemed to go on about the Devil all the time. The rite of renunciation can be arranged differently. Parents and godparents can use their own words to say why they want nothing to do with negative influences in our own times, and how they stand up against them. Or they can express their resistance to destructive forces symbolically, for instance by doing something that demarcates the protective circle of faith from external threats. The congregation might form a defensive circle round the mother and child and say a prayer together, or sing a hymn such as Charles Wesley's 'Love divine, all loves excelling' or 'Christ, from whom all blessings flow'.

This rite implies not only a decision for Christ but the experience of a community protecting the child from evil. The child is born into a world in which he or she will also encounter evil from the start. But where believing people surround the child, he or she will also experience the healing and protective enclosure of the Church, where evil has no power.

It would not be advisable simply to skip this rite of renunciation of evil. It is precisely the awkward aspect of this part of the ceremony that challenges the parents to ask themselves how they can fulfil the meaning of this ancient rite in a way that really means something to them. At one baptism I asked all the children to crowd round the mother and child. I said that if they wanted to they could spread their hands protectively over the child. Then we all sang the same benediction: 'You are blessed. You are a blessing.' The other children gazed at the infant in fascination. It was an immensely happy experience to have them all there. A very warm, loving atmosphere was created, a secure space, an enclosure full of love and security in which that child surely knew that he or she was safe from anything hurtful or discordant. The real meaning of renunciation of evil was immediately apparent. Everyone sensed the special quality of this rejection and of this area filled with love and trust.

Baptized into love

After the renunciation and the confession of faith come the basic rites of baptism: the pouring of water and anointing with chrism. The children should be as close to the font as possible when the water is poured. Children want to see and experience something. The threefold pouring of water over the infant's head always fascinates children. As he pours the water three times, the priest says: 'I baptize you in the name of the Father, and of the Son, and of the Holy

Spirit.' The child is received into the community of the Holy Trinity. He or she is baptized into the love between Father and Son that is poured into human hearts in the Holy Spirit. If it seems appropriate, the baptismal water can also be distributed to those round the font by sprinkling a few drops on them, so that everyone experiences something of the vitalizing and refreshing power of the water and shares in the community of the threefold God.

King, priest and prophet

Anointing with chrism can only be experienced properly if the chrism also sends out a rich fragrance. I do not restrict the anointing with chrism to the child, but also anoint the parents and godparents. They too are royal, prophetic and priestly individuals who also fulfil their priestly role in baptism. During the anointing I also give the meaning of the prescribed formula in my own words. I might say something like this:

> Christ has given you new life through water and the Holy Spirit. May he anoint you as a priest, so that you become receptive to God's love; as a king, so that you live as a free human being, aware of your divine worth; and as a prophet, so that you proclaim the message that God wishes to resound in the world through you alone.

The office that I offer parents and godparents through anointing is not the same as that for the child. I anoint the mother as priestess, queen and prophetess, and the father as priest, so that he can discover the marks of God in the child's life; as king, so that he will live as his own person and not allow his life to be ordained by others; and as prophet, so that he can express God in his own particular way.

Image of God

Then the baptismal garment, a white robe, is put on the child. The rite comments on this by referring to Galatians 3.27, and makes the point that the child puts on Christ himself like a garment and thereby the beauty of God himself. The white robe is a symbol of purity and integrity. It expresses the fact that the child is entirely open to Christ and his glory. We see Christ's love shine forth in the child unobscured by human desires and egotism. By putting the white robe on the child we declare our hope that he or she will always be a clear, unique image of God and lead a sincere, transparent life untouched by danger and temptation.

Light of the resurrection

No one can fail to be moved by the lighting of the baptismal candle. When I light it from the Paschal Candle, I pray that the light of the resurrection illuminating the darkness of death will brighten every night-time in this child's life. I hold the burning candle close to the child and trust that he or she will bring light into the world's darkness, and warmth into areas where cold reigns and human emotions threaten to ice over. Then the children, followed by the adults, light their own candles at the infant's baptismal candle. A single candle has brought a vast amount of light into the church. This new light falls on so many faces that a warm, secure atmosphere results. Evidently the child has helped to make this world a brighter and kinder place. If the light of Christ shines in this child, surely very many people will be comforted and enlightened after meeting him or her. All the members of the congregation usually stand in a circle holding their lighted candles. Sometimes parents prepare something else. They buy floating candles for the children to place on the water in the font. Or they lay out a sea of sand and material on the floor, where the children arrange their candles to resemble lighthouses or beacons lighting the way for those who risk their lives on the seas of this life. The children enjoy gathering round this display as a beam of light from this particular baptism shines into their hearts too.

The *ephpheta* rite

This is the final rite in the baptismal service. Jesus opened the ears and lips of the deaf and dumb. Baptism means that someone can now hear the word of God properly and also proclaim it by mouth. The deaf mute could communicate only in a limited way. He could not relate to other people effectively. Many people today are members of a lonely crowd, unable to relate to others. We relate to people through our senses, with our ears, eyes, mouth, by touching and smelling, with hands and feet. Therefore I extend the *ephpheta* rite to include an opening of all the senses.

Baptism should represent the mystery of human life. A baptized person's life is intended to be meaningful, communicative and lived through the senses. An ability to relate to others is essential for this. Only those who exist with all their senses can establish a good relationship with God, people, things and themselves. I begin by placing my hand on the child's mouth and saying that I trust these lips will pronounce words to awaken life and secure peace, and support and encourage other people. They should be words overflowing with love, capable of healing wounds and of comforting the distressed. Then the father and mother lay their hands on the ears and eyes of their child and express the wishes that they have for him or her.

A rite of this kind is an opportunity to express feelings and wishes that would remain unspoken otherwise. It is very important how children use their eyes: whether they close them to reality, or perceive and wonder at the beauty of this world; whether they see the goodness in every human being; whether their eyes radiate warmth and liveliness or only spread depression. Children must also use their ears to hear what God wants to tell them, and the inner meaning of the words they hear from others' mouths.

They have to listen for intermediate and scarcely perceptible sounds if they are to do justice to other people. They should be so keen to hear what others have to say that people want to seek them out in order to express themselves.

The godparents touch the child's hands and feet in blessing and hope that he or she will use them to do good where there is need, that they will be gentle, that they will give as well as take, and that they will take their life into their hands and enjoy shaping and planning it. Children must follow the right road with their own feet. They have to advance along their own inner way. They must find means of access to others and constantly transform themselves on the road of life until they arrive at the goal of their transformation.

One six-year-old in my church felt he just had to open his brother's nose during baptism. He laid his finger on the infant's nose and wished that he would always have something good to smell and that he would be able to taste good things. Rites of this kind can show parents, godparents and brothers and sisters what life really means, and that the infant should experience life in its fullness. That means life as God intended, with all the possibilities inherent in the senses. We become aware of reality and relate to it through our senses. The senses are also the location where we experience God himself. They enrich our lives and make them productive.

The blessing

After these rites, which may also be interspersed with hymns, the whole congregation says the Lord's Prayer together on behalf of the child. It is very effective if at the same time all present join hands in one or more circles. This shows that God is the true Father and true Mother of this child and of us all, and that God alone can grant us true security and refuge. While praying we show that the Spirit of Jesus is flowing through our hands to unite us in God. Then the mother and father are blessed.

The laying on of hands is the original form of blessing. With this special form of benediction I ask that the mother should be able to offer the child security and loving care, fundamental trust and acceptance throughout her life. I also pray that she should not exhaust her own resources in her love for the child but draw from the well of God's own love, that she should always look thankfully at the mystery of the child, and rejoice in its uniqueness. When I bless the father I ask that he may share in the fatherhood of God, that he may strengthen the child, and encourage him or her in the venture of life. I trust that he will always be there for his son or daughter when he is

31

needed, and that he or she will seek his help and share in his strength. I hope that he will be able to accompany them on all the pathways of their lives, wherever they may lead.

Then I bless all those present. I pronounce the blessing together with the parents, who often choose or write their own words for the occasion. When the parents pronounce a blessing over the congregation, their priestly role is made clear. They gave the child life because God gave them the capability. Now, in this benediction, they want to proclaim something of the fullness of life which God has in store for everyone. A parents' blessing might be something like the following:

> May God who is good and merciful bless you. May he keep his hand outstretched over you and be a light to you on your way. May he strengthen you with his power and be for you a source from which you can always draw. May he always send you the angel you need. May he help you up when life lets you down. May he heal you when old wounds open up. May he go with you wherever you may travel. May he enclose you in his healing and loving kindness. And may he make you a source of blessing for your brothers and sisters. May God of his gracious goodness, Father, Son and Holy Spirit, bless you.

The nature of baptism

The parents and godparents have to discuss with the actual celebrant how they want to adapt the individual baptismal rites. It is more than a question of designing something attractive. Preparation for and of the rite should bring out the parents' understanding of what baptism means. This will enable them to develop an ever-deeper idea of the nature of the sacrament. The rite must reveal the effect it has. An efficient preparation will touch on such questions as: What does it mean to be a human being? What is life? What does it mean to be a Christian? What is the true significance of baptism? What is the mystery of Christian life? What does an option for Christ mean and what does accompanying Christ on his way imply? What effects do the rites have? Are they just an appealing piece of play-acting, or do we really believe in what is going on? How close to us is God? How close to us does Jesus come in baptism and how does he affect our lives? Would I shape my life in the same way without Christ, or does Jesus actually influence the way in which I live, think and behave? When parents get together with the priest to prepare the ceremony appropriately, does it mean anything more for them than a clerical pep talk about the importance of making sure the child has a Christian education?

When they study the rites of baptism many parents rediscover their Christian roots. My intention when discussing the sacrament with them is not to give them a bad conscience in the hope that they will start living like Christians again. Instead, in the course of talking about the rites, I awaken their interest in considering for themselves how they want to see and experience their lives as Christians. Then they begin to realize that the Christian faith is not something far removed from this world, but makes possible a life defined by freedom and dignity, love and security, strength and fixity of purpose. They see that faith really helps them to live their lives authentically, so that they can talk sincerely about the quality of life.

III. BAPTISMAL LIFE

Baptismal renewal

On the feast day which commemorates Jesus's own baptism and during the night of Holy Saturday, the Church invites all believers to renew their own baptismal promises. The Church hopes that this will encourage Christians to start living once again according to the mystery of their own baptism. Since most of them were baptized as infants, the memory of their baptism means little or nothing to them. No matter how often Christians are told they should live by the real meaning of their baptism, for the most part they have no idea what its significance might be.

Those who were baptized as adults will always be able to recall what happened then. Like the early Christians, they can renew and confirm their renunciation of evil and their decision for Christ by remembering their own experience of the sacrament. But what does living on the basis of the real meaning of baptism imply for those of us who were baptized as children? For me, life on the basis of baptism means living a more aware and authentic life. It means existing by the power of another dimension, by the effects of the dimension of grace and not by the yardstick of achievement. It means freedom in the face of the world's expectations, acting from that source within me and not by my own power. The fact that I am baptized makes me ask, throughout my life: What does it mean to be a human being? Who am I really? Where do I come from? Where am I going? What do I want to do with my life? What is the mystery of my life? What does it mean to be a Christian? How does Jesus Christ see my life? What does he say to me today? What opportunities will I have today of living in communion with Jesus Christ? Do I live differently from people who are not baptized? If so, how exactly?

I am baptized

We are told that Martin Luther engraved the Latin words *Baptizatus sum* – 'I am baptized' – on his desk. Whenever he was depressed, and was tempted by doubts about himself and by feelings of inferiority, he looked at this declaration and told himself: 'I am baptized.' For him this meant: 'It's not a question of my achieving anything. It isn't so much whether everything I do is right and just, or I live in the right way in the sight of God himself. The decisive factor is that God has accepted me unconditionally, that he loves me impartially, that God justifies me, and that my justification comes from God and not from my achievements.' Similarly, remembering our own baptism might mean assuring ourselves that we are God's beloved sons and daughters. We all have a profound longing to be loved and to be capable of loving. Baptism tells us that we are loved absolutely, that no part of us is excluded from this divine love. Love is the basic fact on which we can build our life. Furthermore, God's love is not fragile like the love that we receive from human beings. It is not ambivalent like the love our parents give us, for all too often they also expect us to be grateful for that love, or want to keep us firmly clasped within it. Whenever we doubt our own capacities, when we feel inferior, when we reject ourselves, the memory of God's unconditional acceptance of us in baptism can help us to affirm and love our own selves.

The source of life

The primary result of recalling our baptism is not that it prompts us to obey Jesus's commandments and behave as we ought to. A much more important outcome is that it tells us who we really are. We can live just lives only if we constantly remind ourselves who we are. Baptism tells us that we are not only our parents' children but children of God. We possess not merely the characteristics we have inherited from our parents but the divine life that flows within us. We must not remain satisfied with the power we have received in our body and psychological make-up. The inexhaustible wellspring of the Holy Spirit is always flowing in us too. We can always draw on its creative force, even if our own strength fails us. It is a source where we share in God's ever-available and limitless power. The memory of our own baptism frees us from the pressure to achieve, which compels us to do everything by ourselves and to prove our own worth. It also liberates us from the fear of losing our strength.

We sometimes find that we have dried up completely. We seem to have become rigid and ossified. Work has made us stony-hard. We have encased ourselves in armour plating in order to move unhampered through life's challenges. But this has made us insensitive and has cut us off from the flux of life. The creative flow has dried up inside us and it's all a matter of routine. If that happens, recalling our baptism can be a way of coaxing our creativity into new life. We can contact that inner source again and our vitality will begin to flow. Becoming fixed in a set of automatic reactions kills life. Baptism can prevent us from turning into petrified entities, and can dissolve the barriers so that we start to live effectively again.

In communion

Being baptized means not only that I live by the waters of a divine spring but that I am in communion with Jesus Christ. When I examine myself I not only face my own life-history but Jesus Christ as my innermost reality. I have developed together with him in baptism. How does this finding affect my life and my self-image? For me, meditation on my baptism means that I do not feel alone. When I am sitting down at my desk to write this book I don't have to labour over the sequence of my thoughts, for Jesus Christ is with me and in me. I don't have to think about him all the time. I don't have to delve into my Bible continually to come into contact with him. He is within me. If I am fully aware of that, I feel liberated from the pressure of having to weather the storms of my life. I know that I am in a relationship. Awareness of Jesus within me allows love to flow through my physical self. I am not isolated but immersed in a love that concerns me personally but is intended to flow through me and beyond me, into this world. For me, growing together with Jesus Christ means that I am never lonely. It means that even in the solitariness that might encircle me outside this inward relationship I am never without support, never without love, and never without protection.

Holy water

Several individual rites are celebrated in baptism. Everyday rites and practices can also serve to remind me of the real meaning of baptism. One of these is taking holy water. We do this when we enter a church. Some people also have a holy water stoup at home. They begin each day by crossing themselves with holy water. The blessed water is intended to remind us that the wellspring of the Holy Spirit flows within us, that we are not dried up and burnt out, but that God's refreshing and renewing water of life flows in us.

Holy water also symbolizes our being cleansed entirely in baptism. When I use holy water to make the sign of the cross I realize what it means to be quite pure and open to God, washed clean of all obscurity that might distort God's original image in me, wiped free of my past and of my guilt. The blots and blurs I have collected throughout my life have been dissolved. In this moment, here and now, I stand before God, free of everything that might stain and defile me. Holy water stands for the promise that I can start my life all over again, that I can posit a new beginning each day, and that I am not determined by the past, by the wounds of my life-history, or by my guilt and failures. I sign myself with the cross on my forehead, my chest, my left and right shoulders, and thereby acknowledge that God's life and love flow in my thoughts, in my vitality and sexuality, in my unconscious and in my conscious mind, and that everything in me is unconditionally accepted and loved, including those aspects of myself that I want to exclude. By crossing myself with holy water I come into contact with the spring that rises in me and quenches my thirst. I feel that I am immersed in God's own life and love.

The holy water also reminds me that I died to this world in baptism. The world and its standards no longer have any power over me. What the world thinks of me is not important now. I don't have to rely on the world that surrounds me for confirmation. I live in this world, but I am not of it. Then I feel free. Every morning, when I enter the church at five o'clock and take holy water I tell myself: 'Today you don't have to prove yourself. You are not of the world. The yardsticks of this world, such as success and recognition, being liked, having a use-value, don't apply to you. Live by your innermost reality! Live by the power of Jesus Christ!' As I carefully sign myself with holy water, I increasingly realize what it means to be a Christian: to be free, to be loved, to live by God's own reality, and to enjoy an irreducible value.

Putting on Christ

In baptism we put on Christ as a garment. That can sound like a pious assertion without any relevance to my own life. Not long ago, when a priest put on his vestments it was usual to say a special prayer, such as: 'I shall clothe myself in the robes of salvation.' Or when he put on his stole, he would say: 'I put on the robe of immortality.' In my own monastic tradition, it is customary to say our own prayers when we clothe ourselves in habit and hood. When I put on my Benedictine habit in the morning, I say: 'I do not belong to myself, but to God. I am in your and not my own service.' I picture Christ enclosing me like the robe I am wearing. He accompanies me throughout the day. When we pray together we place a hood over our habit; traditionally, this stands for the cross. When I'm not in a hurry and put my hood on carefully, I think about its meaning: growing together with Christ, putting on Christ as my garment, sharing in his form, and being clothed with his Spirit.

A royal person

I can also recall my baptism by holding my head high as I make my way through life, by acknowledging my royal status. This means that I am aware of my dignity and value. If I am in control of myself instead of being run from somewhere else, and if I am truly at peace with myself, I realize what it means to live in my own right instead of being the passive object of other people's commands and of events. By keeping the image of a king or queen, of a prophet, or of a priest before me, I shall begin to experience myself differently. When I do that, I shall think and act differently as well. My mind will no longer be ruled by comparisons with others, or by resentment, annoyance and anger at them and their behaviour. As a royal person I shall also respect their worth. Then I shan't have to worry about them all the time, let alone devalue or insult them in order to feel superior. If I feel right in my own skin I can allow other people the space they need to experience their own dignity and value.

Opting for life

In baptism we made a conscious decision to reject evil. Recalling our baptism always means opting for God and for life. I constantly come across people who are on the point of drowning in self-pity. They can hardly get out of bed in the morning because it's all too much for them to cope with. They just feel sorry for themselves and are entirely focused on their own depressive emotions. I always tell them: 'You have to opt for life. When you get up, step straight into life and not into a depressive mood.'

When I realize that I myself am starting to complain about how difficult everything is, I am helped out of this kind of mood by recalling my baptism. Then I tell myself: 'I have to live, not gripe. I must do something myself to shape the way things are and not let other people suck me into their negativity. I'm going to choose life.'

There are two feasts in the Church's year that remind us of baptism more than any others: the Baptism of the Lord (the commemoration of Jesus's Baptism) on the Sunday after Epiphany, and the Easter Vigil of the night between Holy Saturday and Easter Day. In some places, on the feast of the Lord's Baptism, the priest sprinkles the whole congregation with holy water before the Eucharist. As he does so everyone sings the ancient hymn 'Asperges me': 'Purge me with hyssop, and I shall be clean; wash me, and I shall be whiter than snow.' (Ps. 51). The priest blesses the holy water during the Easter Vigil. He dips the Paschal Candle once or three times into the water in the font, saying: 'We ask you, Father, with your Son to send the Holy Spirit upon the waters of this font.' He holds the candle in the water and continues: 'May all who are buried with Christ in the death of baptism rise also with him to newness of life. We ask this through Christ our Lord.' In our church we place a large basin of water ready for members of the congregation who want to take some of the newly blessed water home after the vigil. Throughout the Easter period it will remind them that they have risen with Christ and that in them, too, life has conquered death.

SUMMARY

Thinking about baptism and its profoundly significant rites will do more than merely help parents to prepare for their children's baptism. The points and suggestions I have made when discussing this sacrament are intended to encourage all baptized Christians to look at the mystery of their baptism and repeatedly consider how it has affected them. The symbols and imagery of baptism should remind all believers of what it means to be a Christian, and face them unforgettably with the deep mystery of being human and of being loved wholly and entirely by God. Then they should begin to grasp anew what it means to share in the divine nature and to have developed together with Christ himself.

Baptism for the early Christians was an overwhelming experience; so much so that they never forgot it and were always vividly aware of their life's true origin. Most of us who were baptized as children and take part in a baptism now will find it inspiring to realize that all these rites were celebrated for us very early in our lives. That awareness will enable us to meditate on the ceremonies and to decide what it means to have been anointed as priests, monarchs and prophets, to have been baptized by water and the Holy Spirit, and to have had our senses opened. Then we shall begin to understand who we really are, what the mystery of our life could mean, and what the mystery of Jesus Christ, with whom we have progressed to a new stage in baptism, might imply for us.

This remembrance of our own baptism could help us to a new awareness of our own Christian identity. We are always in danger of adapting to this world. Sometimes we really do not know why we are Christians at all, and what distinguishes us from others who look for salvation in the general marketplace of spiritual options. Nowadays we need resources that will help us to live as Christians in full awareness of our Christianity, not by turning aside from this world but by living consciously in it, knowing that we are in the world but not of it. We need to discover what our Christian freedom and dignity imply, and to live accordingly. Our existence today is menaced by a vast number of tendencies that inhibit any life worthy of the name, and we need advice on how to be as we can and should be. It is a question of entry to and practice in everlasting life: a life that extends even now into the very life of God himself, and is interwoven with God's own immortal life.

Remembering our own baptism can be a most effective way of reaching a new understanding, day by day, of the real nature of our faith and existence, and thus of living as people more vitally aware than ever before of what it means to be truly Christian.

2

The Eucharist: transformation
and union

INTRODUCTION

The Eucharist is the sacrament we celebrate most often. Priests say
Mass every day. Many Christians attend Mass every Sunday. In
recent years, however, church attendance has declined considerably
in many countries. In that sense, the Sunday celebration of the
Eucharist may be said to have reached crisis point. Young people
complain that going to Mass is boring and say they try to leave as
quickly as possible once it's over. It doesn't 'do anything' for them.
Adults feel that they have been present at a rite that no longer really
concerns them, and that its language passes over the vital issues of
their lives.

There have been many attempts to make celebrating the
Eucharist more varied and lively. But members of creative parishes
often find they are constantly under pressure to achieve something
different. They feel that they constantly have to devise even more
attractive and imaginative presentations of the Eucharist. But then
the emphasis is more on the 'production' than on the mystery that is
being celebrated.

If we ask why the Eucharist has lost its fascination, we soon arrive
at the main question: how are we to express our faith in this
postmodern age?

The problems of the contemporary Church, of present-day society
as a whole, in fact, are concentrated in the question of how the
Eucharist should be celebrated now. Our present age tends to
formlessness. It nibbles at a whole range of ways of celebrating this or
that, or puts obstacles in the way of celebration altogether. The
Eucharist is also a commemoration which offers inspiring accounts of

past events. But our age is totally ahistorical. People don't want to remember the past and learn from it. They want to forget what has happened as fast as they can. The important thing, they suppose, is to experience the here-and-now as hectically as possible. It has been said that nowadays our lives are almost devoid of history and that our attitude to time is short-sighted, and short of breath as well. The Eucharist is a communal celebration. But this is an individualistic age and we find it difficult to experience any sense of true community. All the problems of group dynamics in the life we lead with others emerge in the eucharistic community. We don't feel like going to Mass because we don't get on with many of the people we see there. Another problem is our inarticulacy. Our culture is certainly garrulous, but we find it difficult to convey our faith in language that really moves people. In the end, not just crapulous talk-show chatter but the jargon of corporate brainstorming and ecclesiastical discourse are forms of conversation in which no one actually relates to other people, or meets them in any true sense. Nowadays we keep asking what's in it for us. Everything has to be personally advantageous. If we take part in the Eucharist in this egotistical frame of mind, we shall experience it as pointless and boring, and 'get nothing out of it'.

The question is whether we ought to adapt the Eucharist to our times and whether such attempts have any hope of success. Of course any rite always has to be re-examined and reshaped. But tinkering with it won't make the Eucharist more appealing. It is essential to understand the Eucharist so that it says something to us again and fascinates us. Then the difficulties peculiar to our postmodern age, which are intensified in the Eucharist, will become a challenge to create oases as resources against the laying waste of vast tracts of our world. We need to refresh ourselves at these watering-points before we begin our hazardous journey through the wilderness.

The very inarticulacy of our own times makes it necessary to learn a new language that can touch human hearts and open up new spaces in which people can live effectively. The general inability to relate to others compels us to fashion a new form of togetherness in the midst of this self-centred life. We have to oppose the lack of any historical awareness by retelling the old narratives so that we rediscover ourselves in them and they can help us to exist now in a different and more conscious way. We must counter oblivion by celebrating the main events of our history – Jesus's death and resurrection – so that their relevance to all the instances of suffering in our world is made clear. We have to celebrate liturgy together in order to combat vagueness and obscurity and hold back the spreading wasteland of our times. Then we shall create new oases of vitality in the spirit of an age which records its achievements in the flickering of the latest digital watch. To oppose the tyranny of utility and profit-value we need spaces from which expediency is banished and where we seek only to express our humanity as redeemed Christians. In an age so focused on self, we need places where the rule of ego has been overthrown and our vision is unobscured, where we can look for God, and where heaven opens to reveal our earth in a new light.

My intention in this section of the book is to show daily and Sunday mass-goers ways of experiencing their regular celebrations differently and more consciously, so that they can totally change their everyday lives and find a new pleasure in living. We must constantly rediscover what we are actually celebrating in the Eucharist and why we go to church. Otherwise our churchgoing will be mere routine and we shall be unable to convey its point to our children. If we don't do this, we shall keep using the same old clichés to cover up our doubts. But what do you say if your child asks why you go to Mass on Sunday? What do you 'get out of it'? What exactly are you celebrating? What are you looking for?

I know many people who have a deep longing for the Eucharist. Often enough they can't say precisely what it is that takes them to church. They just know that they need to celebrate the Eucharist to live as convinced Christians. One woman told me that for her the most important thing about it was the opportunity to forget herself in church. When she went to communion she could just drop into Christ, as it were. She could let go of herself and all her problems as she surrendered to Christ's love and lost herself in it. For her, every communion was a moment of absolute freedom and love. In these few but utterly intense moments she came into contact with the very mystery of life. This was what took her to the Eucharist regularly.

In recent decades many non-Catholic Christians whose traditions were not emphatically eucharistic have rediscovered the Eucharist. Their concept of the Eucharist and the Catholic understanding of it have become very close, not only in the form of the service, but theologically. Whereas some churches preferred terms such as 'the Lord's Supper' or 'Holy Communion', and Catholics always referred to 'the Mass', nowadays they and Catholics both use the word 'Eucharist'. Eucharist means thanksgiving. We thank God for everything that he has done to and for us in Jesus Christ. Essentially, this section is addressed to all Christians in a time when many people, non-Catholics and Catholics, attend the Eucharist celebrated in other traditions – Reformed, Anglican or Episcopalian, Orthodox or Catholic. Before the authorities in the various churches reach the point of agreeing on actual intercommunion, Christians of different denominations now invite each other to communion: to experience union with Christ in thanksgiving. I hope that this section, indeed the whole book, will help to make the Eucharist increasingly the sacrament of union, a leaven in the biblical sense that interpenetrates and joins all Christians together.

Nowadays many Christians live in a secularized environment with no comprehension of the Christian faith, let alone of the Eucharist. For instance, I know young people brought up in the areligious atmosphere of the formerly Communist East Germany. They have some idea that the mystery of Christianity is to be found in the Eucharist. But they can't explain to themselves and their unbelieving friends what that actually means. People of that kind are to be found everywhere. The following pages are directed to them too. In the Acts of the Apostles Philip asks: 'Do you understand what you are reading?' (Acts 8.30). Similarly, I want to accompany all those who have begun to look for their true destination in life, and ask them with regard to the Eucharist: 'Do you understand what you are celebrating?' Like Philip, I should like to explain what we are celebrating, so that the reader, like the Ethiopian, can proceed on his or her 'journey with a heart full of joy' (Acts 8.39).

I. THE MEANING OF THE EUCHARIST

I haven't the space here to outline a complete theology of the Eucharist. I shall examine only a few eucharistic symbols and images that help us to understand the Eucharist as a mystery. The eucharistic celebration consists first of the Liturgy of the Word, in which we listen to the word of God and try to grasp its message so that we can understand ourselves more effectively and find out the meaning of our lives. Then the Eucharist reaches its focal point in the Liturgy of the Eucharist proper, in which we are united with one another and with Jesus Christ, who gives himself to us as food and drink in the gifts of bread and wine. Jesus told us that we should celebrate this sacred meal regularly. Luke records Jesus's last meal with his disciples: 'Then he took a loaf and after thanking God he broke it and gave it to them, with these words, "This is my body which is given for you: do this in remembrance of me." So too, he gave them a cup after supper with the words, "This cup is the new agreement made in my own blood which is shed for you"' (Luke 22.19f.).

Memorial and commemorative meal

When the Israelites celebrated a feast, they always recalled the great deeds of God. Israel saw God as an historical God who acts in history and shapes it. His wonderful acts are historical events. The most important feast of all, Passover, commemorated the Exodus of the Hebrews from Egypt. The Israelites saw this Exodus as the fundamental miracle of their existence. God had delivered this little nation from the power of the Egyptians. He had freed the Hebrews from ruthless overseers who had constantly demanded more labour from their slaves. He had liberated them from dependency and an inability to act in their own right. He had led them through the Red Sea and the wilderness, until they reached the Promised Land, the

45

land of freedom and fullness of life. Israel celebrated the memory of these great events in a meal, the Paschal Meal, or Passover. God had commanded the people of Israel to celebrate Passover every year in accordance with a rite that prescribed certain actions. 'And you shall tell your son on that day, "It is because of what the Lord did for me when I came out of Egypt"' (Exod. 13.8).

Essentially, the Eucharist commemorates something that happened in the past so that it will happen to us now. It repeats something that was healing, redemptive, sacred and unique. Alfons Kirchgässner reminds us that repetition in this sense is 'reaffirmation of existence in the flux of change, a confirmation of eternity, assurance for the aimless and uncertain, return to the fullness of life'.

As Christians we celebrate the Eucharist not to recall Jesus's Last Supper, but in remembrance of everything that God has done in Jesus Christ: how he spoke to people through Jesus, healed the sick, encouraged the faint-hearted, called sinners to repentance, and proclaimed the Good News to all humanity. Before all else, however, we recall the death and resurrection of Jesus, in which his whole activity and thinking are, so to speak, intensified. Especially in these ahistorical and unthinking times, it is important to celebrate the memory of redemption as it occurred in the life of Jesus so that we experience it now.

Bernard Rootmensen has explained how our own age reveals its lack of an historical memory in superficiality, oblivion, intoxication and an inability to take the past seriously. The famous Rabbi Baal-Shem Tov remarked once: 'Forgetfulness leads to banishment, but remembrance is the key to redemption.' In the Eucharist we celebrate not only the liberating and illuminating history of Jesus but, through his history, everything that God has done for human beings in history. That is why, during the Eucharist, we listen year after year to the inspiring narratives of the Old and New Testaments. They are like oases in the wilderness, offering us places in which to breathe and recover ourselves. If we ceased to tell one another the great stories of things past in the Bible, the world would lose its soul.

The Eucharist in Luke's gospel

Luke's gospel can help us to understand what we celebrate in the Eucharist. The author of Luke translates Jesus's actions into concepts and terms proper to the world of the Greeks. The Greeks developed the main teachings of their philosophy either in the work of travelling teachers, or 'peripatetics', or during meals (the banquets of Plato, for instance). Luke adopts these two themes and presents Jesus as the divine Wanderer who comes down from heaven to walk with and among humans. As he does so he explains the meaning of their lives. The most beautiful of all itinerant tales is the story of the disciples at Emmaus. It shows clearly how Luke saw the Eucharist. The disciples' hopes have been disappointed and they are in flight, so Jesus explains the mystery of their lives. This is especially relevant to the Eucharist. We go to Mass like people who only too often are running away from themselves, and trying to escape from the disappointments of their lives. Jesus himself approaches us in the readings of the Liturgy of the Word and explains the significance of our own life-histories. The radiance of Holy Scripture should shed light on why everything has happened as it has, the meaning behind it, and where we are heading. To enable the words of the Bible to illuminate our lives, we need an interpretation that translates the biblical symbols into the reality of our own world. If we understand our lives we can handle them appropriately. If we don't understand, we take flight. Many people today are running away from themselves and from the truth of their lives. Jesus invites us to see and understand our lives differently in the Eucharist, in the light of his words and of his liberating and illuminating history. The Eucharist is an interpretation of our lives on the basis of faith in Jesus Christ.

We can find another clue to understanding the Eucharist in the many accounts of meals offered by Luke. For him, the eucharistic meal is the continuation of the meals that Jesus shared with the righteous and unjust, with the innocent and with sinners, during his lifetime. During these meals Jesus enabled people to experience God's loving kindness and friendship for human beings. He offered them divine gifts: love and mercy, unconditional acceptance, forgiveness of sins, and cures for their sickness.

Jesus's meals with sinners and with the righteous are characterized by joy and gratitude for God's healing and liberating presence. Greek philosophers unfolded their teachings to everyone during meals, and Luke describes Jesus as the teacher who proclaims the most important points of his message in the course of meals. His words always remind us of the divine essence within us. Our selves consist of more than the part of us that has to carry out its duties and handle its daily encounters. We possess a divine dignity and value. There is a godly core inside us. The kingdom of God lies within us. We ourselves are God's dwelling-place. That is our essential being and the basis of our worth.

The first meal Luke describes is the one Jesus shared with tax-collectors and sinners (Luke 5.27–39). We are invited to the love feast just as we are, with all our faults and inadequacies. The next meals we are told of take place in the house of a Pharisee. Jesus shows the Pharisees what his message has to do with them. It is about God's love, which he shows to people in his meal, and about the forgiveness which he promises us (Luke 7.36–50). He tells the Pharisees how they have deviated from the love of God (Luke 11.37–54).

Jesus introduces a marvellous eucharistic symbol in the parable of the prodigal, or wasteful and lost, son, which he tells to explain why he accepts sinners and even eats his meals with them. We are like the prodigal son. We are alienated from our own selves and have lost our inner home. We have squandered our inheritance. We have lived beyond our means. Now we have to satisfy our hunger with junk food. And things seem to go from bad to worse. In the Eucharist we pull ourselves together and return to our Father's house. We sense that what we receive there will truly satisfy our hunger. The Eucharist is the festive banquet our Father arranges for us. He is speaking about us too when he says: 'This is my son – I thought he was dead, and he's alive again' (Luke 15.24). And so we should eat and rejoice. We were dead, cut off from our emotions, shut out from life. We lost our true selves. We lost contact with our central point of reference. But in the Eucharist we come to ourselves again and recover vitality by celebrating the Feast of Life. Then we find out who we are and what the real basis of our lives is: that God is waiting for us, and it's never too late to come to our senses and return to our real home.

Jesus shares the last meal before the Last Supper in the house of Zacchaeus, the chief tax-collector. Like Zacchaeus we have inferiority complexes, which we compensate for by scrabbling for as much money and property as possible. We loathe our inferiority and long to be loved for our own sakes and nothing else. That precisely is the experience that should await us in the Eucharist. During this meal Jesus uses the word 'today' twice: 'I must be your guest today' (Luke 19.5); and: 'Salvation has come to this house today!' (Luke 19.9). This mysterious 'today' occurs seven times in Luke's gospel. These occasions correspond to the seven sacraments. What happens in them today happened then. In each celebration of the Eucharist what occurred then comes to pass again. Jesus joins us and shares a meal with us. He tells us his good news. He heals our sickness. We arrive as victims of our lack of self-esteem, like Zacchaeus. We enter as lepers, who can't bear themselves and can't accept themselves. We are the sightless and crippled with all our blind spots and the lameness caused by fear and anxiety. We are bent by, resigned to, deceived by life, and worn down by its burdens. In the Eucharist Jesus helps us up, touches us and says: 'Salvation has come to you today, because you too are a descendant of Abraham and because you too have a divine essence within you!' (cf. Luke 19.9).

In his descriptions of meals Luke indicates what happens in every Eucharist. But for him too the Eucharist is primarily a commemoration of the Last Supper that Jesus shared with his disciples, in which he gave a new meaning to the breaking of bread and to drinking from a cup. Jesus used the Passover rite to show his disciples a new rite. They were to celebrate it regularly after his death in order to renew the memory of his love. Jesus reinterpreted the rites which the Jews celebrated during the Passover meal. The Breaking of Bread points to his imminent death on the cross, where Jesus is broken for us. Yet that isn't a disaster, the failure of his mission, but the way in which his ultimate devotion to us is expressed. He gives himself to his disciples in the broken bread. It is a sign of the love with which he loves us beyond death. It is this love we must realize in each Eucharist. His love is the foundation on which we can build and the source from which we draw life. Jesus interprets the wine as his blood, which is the basis of the new covenant, or agreement. Blood is a symbol of love shed for us. The new covenant, which Jesus recalls at the Last Supper, is the promise of God's unconditional love. The old covenant relied on a reciprocal commitment. God bound himself to human beings on condition that they kept his commandments. But here God binds himself to us out of love. He trusts that the love which becomes evident in his total devotion will transform our hearts.

The question is how we should understand Jesus's symbolic act at the Last Supper. Any philosophical speculation about how Jesus can sacrifice himself in bread and wine will get us nowhere. We can explain the nature of the eucharistic meal only by the experience of human love.

Maria Caterina Jacobelli, an Italian folklorist who has written a book about Easter joy, interprets the mystery of the meal from the perspective of human love:

> Is there a mother or a woman who is a lover, who, when close to the body of her own newborn child or to that of her own husband, has not felt a desire to turn herself into food for this person she loves? Is there a mother who has never longed to receive all over again this body that emerged from her? Is there a lover who, clasping that other body in the embrace of love, has never marked with his or her teeth the flesh of his own wife or that of her own husband? 'I'd like to eat you up with kisses?' Have you never said or heard something like this? It means uniting with the beloved in total oneness, becoming food, changing into life, becoming mutual sustenance, in order to live together in a complete unity that is more complete than sexual union.

Jesus established the Lord's Supper because he wanted to show all people his love in a physical form for ever. It is a token of his love, the place where we shall always be able to rediscover his love and experience it through all our senses. When I eat and chew his body in the form of bread, I can picture that as his loving kiss. When I drink the blood he shed for me in the form of wine, I remember the declaration in the Song of Solomon: 'Your love is sweeter than wine' (S. of S. 4.10).

Many cultures feature sacred meals in which something we sense the need of in every meal becomes reality. In every meal we receive a share in God's gifts, in the gifts of his creation, in the gifts of his love. To that extent we can feel something of God's tenderness and goodness towards us in any meal. The Eucharist is the culmination of everything that people crave in a meal. Whoever enjoys a good meal and has a good appetite can already know union with God in that experience. The Eucharist is intended to show us what happens in every meal: union with the Creator of all gifts. But the Eucharist is also a sacred meal. The early Church compared the Eucharist with the sacred feasts that were celebrated in the mystery cults of the ancient world. A *mysta* or *mystes* was a priest or initiate who took part in the mysteries, or secret rites of divine worship. The participants in these meals believed that they would eat God himself and become one with him as they consumed the sacred food. By eating they not only received the Godhead himself but gave themselves to him. They surrendered their own selves and gave themselves up entirely to the act of eating, in order to experience physical union with God. The religious anthropologist Walter Schubart describes the cultic meal as a 'compounding of the human soul in marital union with the Divinity'. In their communion with God, Christian mystics (Schubart says) 'hymn the sweet savour of the God they taste'. Sometimes during communion nowadays we sing the ancient Latin words: *Gustate et videte quoniam suavis est Dominus* (Taste and see how sweet the Lord is).

Communion is the physical experience of God's love. In every Eucharist we intensify our awareness of this love of God radiating in and from Christ so that we can live by this love, immerse ourselves in it, and become sources of love for others.

The Eucharist in John's gospel

The author of John's gospel, the mystic among the evangelists, has a unique concept of the Eucharist. He tried to show his contemporaries the meaning of the Eucharist in terms of their own intellectual and philosophical interests. They were fascinated by *gnosis*, by gnostic ideas. Gnosticism was an influential movement at the end of the first century AD, rather like our own new-age tendencies in many ways. Gnostics longed for illumination, for true life. They were convinced that there must be something beyond all they knew. John answers them by directing them to the Bread of Heaven God offered them. Jesus himself is this Bread of Heaven. 'I am the bread of life. Whoever comes to me will never be hungry and whoever believes in me will never again be thirsty' (John 6.35). We must not consider the Eucharist apart from Jesus's whole life. The true everlasting life which God gives to people is evident in Jesus, in what he said and in what he did. Jesus as a person whole and entire is the bread that comes down to us from heaven. This bread satisfies our hunger for real life.

John interprets Jesus's life and the action of the Eucharist against the background of the Exodus from Egypt. On their way through the wilderness God gave the Israelites bread from heaven to strengthen them as they travelled onwards. Israel's journey through the desert is like our situation now. We are continually on the way from the land of dependency, alienation and deception to the Promised Land, the land of freedom, the country where we can be entirely ourselves. But on our way we, like the Israelites, long for the fleshpots of Egypt. Our hunger for worldly nourishment is often stronger than our hunger for freedom, life and love. On this way of our longing for true life Jesus offers himself to us as the Bread of Life: 'I myself am the bread of life ... Whoever eats this bread will live for ever' (John 6.48,51). Whoever trusts in Jesus will experience true life. His or her hunger for life will be satisfied. Now, however, at the high point of his explanation of the meaning of the Bread of Life, Jesus says that the bread he will offer is his body, which he will give 'for the life of the world' (John 6.51). The revelation of his love culminates in his death on the cross. Jesus loved us infinitely on the cross. At this culminating point of his love he wants us to share in each celebration of the Eucharist. In the eucharistic bread he offers us his body and gives us his love in physical form. That was unacceptable for the Jews of his time. Today, as well, many people find it incredible. They find it difficult to associate the Eucharist with the terms 'body and blood'. Blood reminds them of brutal scenes in which blood is shed. One woman told me that she couldn't drink from the chalice when the priest offered it to her, saying: 'The blood of Christ.' It reminded her of the slaughter of pigs on her parents' farm. Many people nowadays react similarly. But Jesus answers them in exactly the same way as he did the people then who just couldn't handle the notion: 'My body is real food and my blood is real drink. Whoever eats my body and drinks my blood shares my life and I share theirs' (John 6.55f.).

Jesus's way of talking is not 'bloodthirsty' but the language of love. When we speak the language of love nowadays we also talk of individuals whose hearts bleed for others. For Jesus, body and blood are symbols of his sacrifice on the cross. That was a natural part of the harsh reality of torture and punishment in the Roman world. But for Jesus sacrifice on the cross is the expression of his total and unending love. John uses the Greek word *telos* in this context. *Telos* means 'goal', 'turning-point', 'pivot'. Our fate turns on the pivot of the cross. There, love finally conquers hatred. *Telos* also means: 'initiation into mystery'. On the cross Jesus initiates us into the mystery of divine love. John sees the Eucharist as initiation into God's love, which alone makes our lives truly worth living. By eating (here John refers to 'chewing') the bread and by drinking from the cup we enter into inconceivably profound communion with Jesus Christ. We remain in Jesus Christ and he remains in us. We shall be indistinguishably one with him. We shall be filled and fulfilled by his love. As we are penetrated by it, we experience the nature of real life:

to be loved entirely, to be wholly suffused by divine love and by eternal life.

In the Eucharist we should experience what real life is. This means a life that satisfies our innermost longing. Eternal life is not primarily life after death but a new quality of life that we are meant to experience here and now. It means tasting life in a new way: the taste of a love that makes our life really worth living. The true life we are given in the eucharistic bread is not destroyed by death but in death is revealed as divine life, which is imperishable. The personal relationship with Jesus which we experience in the Eucharist outlasts death. Love is stronger than dying. John's gospel makes several references to the Song of Solomon. There we read: 'Love is strong as death, jealousy is as cruel as the grave. Its flashes are flashes of fire, a most vehement flame. Many waters cannot quench love, neither can floods drown it' (S. of S. 8.6f.). We ought to experience the reality of these words with all our senses in the Eucharist, especially with the sense of taste. We should chew Jesus's love and feel his kiss as we do so. And we should drink a deep draught of his love, so deep that it suffuses our whole body and fills it with the taste of love.

In popular tradition blood is the location of our temperament. If something is in my blood, then it corresponds to my innermost nature. If something enters my body and blood then I have internalized it whole and entire. By eating and drinking the Body and Blood of Jesus we participate in his innermost nature; and this means in his love, which is stronger than death.

Since time immemorial, poets have seen love and death as connected. Only when facing death does love reveal its essential nature and its power to vanquish death. If we were to replace the shocking language of the eucharistic discourse in John's gospel with gentler terminology, the love intended to suffuse us in the Eucharist would lose its real power. Jesus does not offer us a 'la-la-la' love but a love that conquers death and culminates in his ultimate devotion to us on the cross.

The second symbol that John uses to explain the mystery of the Eucharist is that of washing feet. John describes this at the point where the other gospels record the institution of the Eucharist. John sees the washing of feet as a demonstration of Jesus's will to love to the point of absolute devotion (John 13.1ff.). We experience this absolute love in the Eucharist. It is enacted there just as it is expressed in the symbol of washing feet. We arrive with dusty and grubby feet, like the disciples. On our way through the world we have been stained with sin and guilt. We have made our feet sore and injured. So many people have wounded us in our Achilles heel, have repeatedly stabbed us where we are most sensitive. In the Eucharist Jesus bends down to us to touch us tenderly where we are most easily hurt, on our Achilles heel, and to heal our wounds. He bends down to wash the dirt from our feet. He accepts us lovingly, quite without reserve, precisely where we think we are most unacceptable, and know ourselves to be filthy and unclean.

The washing of feet is a symbolic enactment of what happens in every Eucharist. In John's account, too, Jesus asks the disciples to do the same for him. They are to wash one another's feet. Jesus's request not only means that we should serve one another but is essentially an image of the Eucharist. By holding the sacred meal, listening to what Jesus says, and recalling what he did, we behave towards one another as Jesus behaved towards us.

Remembrance for John is primarily commemoration of Jesus's love which he offered us totally in his death on the cross. But the Eucharist signifies not merely commemoration but action. We wash one another's feet in the Eucharist by opening ourselves to Jesus's love, and by not reproaching one another for our mutual guilt but accepting one another unconditionally with the same love that we experience through Jesus. According to John's gospel, the Eucharist is also the place where we should show one another our wounds. We approach the Eucharist not as guiltless but as hurt and grimy individuals. We should not conceal our injuries. We can display them and show them to Christ together. He will wash them and his love will cure them.

At the Last Supper with the disciples, Jesus makes a long farewell speech which discloses a third aspect of the Eucharist as John sees it.

John understands the Eucharist as the place where the risen and exalted Lord appears among his disciples and addresses them. The scene on Easter Eve when Jesus appears among the frightened disciples behind closed doors describes what occurs in every Eucharist. There Jesus, now with God, appears in the assembled community and speaks to them in the language of love. What he says is similar to the statements in his farewell speeches: words radiating his love, which has vanquished death. These words cross the barrier of death, come from eternity and open heaven over us. They join heaven and earth and efface the boundary between death and life. John sees the human inability to love as humanity's most urgent need. What people generally call love is merely clutching at others, clinging to them. Jesus came among us to make us capable of true love. The Eucharist is where we are intended to perceive God's love in Jesus's words, so that we can become capable of loving one another truly again.

Jesus not only addresses the disciples but shows them his hands and side (John 20.20). His pierced hands and opened side are signs of his absolute love for us. In the broken bread we touch the maimed hands he held out to be tortured for us, not abandoning us when they were nailed to the wood of the cross. In the wine we drink the love that flowed for us from his lanced heart. When we touch his wounds in communion we should trust in the miracle by which our own wounds will be healed. In his punctured hands we meet the Jesus who acted for us, who healed the sick and encouraged the faint-hearted. There, the whole history of Jesus becomes our present moment.

The Eucharist as transformation

Medieval theologians were interested mainly in the mystery of the transformation of bread and wine into the Body and Blood of Jesus Christ. This central concern gave rise to the concept of transubstantiation as we know it.

Cardinal Ratzinger explains the abstract notion thus: 'The Lord takes possession of the bread and wine, and so to speak raises them from their basic everyday reality to a new mode of being.' Ultimately, this new order of being is the manifestation of Jesus's love. Essentially, in their most profound significance, bread and wine express Jesus's love. They become something different: the Body and Blood of Jesus, signs of his loving sacrifice on the cross. Modern theologians have tried to express the mystery of this change by using various metaphors. When I choose a book as a gift for a dear friend it contains some part of my love. It is filled with my own thoughts and feelings. If I find someone truly worthwhile and precious, no ordinary present will do; instead, I look for something that will wholly and fittingly remind him or her of me and my affection. Jesus chose broken bread because it most effectively expresses the way in which he allowed himself to be broken in death out of love for us, so that we should not be shattered by the unloving world round about us. He chose wine because it most intensely expresses what he told his disciples in his farewell speeches: 'There is no greater love than this, that someone should lay down his life for his friends' (John 15.13).

We should not restrict the transformation effected in the Eucharist to bread and wine. We display the entire creation before God in the gifts of bread and wine. In the Eucharist we express the truth that the whole world is already utterly suffused with Christ, and that we encounter Christ in all that is. In the bread we also place our everyday existence before the altar. We display everything that annoys and irritates us day by day, the whole unrelated array of things inside us, the confusing multitude of concerns that so often seem about to tear us apart, and all our efforts and labour. The bread is also a symbol of our life-history. It consists of the grain from the ear of corn that has grown in sun and rain, wind and wild weather. We lay ourselves on the altar together with everything that has developed in us and everything that hasn't worked out as well as we would have liked. We don't focus on the wounds of our past life but we don't try to escape them. We offer them to God in the bread. He will send his Holy Spirit over our life and say: 'This is my body.' In the Eucharist God will change everything we bring to him into the body of his Son.

In the cup we offer God not only wine but all the world's joy and suffering. The chalice stands for the afflictions of humankind but also for our longing for true ecstasy, for a love that totally enchants us and elevates us in body and soul. In the chalice we take up our life together with everything that has collected within us, all our pains and desires, joy and suffering, and hold it up for everyone to see. Everything in our chalice is worthy to be raised in the presence of God. Everything can be changed into the blood of Jesus, into love that has become human, and longs to penetrate everything within us.

I realized in a dream I had once that our whole life is transformed in the offerings of bread and wine. I dreamed that I was celebrating Mass together with our Abbot. We adapted the rites, each in his own way. During the offertory we held our watches over the bread and wine so that galloping time would be transformed. Our work, time, restlessness, problems, distraction, cares and everything else were placed on the altar and transformed by God's Spirit flowing down on the offerings, as we asked.

Some people think that because the Eucharist is the feast of God's love, it cannot or should not be celebrated every day. But we can confidently celebrate each day the transformation of our world, our life-histories, our relationships, our work, our worries and our daily grind. When we do so, we express the truth that even during every day's mundane events we are not alone, and that the Eucharist is intended to affect and change even the most banal aspects of our lives. If I believe that in the bread and wine God transforms my world too, I can work more freely, hope with sure trust that everything will not remain as it is, that old conflicts will be resolved, and that everything burdensome will be become lighter.

Every day I can offer something new to be changed. I can ask for the particular thing that concerns me at this moment, or that oppresses me, or makes me less effective, and is an obstacle to leading an effective life, to be transformed. The Eucharist is an expression of my hope that celebrating Jesus's death and resurrection will coax even the stubborn and petrified aspects of my self into new life.

The Eucharist as a sacrifice: an introduction to love

The Catholic Church has always seen the Eucharist as a sacrifice. The Reformers rejected the idea of sacrifice. They thought of the Eucharist only as a meal, as the Lord's Supper. We know now that the Reformation was right to protest against an erroneous notion of sacrifice. Many Catholics today also find the word 'sacrifice' difficult to accept. They are reminded of their schooldays, when they had to make as many sacrifices as possible in order to please God. Or they associate Jesus's sacrifice on the cross with the idea that God demanded this sacrifice from his Son. We must reject errors of this kind and ask what sacrifice does signify in this context.

For one thing, sacrifice means raising something earthly into the realm of the divine; giving it to God because it belongs to God. Sacrifice in this sense is very applicable to our present-day world, in which everything has a mundane use-value, and we have to get something out of it. In the Eucharist we assign our lives to God, from whom we received them. We remove them from the context of the pragmatic and advantageous and put them in their truly meaningful context. They belong to God. We create a free area in which we don't have to make things pay, achieve anything, produce anything. We hold out our lives in the divine realm where they really belong, and receive a God-given presentiment of who we really are.

Sacrifice also means total devotion. When the Bible says that Jesus's death is a sacrifice, it doesn't mean that Jesus fulfilled his love by dying. The Bible certainly doesn't say that God demanded the sacrifice of the cross from his Son. Jesus did not come on earth to die for us but to tell us the good news that God who loves us is close to us. Of course, when he realized that conflict with the Pharisees and Sadducees could result in his violent death, he did not flee but maintained his love for his friends to the point of death. Jesus did not think of his brutal death as failure but as devotion to his friends. He explains this when he talks about the Good Shepherd: 'I am the good shepherd ... And I am giving my life for the sake of the sheep ... No one is taking it from me, but I lay it down of my own free will' (John

59

10.15,18). Accordingly, Jesus's death expresses the love with which he loved us unconditionally, and to the end. It also demonstrates the freedom and total resolution with which he devoted himself to us. By celebrating his death and resurrection in the Eucharist, we place ourselves under the love which he felt for each one of us personally. By celebrating his sacrifice on the cross we assure ourselves that Christ's love touches and transforms everything in us that is hostile and contradictory.

Occasionally the liturgical texts also mention the Church's sacrifice. This does not mean that we achieve something to satisfy God but that we learn the practice of love through Christ's love. We should think of sacrifice more in the sense of 'sacrificing ourselves in the pursuit of something', 'giving ourselves up to something entirely'. Sacrifice means practising the way of love that Christ took before us. By celebrating the Eucharist we acknowledge our readiness to take Christ as our model of dedication. Then we show that we want to love God and our neighbour in the same context of destiny and purpose as Jesus Christ, and to be shaped by Christ in the mould of his love.

When it defines the Eucharist as a sacrifice, the Church stands in the same long tradition as all those religions which conceive of sacrifice as the high point of divine worship and as the source of renewal of life. Jung says that Catholics who interpret the Mass as a sacrifice have the advantage of believing in the value of their own lives. They sense that their lives mean something as far as this world is concerned. By learning the practice of love through Christ's love, and by offering themselves to God as a 'sacrifice' together with Christ, they suffuse the world with Christ's love. Then they contribute to the transformation of the cosmos, to its 'amorization', which is Teilhard de Chardin's term for the permeation of the cosmos with love (*amor* being the Latin for love).

It is inappropriate nowadays to focus our understanding of the Eucharist on the notion of sacrifice. On the other hand, we should not simply discard this ancient and venerable concept, which appears in all religions and is used constantly in the Bible and in

Christian tradition. To do so would mean running the risk of interpreting the Eucharist in a banal and far too circumscribed context of reference. Our lives are too often dry and empty. The Christians of the primitive and early Church believed that their lives were renewed by the force of Christ's love, which empowers the fountain of love in each of us to flow effectively again.

The Eucharist as a mystery: God's vision of humankind

The Eastern churches see the Eucharist primarily as a *mysterium*, or initiation into the secret things of God. This initiation occurs by representing the 'fate' of God in various rites. The early Church in the East understood the Eucharist against the background of Hellenistic mystery cults in which the *mystes* (participants in the celebrations of the mysteries) were initiated into the divine fate. In the Mithraic cult the celebrants took part in the life and death of Mithras and thus shared in his saving and transforming power.

The Greek Fathers of the Church conceived of the Eucharist similarly. For them, we celebrate the fate of Jesus Christ, his Incarnation, miraculous deeds, death and Resurrection. Through this celebration we share in his divine life, which conquered death. Our lives are, so to speak, assumed into the nature of divine life. This assured the early Christians that their lives would be successful just as Jesus's life had succeeded, even beyond the cross. Nothing – this was the experience of Christians in the Eucharist – can separate us from Christ's love. Even death has no power over us. We shall be taken up into the way taken by Jesus Christ. This will lead us to true life, which means to fullness of life characterized by complete joy and perfect love.

Nowadays the word 'mystery' means little if anything to many people. We might replace it with the term 'vision', in the sense of God's vision of humankind. We are not alone in having dreams or visions of what our lives might be. God, too, had a vision of human beings, which became reality in his Son Jesus Christ. This was the ultimate demonstration of God's goodness and loving kindness to us (cf. Titus 3.4). The Greek word *philanthropia* = 'love of humans' (in this context) was translated into Latin as *humanitas* = 'humanity' or 'human image'. The image of humankind as envisioned by God was revealed in Christ. It is the image of a person who is wholly one with God, and permeated with God's goodness and love. The eucharistic rites represent the mystery of the Incarnation of Jesus Christ, God's vision of us human beings becoming one with him. The various actions of mixing (for instance, the commingling of water and wine and the immersion of bread in wine) express our becoming one with God like Jesus.

In the Eucharist we celebrate not only Jesus's Incarnation but his death and Resurrection, the culminating points of his Incarnation. Even the dark abysses of death are transformed by Christ. Even in death we cannot be separated from union with God. By representing the mysteries of Jesus's incarnation and of his death and resurrection, the Church enables us to share in them. Then we are received into the mystery of the way Jesus followed, which leads us to union with God. It also assures us that we can no longer be separated from Christ's love, which makes us indistinguishably one with God.

The Eucharist as the Breaking of Bread

In the primitive Church the Eucharist was called the Breaking of Bread. Luke says of the first Christians in Jerusalem: 'Day by day they met by common consent in the Temple; they broke bread together in their homes, sharing meals with simple joy' (Acts 2.46). The breaking of bread reminds Christians that Jesus had broken bread at the Last Supper and during his meal with the disciples at Emmaus. When the priest breaks the bread the celebrants recall Jesus's death, in which he allowed himself to be broken out of love for them. The breaking of bread represents the culmination of Jesus's love in his sacrifice on the cross. But it also refers to all Jesus's meetings with people in which he shared his healing and liberating self, his time, his strength and love with them. The breaking of bread shows that Jesus did not live for himself but that he broke himself throughout his life in order to share himself and his love with us. Jesus is essentially 'for being' and 'for life'. In the breaking of bread we express our innermost desire that someone should be there for us whole and entire, and to such an extent that he commits himself to us and loves us to the point of death.

When breaking bread the first Christians also recalled the accounts of the multiplication of loaves that we find in all the gospels. The structure of these descriptions of Jesus breaking loaves and giving a blessing is the same as that of the Eucharist. In Mark we read: 'Then he took the seven loaves into his hands, and with a prayer of thanksgiving broke them, and gave them to the disciples to distribute to the people' (Mark 8.6). The breaking of bread here is about sharing. The disciples are to share their bread with the listening crowd.

Dividing and sharing make up an important symbol of the celebration of the Eucharist. The Eucharist is not only an invitation to share our possessions with others, and to give the hungry our bread. Inherently it is a celebration of sharing. We share our time and space with each other. By committing ourselves to this celebration in common, to singing and prayer, and to the people who are eating with us, we share our lives, wishes and aspirations, feelings and needs, fears and hopes with them. By sharing our lives in the Eucharist we create an opportunity for fellowship and hospitality to prevail, resulting in commitment, warmth and mutual concern. Sharing is healing. Sharing makes something fractured whole. The bread we break for each other allows us to hope that what is torn and riven within us will be repaired to the point of wholeness. Then our fragmented lives will come together again. The breaking of bread is also an invitation to break ourselves open for each other, to shatter our emotional armour and open our hearts for each other.

II. CELEBRATING THE EUCHARIST

Many people find the Eucharist boring because it always follows the same pattern. They crave variety. Yet even though feast days or special occasions such as small-group celebrations justify certain changes in specific rites, by its very nature the Eucharist should always be celebrated in the same way. We shouldn't succumb to the pressure of demands for novelty and keep trying to 'stage' it differently, while ignoring the real essence of the Eucharist.

Some people also celebrate the Eucharist every day without any awareness of the significance of individual rites. All the eucharistic rites are intended to represent certain aspects of Jesus Christ's love. They are designed to show us what Jesus did in and for us, and carries out again in us in each Eucharist. Furthermore, the eucharistic rites are rooted in ancient ideas which are to be found in some form in all nations, and express our longing for the transformation, sanctification and redemption of our lives. Therefore I shall describe and explain the rites one by one. At certain points I shall suggest some ways in which this or that rite could be celebrated with a special emphasis for a particular purpose.

Introductory Rites

Every act of worship begins with an introduction that allows entry to the closed, secret and holy area. The Introductory Rites of the Eucharist (or 'fore-Mass') provide us humans emerging from the bustle of our age with the key to the doors of a sacred space. In the liturgy we enter another world. If we wish to gain access to the sacred area of the liturgy, we must detach ourselves from all other preoccupations. Thus the liturgy of St John Chrysostom begins with the hymn: 'All earthly cares let us abandon, the Lord of creation to receive.' So many people today complain that the Eucharist seems to bear no relation to their lives. But it is in the nature of divine worship to transfer us to another world. It is good for us to leave this world whose concerns too often hold us fast, and to enter the eucharistic space, a world where we can discover who we really are and experience ourselves as our souls require.

Our world is so often 'soulless'. The Eucharist nourishes our souls and enables us to contact them, so that in the everyday world we can live an 'ensouled' life, conscious of our divine worth, and assured that we are more than the world that seeks to imprison us.

Like all forms of worship, the Eucharist contains a number of introductory rites. The celebration starts with the 'Introit', or entrance hymn. The congregation sing as they enter the mystery of love which God wishes them to perceive in the Eucharist. The priest has already prepared for the celebration when putting on his vestments in the sacristy. As he takes up each piece of sacred clothing he says a special prayer. Together with the acolytes or servers he has silently composed himself for the sacred action. Then the doors to the church are opened. At this point priests in the Eastern Church say: 'Now, Lord, I shall enter your house and pray to you in your temple in holy awe.' Then the priests and servers bow before the altar and mount the steps.

The priest kisses the altar. His kiss expresses tenderness and love. A kiss is the most intense form of touch we can offer each other. The altar symbolizes Christ. When kissing the altar the priest touches Christ in order to receive his strength and love. By this he shows that he does not celebrate the Eucharist by himself but by virtue of Christ's strength and love. He kisses the altar to inhale the divine atmosphere and drink from the fountain of life. The priest touches the altar several times during the Mass to make sure that he is acting by the power of the altar.

The Sign of the Cross is the key that opens the doors to the space of love for Christians as they enter the Eucharist. When the early Christians signed themselves with the cross, they showed that they belonged to God and not to the world, that no earthly ruler could dominate them. For them it was an honourable distinguishing mark. By making this sign they engraved Christ's love on their bodies. We bless ourselves when we make the sign of the cross. First we touch our forehead, then our chest, then our shoulders, left then right. By this we show that Jesus Christ loves everything in us: our thoughts, vitality and sexuality, our unconscious and conscious mind. And so we begin the Eucharist with the sign of love, to show the real purpose of the celebration from the start. The Mass is about really experiencing Christ's love. We accompany the sign of the cross with the Trinitarian formula: 'In the name of the Father and of the Son and of the Holy Spirit.' For many people this has become something like a mere rhetorical embellishment. But it is very meaningful, for as we say these words we acknowledge the fact that God is not some distant and unapproachable deity, but the God who is open for us, and allows us to share in the very movement and system of his love. The significance of the words can be emphasized by extending them, as in the Syrian church, and by making the sign of the cross very slowly and deliberately: 'In the name of the Father, who conceived of and created us, and of the Son, who descended into the depths of our humanity, and of the Holy Spirit, who turns dark to light, and who transforms the unconscious and unknown in us so that it is directed to God.'

After the sign of the cross, the priest greets the congregation with the assurance that the Lord himself is with them, together with his peace, grace and love. This is to make clear that it is not the priest who presides over the Mass, but Christ himself who is among us as the actual source of the celebration.

Then, after a brief introduction to the Mass of the day, comes the Penitential Rite. Many people today find this off-putting. They think they are being asked to feel like poor sinners whom the Church somehow wants to humiliate before generously pronouncing an absolution over them. But the meaning of the confession here is that we come to this encounter with Christ along with everything in us: with our light and dark sides, successes and failures, hits and misses, and guilt. We mustn't humiliate ourselves. Instead Christ invites us to bring with us those aspects of ourselves that we would rather leave outside because we dislike them so. Confession will encourage us to celebrate the Eucharist as whole people and to take more than our 'pious' side to the meeting with God. Even at the beginning of the celebration we are told that the Eucharist is the experience of God's forgiving love, which accepts us unconditionally.

The congregation, especially a small group, can shape the greeting and penitential rite in a particular way. They might open the service with a meditation dance and announce special intentions for the celebration. Instead of the formal confession they can mention their own problems or dangers for their environment, or represent them in dramatic form. During a course at Pentecost one group mimed a pool which they could enter, and showed what could be left there, and what could be washed away.

Sometimes I arrange the penitential rite as a sequence of three gestures. First people cup their hands, and I say a prayer, something like the following:

In our hands we hold out to God everything we have taken into our hands, and shaped and formed with our hands, and everything that we have succeeded in doing, but also our failures. We hold out the hands we have offered to others and we have held back from others. We hold out everything that has marked our hands, so that God can bless all this with his kind and loving hands.

Then we turn our hands palms downwards:

We are letting go of everything to which we cling. We are burying everything that is in the past: everything that oppresses us, everything for which we reproach each other. In this gesture we show that we no longer intend to use the past to accuse others or to excuse our own inadequacies. We also let go of our guilt. We bury it so that we can rise again with Christ from the grave of our self-deprecation and self-pity.

Then we hold out our hands to each other, and offer God our relationships together with everything that unites and everything that separates us:

We hold out to God our good relationships so that he can bless them. And we show God the relationships that are blocked by misunderstanding and emotional troubles, so that his healing love can flow between us again.

It can be left to the group's creative imagination to shape this rite appropriately, but no pressure must be exerted. This kind of adaptation is very suitable for specific feast days and group services.

After the penitential rite comes the Kyrie. Essentially, this is a series of invocations of the glorified Lord. When these are sung in Greek I feel that the glorified Lord is present among us in the singing itself. We are addressing Someone in our midst. Our singing makes his image all the clearer. It is like a lover serenading his beloved. As he sings she appears before him and he feels deeply united with her. In group services I ask the participants to address Christ by the name or in terms of the image that occurs to them spontaneously: 'Christ, our Brother. Christ, Good Shepherd, Friend of the Poor, Lover, Light of the World.' It is amazing to discover how many names for Jesus people like to use. As each person addresses Christ with his or her special name for him we realize all the more surely who is present among us. This helps to produce an inward relationship to Jesus who is in our midst to fulfil our deepest longings.

On Sundays and feast days, though not in Advent and Lent, the Kyrie is followed by the Christmas hymn 'Gloria': 'Glory to God in the highest, and peace to his people on earth.' This is a joyful song about the mystery of our salvation. Then comes the Opening Prayer, when the priest asks the people to join in a brief prayer connected with the Mass of the day.

The Readings

The Liturgy of the Word begins with the First and Second Readings and the Gospel. The arrangement and choice of readings were introduced after the Second Vatican Council, and provide a rich selection of biblical texts. The Word is effective in its own right. We must be attentive in order not only to hear the words through our ears but to ensure that they drop into our hearts. Then we must be silent so that the Word can sink into our hearts. When the Word enters our hearts it will do its work there, but to ensure that it is received in the first place the reader must speak the words from the depths of his or her own heart. People have to sense that this is a committed reading, that the reader is moved by the texts. What is said in the readings and Gospel is not intended primarily to tell us what we should do but who we are. The mystery of our lives is expounded in the readings from the Old and New Testaments. In the Gospel, Jesus Christ himself appears in our midst. He speaks to us himself and acts on and in us as the text proclaims. Before the priest proclaims the Gospel for the day he signs the book and then himself on forehead, mouth and breast, and the faithful do the same. This threefold gesture states that every word is an expression of the love with which Christ loved us to the point of ultimate devotion, and that we want this love to affect our thinking, speaking and feeling.

To make sure that the Word means even more to its hearers, the priest or specially commissioned men and women comment on it in a sermon. The sermon should emphasize and make the congregation more aware of what we are celebrating in the Eucharist. If no sermon is preached, it is helpful sometimes to say a few words (a homily) about the relevance of the readings or Gospel to our lives. This can be done, for example, during the introduction to the Prayer of the Faithful, or Bidding Prayer(s). What is announced in the Gospel becomes reality in the Eucharist, and is represented in the sacred drama. We shall encounter Jesus physically in communion. This contact with him can heal our wounds, dissolve our fear, turn our sadness into joy, our rigidity into vitality, and our coldness into love.

Prayer of the Faithful, or Bidding Prayer(s)

On Sundays we say the Creed after the sermon, in order to 'confess' or acknowledge our faith. Many people find this too abstract a practice. But every sentence in the Creed expresses the mystery of our lives redeemed by Christ.

Then come the Bidding Prayers, Intercessions, or Petitions (known collectively as the Prayer of the Faithful), in which we bring the whole world into the context of our worship. On special occasions, these prayers are an opportunity for the creative abilities of the congregation to get to work. If appropriate, members of the congregation can devise and say their own spontaneous bidding prayers. In group services or on feast days when light is a central theme (such as Candlemas, the Immaculate Conception, Christmas, St Lucy, and so forth), the priest can invite members of the congregation to light a candle or a night light for some particular purpose and to place it on the altar or before an icon. During services for a specific profession or an association, some representatives of the group or organization could associate their petition with a symbol by choosing something characteristic of their vocation or group activity, bringing it to the altar and praying appropriately.

In group services I sometimes combine the preparation of the gifts and the bidding prayers by circulating the paten or dish on which the unconsecrated hosts are collected. Each person takes the paten and, either silently or in his or her own words, places (as it were) a concern or interest in the dish. He or she might say, for example: 'I am putting my dullness of heart, my inner commotion, my anxieties, my inadequate self-esteem in this dish. I want to place my sister here, because she is so worried about her children,' and so on. Then the paten is handed to the next person, and to the next, until it comes back to me. Then I raise it and say a prayer over everything that we have put in it. And I ask God to change everything there when he changes the bread into the Body of Christ.

Preparation of the Gifts, or Offertory

The Preparation of the Gifts begins with the Procession with the Gifts, or Offertory Procession, which is not so general a practice as in the past. Its deep meaning is that we actually bear our world before God. When the celebrants or representatives of the congregation take the paten(s) and chalice(s) slowly and carefully to the altar, they bring before God the paten revealing the fracture of our world and the chalice disclosing the suffering and longing of all humanity.

The Eucharist is more than a pious private celebration by a group of Christians. A changing effect for the whole world will radiate from the transformation of the bread and wine. Christ died for the whole world and, as he rose again, raised it too. Christ is among us and working in us now, so the scope of our Eucharist is nothing less than the entire cosmos.

The Elevation of the Gifts is one of the main symbolic enactments of this process. This gesture extends the offerings into the divine realm. We acknowledge the truth that everything comes from and belongs to God. We praise God for the good things which he gives us every day and in which we can know his loving kindness physically. But in this elevation we also appeal to God to ensure that his healing and liberating power will work its mighty effects throughout his creation now, reconciling all that is disjointed and repairing all the fractures between us. As we reach into God's presence with the gifts, we offer our lives to him, knowing that he alone can make our existence true and whole.

Another easily overlooked rite is prescribed during the Preparation of the Gifts. The priest pours wine and a little water into the chalice and says: 'By the mystery of this water and wine may we come to share in the divinity of Christ, who humbled himself to share in our humanity', or similar words. The Commingling, mixing of water and wine, stands for God becoming human in Jesus Christ. Just as God took on a human nature, so we share in God's nature through the Eucharist. We become one with God just as water and wine have become one indistinguishably. Water and wine are inseparable now. Now we cannot divide the divine from the human within us.

Rites of mixture appear in almost all religious cults. They express the union of separates in order to restore the original unity of Paradise, where there is no division. 'The wolf shall dwell with the lamb, and the leopard shall lie down with the kid, and the calf and the lion and the fatling together ... The cow and the bear shall feed; their young shall lie down together; and the lion shall eat straw like the ox' (Isa. 11.6f.). Neither the mixture of water and wine, nor the union of God and human in Jesus Christ, nor that worked in us through him, can be reversed. Ignatius of Antioch (d. 110 AD) writes: 'We are his Body and Spirit mixed.' Cyril of Alexandria (d. 444 AD) says: 'Though our physical nature makes us perishable, this admixture will cancel that fragility and endow us with the unique quality of his (Christ's) Nature.' The mixture of wine and water shows how seriously we take God's becoming human, his incarnation, in the Eucharist. It gives us a new sense of the meaning of our existence. To know that God's life and love are flowing in me and can no longer be separated from me gives me a more fitting idea of my dignity and value as a Christian.

The Eucharistic Prayer, or Canon of the Mass

After the Preparation of the Gifts comes the central rite of the Eucharist, the Eucharistic Prayer. It is introduced by the Preface, a hymn of praise for God's saving action towards us. The congregation answer the Preface with an acclamation, the 'Sanctus', or 'Holy, holy, holy', thus joining in the angels' song of praise. This shows that the celebrating community is not closed in on itself but a window is opening into heaven for its members, so that they can participate in the heavenly liturgy. I always find it very moving when we concelebrate in the abbey and sing the 'Sanctus' standing together round the altar. Then I feel that I am singing it in the company of all my brothers who lived and praised God here in the past, that heaven is opening above us, and that heaven and earth are touching each other now.

Then the priest says the Eucharistic Prayer, for which several versions are prescribed. In its first part (the 'Post Sanctus') the Eucharistic Prayer continues the praise initiated in the Preface. Then, in the 'Epiclesis', the Holy Spirit is asked to descend on the gifts of bread and wine, to change them into the Body and Blood of Christ. The priest extends his hands over the gifts to shows that the life-giving Spirit of God is poured out over bread and wine in order to transform them into Christ's Body and Blood. Then comes the Consecration, which always follows the main lines of the formula handed down by the evangelists and St Paul.

After the consecration the priest elevates the Host and the chalice containing the Wine so that everyone can see them. Everyone must be aware of the mystery of Christ's presence among us, and everyone must look up at him. 'For it was *life* that appeared before us' (1 John 1.2). Here this statement is reality. The meaning of this rite has always been sharing in the mystery of the Lord apparent and perceived. The Israelites' snake-bites were healed when they looked at the brazen image of the serpent. When they gazed at the Host the faithful in the past hoped that their wounds would be healed by its sacred power. When the consecrated Host was shown to the congregation the line from the Psalms became reality: 'Restore us, O God of hosts; let your face shine, that we may be saved!' (Ps. 80.7). The priest always follows the elevation by genuflecting, by kneeling in prayer before the mystery of God's love which now shines forth for us in Jesus Christ. The congregation answer the priest's 'Let us proclaim the mystery of faith' with the words: 'When we eat this bread and drink this cup, we proclaim your death, Lord Jesus, until you come in glory', or 'My Lord and my God', or a similar formula, depending on the country and occasion.

The consecration proper is followed by the 'anamnesis', a prayer in which we consider all God's redemptive and liberating acts in Jesus Christ, recalling especially Jesus's Death, Resurrection and Ascension. Everything that God has done in Jesus Christ is now here among us and for us. The effects of his healing, liberating and saving power will be felt in us and in the whole world. This prayer is followed by petitions for the Church, for the parish or community assembled here, and for the dead with whom the congregation are united. The Eucharistic Prayer closes with the 'doxology', or praise, and the congregation answer with the 'Great Amen'. During the doxology the priest elevates the gifts of bread and wine to show that Christ himself is the actual Celebrant and Petitioner. God will bestow glory and honour on everyone through Christ. Earlier, the priest held the Host over the raised chalice. This has a deep meaning, for the round Host stands for the Sun who in the Resurrection has vanquished all darkness for ever. The chalice containing Jesus's Blood symbolizes the depths of the soul into which the Sun casts his light, and the countless ranks of the dead who are transformed by the resurrection. The chalice also stands for the maternal earth from which Christ rises as the Sun.

Altogether, this brief rite expresses the mystery of the Resurrection. On the morning of the Lord's rising from the dead, the women came to the tomb 'just as the sun was rising' (Mark 16.2). In the Resurrection Christ has risen as the true Sun. 'The people who sat in darkness have seen a great light, and for those who sat in the region and shadow of death light has dawned' (Matt. 4.16). Now Christ's sun shines out over all those many tombs where we dwell, over the graves of our fear, our resignation and our depression. God will give everyone honour and glory in the risen Lord. Through him and in him we ourselves share in God's glory.

The Communion Rite

The Lord's Prayer introduces the Communion Rite. The Fathers of the Church tell us why we say the Our Father before communion, especially with regard to the two petitions: 'Give us this day our daily bread' and 'Forgive us our trespasses as we forgive those who trespass against us'. From Origen onwards, the Fathers maintained that the eucharistic bread was the form of bread appropriate to our spiritual nature. Augustine sees the plea for forgiveness as a form of washing one's face before approaching the altar. In our abbey not only the priests but all the monks pray the Our Father either with hands raised or with hands extended and cupped. Many laypeople use the same gestures. Of course you always have to be well aware of the type of congregation before recommending any such practice. Some people are nervous about gestures because they have to show their feelings. Individuals have to know that they are completely free in this respect. There is no compulsion to follow the crowd. But if everyone finds certain gestures acceptable in a liturgy, the effect can be powerful and impressive and make a service much more intense and profound. Our open hands, for instance, can make us all sense the Spirit of Jesus flowing into our world and permeating it with his love.

After the Lord's Prayer, the priest prays for peace in the world and invites everyone to offer the Sign of Peace. Here, too, I advise caution and respect for the inhibitions some people have about approaching one another. In group services there is always a danger of majority pressure forcing people to embrace each other and make a sign of peace when they find it embarrassing. With goodwill, however, this sign of peace can express our joint celebration and our readiness to accept one another, for we intend to unite in communion with Christ and with the whole congregation.

The Sign of Peace is followed by the Breaking of the Bread, or Fraction of the Host. The congregation are often unaware of this apparently minor action by the priest. But it is an important part of the rite. The early Christians often called the whole Eucharist the Breaking of Bread. The breaking of the bread is a symbol of Christ's readiness to be broken on the cross for us, so that life can no longer break us. He broke himself open in order to heal our fractures and unite the fragments of our lives. The breaking of the bread reminds us that we too are shattered and injured people, but that the resurrected Christ towers over all our fragments to make everything true and whole again.

After the breaking of the bread, the priest dips a tiny piece of the Host in the chalice. The early Christians saw this action, known as 'tincture', as an image of Christ's Resurrection. Body and Blood are symbols of Jesus's sacrifice on the cross; similarly, the immersion of the bread in the wine stands for the union of Jesus's Body and Blood in the Resurrection. I see this as a moving symbol of the healing of the cleavages in my life when they are immersed in Christ's love, which fills the chalice. My life is restored to wholeness when it is dipped in the blood of Jesus, who died and rose for me.

The Fathers called the bread dipped in the wine *fermentum*, or 'leaven'. They interpreted this brief action as a symbol of the union of Christ's earthly and heavenly nature. At this point in their liturgy the Syrian Jacobites say the following prayer: 'Lord, you have mingled your Godhead with our humanity and our humanity with your Godhead, your life with our mortality . . . you take on what was ours and have given us what is yours so that our souls may live and be healed.'

The commingling of bread and wine also recalls the union of man and woman. Jung sees bread as female and wine as male. Accordingly, this action expresses our longing for union, for the sacred marriage in which anima and animus are no longer opposed but fertilize, or fructify, each other, and become one in the unity for which God made us. The bread and wine stand for solid and liquid, and for all contraries in this world. They become one in the process of immersion. Similarly, all those aspects of ourselves that so often conflict with each other are always capable of uniting to form a whole. The liturgy of St Basil the Great calls the mingling of the bread and wine the moment of 'sacred unification'.

Then the priest elevates the Host, saying: 'This is the Lamb of God who takes away the sins of the world.' These are the words with which John the Baptist told his disciples to follow Christ. In the bread the priest shows us Christ, the Redeemer and Saviour, who loved us infinitely. These words invite me, just as I am, to look up at Christ and find my salvation in him. Neither my sins nor my feelings of guilt need stop me now from actually experiencing God's love in communion. When I hear this reference to the Lamb of God, I always hear, too, the words with which John ended his testimony on behalf of Jesus: 'Now I have seen this happen and I declare publicly before you all that he is the Son of God!' (John 1.34). Everyone answers with the words of the centurion to Jesus when he said he would heal the officer's servant: 'I am not worthy.' Many people find these words difficult to say. They associate saying they're not important enough with their experiences when their parents or the Church made them feel 'small'. I can quite understand how these people feel. But I don't think that these negative echoes justify dismissing the quotation. One non-Catholic Christian told me when we were discussing these words that this was his favourite among all the sayings in the Catholic liturgy. We shouldn't feel inferior when we repeat this statement but see how it deepens our awareness of the mystery of communion, when we receive the Son of God. This is not a fragment of bread, although some people nowadays receive it as carelessly as if it were just that. It is Christ himself who is coming to heal me. The centurion who said he wasn't important enough for Jesus to enter his house wasn't abasing or humiliating himself. He explained to Jesus that he had soldiers under him: 'I can say to one man "Go" and I know he'll go, or I can say "Come here" to another and I know he'll come' (Matt. 8.9). Yet he sensed that he was honoured by Jesus's visit to his house. He felt that he was not worthy to receive him under his roof, and that it would be sufficient if Jesus were merely to 'give the order', or 'just say the word' (Matt. 8.8). That was all that was needed. Then his servant would recover. The liturgy changes the word 'servant' to 'my soul'. The soul is the servant of life. If our soul is sick then the whole person is affected and impaired. The words we use to answer the priest's invitation are also an expression of respect for Jesus, who is visiting us and about to enter our house. Our response also shows our trust that Jesus will heal our soul in communion, that the encounter with Jesus will free us from confusion and make us whole and well, and that our wounds will be transformed by union with Christ.

Then the priests and lay assistants distribute communion. Communion should be experienced as a meeting with Christ, so the priest shows the Host to each person and says: 'The Body of Christ.' The intention is that the communicant should recognize Christ himself in this piece of bread, for Christ himself is entering his or her house in order to heal his or her innermost being. In the fourth century Cyril of Jerusalem described how we should receive communion: 'When you approach, do not go stretching out your open hands or having your fingers spread out, but make the left hand into a throne for the right which will receive the King, and then cup your open hand and take the Body of Christ, reciting the *Amen*. Then sanctify your eyes with the utmost care by touching the Sacred Body, and receive It.' To receive Christ on your open or in your cupped hand is a respectful way of taking the sacrament. Fourth-century communicants also touched their eyes with the Body of Christ. If their lips were still moist after receiving the Blood of Christ they touched them with their hands to sanctify their eyes, forehead and the other senses. In the communion rite Christians at that time signified their awareness that Jesus also touched their blind eyes so they might see, and opened their ears so that they might speak and listen in the right way. They showed that they were meeting Jesus Christ through their senses.

In the Middle Ages, fear of infection led to withdrawal of the chalice from the laity. But there were other ways of protecting communicants. In some places they dipped the bread in the chalice. In Rome they used tubes or reeds like our present-day straws to drink from the chalice. Nowadays, when appropriate, the chalice should be offered to everyone, for instance during group Masses, at weddings, at weekday Masses, on Holy Thursday and on Corpus Christi. In Christ's Blood we drink God's love become flesh so that it can permeate our entire body and suffuse us with the taste of love. As I take the chalice I can think of Christ's healing power flowing into all the wounds and sick areas of my body and soul. Or I might recall these words from the Song of Solomon: 'Your love is sweeter than wine', (S. of S. 4.10) and realize that I am experiencing Christ's love physically.

After the prayer of the faithful the priest may say something like: 'Whoever eats this Bread will live for ever.' I like to repeat some words from the Bible during Communion. This will show that what is described in the Bible is happening to us now. If the reference is to an account of healing I sometimes say: 'I want to be whole!' or: 'Jesus said to the cripple: "Stand, pick up your bed and walk!"' When the chalice is offered, I recall the healing of the woman who had had a haemorrhage for twelve years (Mark 5.25–34): 'The Blood of Christ to save you from bleeding'; or: 'May Christ's Blood heal your wounds.' Or I quote from a parable that throws light on a quite different aspect of receiving communion. This will help to ensure that communion is not seen as always the same rite but in the sense that Jesus can always meet me in a different form and affect me in another way. This will remind me that he treats me now exactly as he treated the sick people and sinners of his own time, and that in communion I receive his words become flesh so that in the depths of my heart that flesh will transform my own body and soul as it did theirs.

After communion it is appropriate to observe a period of silence, so that our union with Christ can also penetrate our hearts and occur through all our senses. These moments of quiet can give us time for a personal conversation with Christ, who is in us now. They can also allow us simply to recollect what we have celebrated, the penetration of Christ's Body and Blood into my entire body and into the innermost layers of my soul; and the mystery of communion, of God becoming indistinguishably one with me. Now I must put into practice in my life what God has done for me here. If God has become one with me, then I can be reconciled with myself and with my life, and reach a new personal harmony. If Christ is in all of us, I too must try to feel an inward sympathy for everyone, and to feel united with them.

The Concluding Rite, or Dismissal of the Faithful

After a suitable time for silent recollection, the priest recites the concluding prayer, blesses the congregation, and dismisses them in peace. The faithful should return to their everyday lives as blessed people, and become sources of blessing and peace wherever they are. They should be channels for the peace of Christ entering the world. They have not only celebrated the Eucharist on their own behalf but are 'ambassadors' who are to proclaim on Christ's behalf: 'Make your peace with God!' (2 Cor. 5.20).

At a group Mass I sometimes invite those present to bless each other by making the sign of the cross on their neighbour's hand and expressing a particular wish for him or her. The hand with its many lines is a symbol of our life. It is said that if you can read a person's hand you can discern the truth about him or her. We sign the cross on these lines inscribed in the hand to acknowledge the fact that all lines are enclosed in God's love, that God can transform all roads into pathways of salvation, that he extends his loving hand over us to protect and heal us, and that we are carried and cradled in the hand of God.

The eucharistic celebration closes as meaningfully as it began. The Concluding Rite is like a key turned to make sure that the doors are really shut and that the participants have really prepared for their departure. The Eucharist concludes with a blessing, so that all those who have celebrated it can return to the everyday world bearing a blessing. They are released with the words: 'Go in the peace of Christ', or 'The Mass is ended, go in peace', or 'Go in peace to love and serve the Lord.' The peace of God which they experienced in the Eucharist is to accompany them on their way. They will not return to their familiar surroundings unprotected. Those who were present at the mysteries within the church will carry its effects with them, and in that sense the church door never truly closes behind them.

The priest kisses the altar again in order to take its power with him and say a loving farewell to Christ. Now the love of Jesus, which is celebrated on the altar, should be impressed on his conversation and behaviour and flow into all his encounters. The congregation sing a final hymn or leave as the organ plays. Many people remain seated for a while in silence, so that the mystery of the sacred celebration can penetrate their bodies and souls, and they can assure themselves that they will make their way out not as they entered but as transformed individuals who can now change the ordinary world around them.

III. EUCHARISTIC LIFE

It is very important to me, as a priest, to celebrate the Eucharist every day if possible. I never find it tedious. The mystery of the transformation of bread and wine into the Body and Blood of Christ and my becoming one with Christ in communion never fails. I need to celebrate the Eucharist as an introduction to my daily life, so that I can experience each day's events from this central point of my faith.

I find it difficult to describe the effect of the Eucharist and of its transforming power on my ordinary existence. But I certainly experience the Eucharist as a kind of oasis which I come upon day after day and where I can drink from the source of life. It is the daily sustenance that gives me strength to face the demands of the next twenty hours.

Life and the words of the Eucharist

Each person lives by the Eucharist in a different way. Some people find it important to meditate on the eucharistic readings and to choose a daily passage that will accompany them throughout the day. Such excerpts consist for the most part of words taken from the eucharistic celebration and applied to everyday life to mark it indelibly. The quotations usually chosen act like a pair of spectacles through which I view everything that happens. But the words heard during the Eucharist are more than an arbitrary selection of phrases from Scripture used for meditation. They are words proclaimed throughout the world this very same day. They are words which have become all the more important because the Word has become flesh in the Eucharist. They have become actual in the Body and Blood of Jesus. I not only heard them with my ears but ate and drank them, and incorporated them in my body. I have become one with them. Now these words are intent on becoming incarnate in my everyday life. They want to take on flesh in my existence and to transform it.

Living through communion

Other people are more inclined to live on the basis of their communion experience. They find it essential to remember throughout the day that they are not acting alone but that Christ in them is the very source of life and love. They constantly recall how they became one with Christ and that they lead their lives on the basis of their inner relationship with him. They perceive Christ not only in themselves but in their brothers and sisters. This changes the way in which they treat them. They believe that they encounter Christ everywhere. In communion they also became one with all people, for whom Christ died and whom he encircles with his love.

The memory of the Eucharist can penetrate everyday conflicts and remind us that everyone has a good centre, that everyone longs to be like the Christ within, and that ultimately we all suffer from some form of antagonism. Faith in Christ in others helps us to believe in the goodness in others and to detect it in them.

The daily altar

Yet others consider it important to see the altar on which their own self-offering is made as their daily life. They celebrated Jesus's sacrifice for them and their own offering of themselves to God on the altar in church, and now put this into practice in the loyalty with which they carry out their everyday tasks, devote themselves to their profession or vocation, and serve the people for whom they have become responsible in the family, at work, or in the parish. Their work becomes a kind of divine service, a continuation of the Eucharist. Ultimately, all work is a matter of devotion and sacrifice. We give ourselves up to a task or to a service. We sacrifice our strength and attentiveness to people and things. The sacrifice of the altar continues in, and extends into, our everyday labours and our world. It is often more difficult to carry out the sacrifice of dedication on the altar of our daily lives than to celebrate it to the accompaniment of festive hymns under a lofty church roof.

Work is concerned with transforming this world so that it grows more and more open to Christ and people can recognize Christ in it. It is as if they were uttering the words of the *epiclesis* spoken over the bread and wine in the Eucharist, but now over their work, their discussions, their desk and their household tasks: 'Father, may this Holy Spirit sanctify these offerings. Let them become the body and blood of Jesus Christ our Lord.' The Holy Spirit, who has changed the bread and wine into the Body and Blood of Christ, also transforms their everyday life. They can say over all their endeavours: 'This is my body . . . This is the cup of my blood.' In all they do, they meet Christ as the basis of all existence.

The transformation of our everyday life through the Eucharist also continues another form of encounter with things, with people and with the creation. We show the people whom we meet the same respect with which we received Christ in communion. Christ himself wants to enter us in them too. St Benedict lived on the basis of this eucharistic piety when he required the cellarer to handle all the monastic containers and tools as if they were sacred altar vessels. He had to treat them as carefully as the Body and Blood of Christ in the Eucharist.

Ultimately, in everything we touch we come into contact with the love of Christ, which flows through the entire creation.

The Eucharist and everyday meals

Anyone who takes the Eucharist seriously will also eat his or her meals in a totally different way. Some part of the mystery of the Eucharist shines forth in every meal. What we eat consists of God's gifts to us, interfused with his Spirit, with his love. Therefore we should eat our food with care and attention. Ultimately, every meal is a celebration of God's love. God cares for us and loves us. Only if we chew our bread slowly and consciously can we become properly aware of how good it tastes. As we taste it we begin to sense something of the love of God that makes the flavour of our lives so very distinct.

People have always seen eating as a mystery. Accordingly, the Sacred Meal is the summit of all meals. The Sacred Meal also casts its light on everyday eating, which is more than the mere satisfaction of our hunger. We are not just stuffing ourselves indifferently until we reach saturation point, but consuming victuals. These are substances which not only sustain but convey life, and in which we encounter an aspect of the life God gives us. St Benedict placed monastic meals in a setting that brought out their ritual aspect. They are like an *agape*, a continuation of the love feast celebrated by Christ and his disciples.

This is expressed in the graces, or prayers before and after meals, but also in the readings during meals in which, while we eat God's gifts, we hear the word of God reminding us that everything comes from him and is suffused with his love.

Eucharistic devotions, or visits to the Blessed Sacrament

For some people visits to the Blessed Sacrament are their preferred way of living on the basis of the Eucharist. They return to a church during the day and kneel before the tabernacle or wherever the Host is reserved. They believe that the eucharistic wafer or bread kept in the tabernacle is Christ himself. By meditation they enter the space of the love in which he offered himself for us. The eucharistic bread reminds them of the love with which Jesus on the cross loved them to the point of death and beyond. Then they put their everyday lives in that space, with all its conflicts, and with their aggression, dissatisfaction, wounds and disappointments. Then, sometimes, they experience a transformation of their daily lives, and their upset minds and distraught emotions are calmed.

Many churches still practise a form of eucharistic devotion during Benediction, when the eucharistic bread is placed in a monstrance and displayed to the congregation. They contemplate the round Host visible before them and pray out of their conviction that it is Christ himself. As I look at the Host I come to realize not only that this bread is now the Body of Christ but that this transformation embraces the whole world. Christ has become the innermost mid-point of all reality. As I gaze at the transformed bread I see this world with new eyes, and everywhere I look I recognize Christ as the very ground of all that is, and know that his love runs through everything.

This was the decisive experience for Teilhard de Chardin, the French Jesuit and anthropologist. Meditation on the Eucharist showed him that Christ's love flows from the Host into every part of the world. When I become one with the Host which I contemplate in meditation, I realize that Christ is in me too. Then I try to picture him entering and filling all the rooms in the house of my life, even those where indignation has lodged or that are littered with the everyday garbage of life's confusion.

Eucharistic meditation is a liturgy of the heart and a continuation of what we celebrated together in the Eucharist. It is more than mere looking, for when we look at the Host we retrain our contemplative understanding until it becomes a new vision of the reality of our lives.

Reminders of the Eucharist

Spiritual tradition offers us many reminders of how to live on the basis of the eucharistic mystery. Church bells, for instance, invite us to attend Mass. Many people who have no time to go to Mass on working days are reminded of it when the bells ring out. This thought alone will alter their everyday thinking. In my church the bells ring during the consecration too. This challenges many people to concentrate for a moment and consider how the transformation of the elements during the Eucharist changes their actual daily lives. Others are reminded of the Eucharist whenever they walk or drive past a church. I was always impressed when my father removed his hat on passing a church. He was showing his respect for the Eucharist, which was celebrated in that church every day.

Not so long ago it was customary to make what was a called a 'spiritual communion'. When people had no opportunity to attend a Eucharist, they would transfer themselves spiritually to the celebration of Mass in order to sanctify their lives through the Eucharist and offer themselves to God together with Christ. The purpose of this traditional devotion was to see everyday life as eucharistic, as an occasion for thanking God and as an offering to God.

The decisive aspect of all such devotional reminders is that the Eucharist should not be restricted to the short space of its actual celebration but take effect in our entire lives, transforming everything within us and round about us. Then, wherever we are, we encounter the love with which Christ loved us unto death and beyond.

IV. THE EUCHARIST AS A SACRED DRAMA

In the Eucharist we celebrate the very centre of our faith. But this also means that all the problems of our faith and our difficulties in living together are concentrated and intensified here. It is not a question of devising a few cosmetic effects to make the Eucharist more attractive. What is really called for is learning how to express our belief as people living in the present-day world, so that we rediscover ourselves and our ultimate longing and purpose in the Eucharist, and experience Jesus Christ as our Redeemer and Saviour, as our Liberator, and as the one who shows us what our lives mean.

The Eucharist is a sacred drama. But how are we to enact it so as to reach people today? This does not mean adapting it to contemporary taste. Surprisingly, what seems alien and intractable can prove thoroughly appealing to people nowadays, as long as it is presented appropriately and thoughtfully.

The author of Luke's gospel was a Greek, and someone fascinated by theatre and plays. He described Jesus's death on the cross, which is celebrated in every Eucharist, as a sacred spectacle. The effect of this drama was to move people so profoundly that they experienced an inward conversion: 'And the whole crowd who had collected for the spectacle, when they saw what had happened, went home in deep distress' (or: 'underwent a change of heart') (Luke 23.48). It is a matter of enacting the sacred spectacle of the Eucharist nowadays so that the people who have assembled in the church – often enough no more than spectators – are deeply moved and go home with changed hearts: as people who have realized who this Jesus Christ is, that he gives them true life and heals their wounds, and that he supports them and shows them a way to live meaningful lives in this world.

We should not expect every celebration of the Eucharist to affect us profoundly. But every Eucharist should make clear that the mystery of God and of humanity is being celebrated here and now. Then, as the Greek author of Luke understands, each celebration of the Eucharist will help to bring the healing, saving presence of Jesus Christ into this malign and calamitous world. Then we shall re-enter everyday life after each Mass as more upright beings who are able to deal justly and effectively with the things of this world.

3

Confirmation: responsibility and strength

INTRODUCTION

Of all the sacraments, confirmation is probably the one that makes Christians feel most doubtful and uneasy. Nowadays many priests, teachers and catechists find it very difficult to motivate young people to receive the sacrament. Boys and girls ask what it's going to do for them. When they make their first communion they have some idea of its implications. But confirmation seems somehow vague and woolly. Many mothers and fathers of candidates are at a loss to explain to their children what confirmation is exactly.

For some years now there has been much discussion among the clergy about the right age for confirmation. Individual priests and pastoral theologians have different opinions, and practice varies from one parish to another. People see the sacrament differently. Some think of confirmation as the culmination or completion of baptism. They believe it is quite acceptable to confirm children even before their first communion; indeed, this was the general custom among Catholics for many years. Others see confirmation as the sacrament marking the threshold between childhood and adulthood: as the 'sacrament of maturity', of development as a Christian, of responsibility, of acceptance as a full member of the Church, and as a kind of commission for entry to the world.

If confirmation is understood as a rite of initiation into adulthood, then it seems appropriate to administer it to candidates between 14 and 18 years of age. At a recent conference of pastoral workers I realized how varied the methods of preparation for the sacrament could be, and in how many different ways confirmation was interpreted by those immediately concerned with preparing children to receive it. Parish workers put an immense amount of imagination and creativity into motivating young people for confirmation and making its mystery seem attractive. A curate here will invite boys and girls to an hour-long discussion of the meaning of faith. An organizer there will arrange special courses or workshops. And so on. Clearly, there is no one method or prescription for confirmation. It's always a question of the enthusiasm, expertise and effective conviction of those charged with preparing the young to receive it.

My intention in this section is not to push one particular form of preparation as the universal model. Instead, I want to invite candidates' parents to think about the sacrament, and to ask themselves what confirmation means for them nowadays and whether they can see it as a basis for living. I want to encourage them to talk about it with their children. I have in mind all men and women who have the task of helping young people to receive the sacrament, which means catechists, youth workers, priests and nuns and others conducting courses and classes, and working out with young people the best way to arrange the actual confirmation rite.

Most Catholic Christians have been confirmed. But very few of them ever think about what it really means to them and could mean in their lives. How can I live on the basis of my confirmation in today's world? Does the sacrament really mean anything to me, or could I live just as responsible a Christian life without it? If confirmation is the sacrament of mission, what is my mission in life? Do I have anything like a mission anyway? Or is it enough just to observe God's commandments? What exactly is confirmation 'in its own right'? In the following pages I shall consider how confirmation might influence the way in which we live and how it might become a beneficial reality in our lives.

I. CONFIRMATION AS INITIATION

Introduction to the art of living

Confirmation is the sacrament of initiation. There are initiation rites of this kind in all cultures, most of which locate them at the start of adult life. In some tribes and nations, initiation into puberty comprises a series of dramatic trials which young people have to undergo. They are separated from their mothers, taken into the bush, and isolated there. Some Australian Aboriginal tribes knock out a single tooth from a boy's mouth to show that he has died to childhood in order to rise again as an adult. Sometimes the children are smeared all over with mud so that they look like ghosts. Other tribes cut the boys and draw off some of their blood. They are placed in huts in the bush, where they must stay fasting for a few days. Originally, these bush huts symbolized dragons or serpents which swallowed the boys so that they would die and re-emerge into life. Some tribes see isolation in the huts as a return to the mother's womb for rebirth.

When a young man preparing for confirmation read the manuscript of this section of the book, he became very interested in these initiation rites. He wanted to know more about the light tap on the cheek which used to be part of the rite of confirmation, and wondered why it had disappeared. He found confirmation nowadays boring because nothing spectacular happened in it. He clearly sensed that confirmation had a function similar to that of the often very demanding and painful initiation rites. The tap was reminiscent of those rites. The practice has been said to originate in an ancient legal custom. When carrying out some legal act, such as transferring a boundary-stone, it was usual to take boys along and to beat them on the spot. The reason for the thrashing was to ensure that at a later date the boys would remember the exact position of the boundary-stone. Similarly, the tap was intended to help those who had been confirmed to remember that they had received the Holy Spirit, and to grasp the significance of that reception. Since God's Spirit is intangible and passes our comprehension, something more emphatic than words, a physical experience, was needed to stress what was happening. The medieval theologian Durandus of Mende (d. 1296), for example, justifies the tap on the cheek because by it 'the candidate will remember all the more forcefully that he has received the sacrament.' This symbolism has entered another confirmation ritual. In the ancient rite, the sponsor was expected to tread on the candidate's foot. Clearly, this painful experience was designed to induce a lively memory of reception of the sacrament and of another Spirit's presence in you. These old confirmation rites, with their reminiscences of ancient tribal initiation rites, preserved the awareness that the path of human growth and development is painful, and that it hurts to experience the tension between the Holy Spirit and your own spirit.

The question is how we should arrange confirmation and preparation for the sacrament today as a form of initiation into adulthood. It would be pointless simply to restore the tap on the cheek by the bishop, which was removed after the Second Vatican Council. People would see it only as an incomprehensible relic of olden times. Yet these two rites show us that we shouldn't be too cautious and delicate in dealing with young people. We have to offer them something that demands an effective response. Young people want to be challenged. Nearly thirty years of working with them has made me well aware of this.

On courses with young people we sometimes made it their responsibility to get up as early as 5.15 in the morning. They did so willingly. They also found an adventure trip under canvas in the mountains an interesting and lively way of preparing for confirmation. One commentator said on the radio the other day that young people nowadays were in sore need of initiation rites, and that in his opinion the first reefer they smoked or getting stoned fulfilled precisely that function for many of them. For others it was the first drive over the speed limit in someone else's, usually a parent's, vehicle. These were replacement rites, chosen because society offered no appropriate alternatives. The attraction of occult practices and ceremonies for this age-group certainly points to the lack of genuine initiation rites. The Church has to rethink the whole problem of answering this need appropriately.

Some sociologists talk of the contemporary 'experience society'. Many young people are just waiting for life to start 'kicking in'. They want to 'have a real trip', 'get something out of it', 'get a proper hit',

91

'live it up', and so on. The Church should seize the opportunity offered by confirmation to introduce young people to the art of existence, of living intensely, instead of letting them go on searching for a succession of new kicks just to convince themselves that they exist at all. But any such introduction to life would have to provide or accompany deep experiences of some kind. To restrict it to talks that tiptoed all too cautiously along the borders of real life would be useless.

There have been several attempts to introduce confirmation candidates to the art of living. One of these takes the form of group courses spent away from home, often in camps. But the candidates have to be challenged, if only by rising early or learning how to meditate. Young people find it difficult just to sit still and be inside their own heads. But it's part of growing up to get to know and accept yourself in silence, and to learn how to be alone. One way of getting used to this which impresses many young people is a 'day in the wilderness', during the course. They have to spend a day alone, relying on their resources, living off the land (from what they find in nature). They mustn't speak to anyone but walk on their own with regular stops for rest. During these pauses they are simply there, communing with their own senses, drinking in what they hear and feel around them. Strange to say, many young people today have no real awareness of their own bodies. They need some external stimulus just to acknowledge that they're actually there. Something like this solitary walk is needed so that they can teach themselves how to open their senses to perception of the life round about them in the natural world, so that they see, hear, smell, taste and feel it.

In our monastery we have found it very effective to invite confirmation groups to stay here for a few days. After agreeing out of curiosity to share the rhythm of monastic life, young people are surprised to find it a considerable challenge. But many of them enjoy it. They make sure that they get up at 4.40 in the morning to be in the chapel on time. They learn that the men there are really trying to live as Christians in a more determined way. This is a challenge to the candidates' often superficial experience of being a Christian, and elicits a host of questions about how and why people live like that, what the meaning of life is, what really makes you happy, and so forth. We must remember that places with a spiritual tradition behind them have the power to vitalize a confirmation group and start them on a spiritual quest.

Another challenge would be trying to define their own identity. Who am I? Am I just the son or daughter of these parents? What is my real identity? What is the unique image of God that I am intended to be? What do I feel? What do I think when I stop accepting what other people say? What do I really dream of in life? What would I like to do with my life? What would I like to get done in this world if I had the power? It's important, too, to be aware of the emotions that can well up in us when we're alone. How do I cope with being on my own? Am I someone only if I'm with other people, and if others acknowledge and approve of me? Am I capable of standing up for myself and for my opinions?

It's also possible to introduce physical exercises in self-awareness. I have often used the following exercise with young people. We stand with our feet about a foot apart. I say something like: 'I have a standpoint. I can stand. I can stand up to something. I can stand up for myself. I can be myself, standing here like this.' The young people see whether these statements fit the posture they've assumed. Then we stand to attention, feet close together, with our shoulders drawn up tight. They realize immediately that you can't be yourself like that. Then we take up another pose, with feet really wide apart, in a frozen stagger like cowboys in a western or the toughest kids in the block. We're clearly trying to be something we're not, trying to prove who we are. But we're unsteady. We could easily fall over.

Confirmation is connected with the Latin verb *firmare*, which means 'to make firm or fast, strengthen, fortify, support, encourage, animate, strengthen in resolution, secure, affirm, help to stand firm'. Confirmation is intended to strengthen young people in their Christian life and support them through the Holy Spirit, so that they can stand up for themselves in this world, so that they can find their own standpoint, and live a Spirit-centred life in an often unspiritual, uninspired and spiritless world.

93

In baptism we are reborn in the fountain of the Holy Spirit. Through confirmation we shall be strengthened in our new existence, so that we are led by the Spirit of God, not by the spirit of this world. We receive a share in the power of the Spirit so that we can deny the world any power over us, and help to shape it instead as God wants it to be.

Taking responsibility

Confirmation may be thought of as the sacrament by which a young person is transformed into an adult. Young people are no longer to be seen merely as their parents' children. Rebirth through the Holy Spirit should help them to discover their own identities and to assume responsibility for themselves and for their own lives. It's usual nowadays to refuse any responsibility for your life. People shift the responsibility – and guilt – onto their parents. As for me, they say, well, I haven't been given sufficient self-confidence, I'm not intelligent or gifted enough, I haven't had the opportunity, and anyway I just can't handle life.

Pascal Bruckner, a French philosopher, has identified infantilization and victimization as the two main attitudes of our times. Many people remain in a perpetual childhood, only expecting something from others, from their mother, from society, or from the Church. So many people are infantile, and want to be looked after like children, refusing to take responsibility for others. Only one person counts. This attitude is usually accompanied by a feeling of victimization. 'Victims' in this sense are people who always ascribe the guilt for their misfortune to others. My parents are responsible for my depression and for my inability to take control of my life. Teachers are responsible for my inability to develop my capacities. The Church is responsible for my lack of faith. If I go on feeling victimized, I refuse to assume responsibility for my own life. Because so many people today won't take responsibility for themselves, they also refuse any kind of accountability for others in the Church and in society.

But part of being an adult is being responsible for myself. It isn't decisively important how I have developed, what I am, or what influences parents and teachers had on my upbringing and education. I have to accept that I've become who I am, and then start being accountable for my own life. Otherwise I shall be a perpetual plaintiff, always pointing out others' mistakes. Or I shall adopt the role of the permanent spectator, who just watches life unrolling before him or her without engaging in it. Preparation for confirmation must contain some practice in taking responsibility in various ways.

My primary responsibility is for myself. I am responsible for my personal development, for my appearance, for my inner mood. I am responsible for my innermost feelings and decisions, because I am the one who opts for a lifelong attitude of disappointment and misfortune, or for life. I am responsible for the thoughts I dwell on, for keeping my room tidy, and for using my time meaningfully.

When my nephews and nieces were confirmed, my sister discussed with them what the responsibility they were learning about might mean in everyday family life. On the day they were confirmed she gave them copies of the key to the house, and from that day on each of them was made responsible for some aspect of the household. The children realized that when they were confirmed their role in the home had changed. It's rather pointless to introduce candidates to adulthood in the parish if they have to carry on as before at home. Parents should see confirmation as an opportunity to discuss responsibility for family life with their sons and daughters, and what each of them thinks is the meaning of growing up and of maturity.

Young people can also exercise responsibility in the confirmation group or class. Each of them can be in charge of some aspect of it. They should also learn how to take responsibility for each other, both in the confirmation group and in their classrooms. Who are the weaker members who need help? Is there an outsider whom the class picks on or bullies? Are there any foreigners or immigrants in the class who are isolated? Each confirmation candidate could take responsibility for another young person.

Receiving new abilities

The development of new moral and spiritual capabilities is part of the experience of rebirth in the Holy Spirit. Luke's gospel repeatedly tells us how Jesus proceeds and carries out his mission in the power (*dynamis*) of the Holy Spirit . Luke sees baptism as Jesus's reception of the Holy Spirit. Jesus has received the Spirit when he enters the wilderness and is tempted by Satan. That is where he undergoes his initiation into the office of Messiah. After his temptation, we are told: 'Jesus returned in the power of the Spirit into Galilee' (Luke 4.14). Then he went to the Nazareth synagogue, and stood up to read from the Prophet Isaiah: 'The Spirit of the Lord is upon me, because he has anointed me to preach good news to the poor. He has sent me to proclaim release to the captives and recovering of sight to the blind, to set at liberty those who are oppressed, to proclaim the acceptable year of the Lord' (Luke 4.18f.).

Young people receive the Holy Spirit in the sacrament of confirmation in order to carry out their mission in the world and in the Church. The Spirit enables the candidates to acquire new behaviour and to develop new abilities. Therefore preparation for confirmation should include a challenge to young people to work out their ideas of what they intend to set about in their lives and which aspects of their lives they could take charge of themselves. Young people should discover their own charisma, the nature of their own power, talents and capacities to inspire others: What can I accomplish? What am I capable of doing? What do I feel I am called to do? What is my vocation? What is my mission? Confirmation is intended to divert young people's attention from satisfying their own needs, so that they are not forever asking: 'What do I get out of it?' They should ask instead: 'What contribution can I make? What am I called to do? What are the tasks before me?' This change of outlook is good for the young. It frees them from endless self-obsession and challenges them to develop their capacities and to dedicate themselves to something that fascinates them.

Confirmation as the strengthening of Christian life includes training in healthy self-discipline. This begins with young people dividing their days meaningfully, clearing and arranging their rooms effectively, and caring for and shaping their own minds and bodies. It also includes examining their behaviour to date and asking themselves if they have only followed old patterns adopted from their parents. In what respects do they merely copy their parents or the role-models they idolize, and when do they act independently? Is there a personal mark they would like to leave on this world? What is right for them? Self-discipline really means training in the use of inner freedom. In what respects am I dependent on fashion and advertising, on what others say, on the approval of others? When can I say No? Can I go without things or do I have to satisfy every urge immediately? Those who can't do without things will never develop a firm individuality.

The Spirit awards us new abilities so that we can use them for the good of humanity. Jesus sees his anointing by the Lord's Spirit as a commission and mission for his work in the world. We all have a mission. We can all get something done in this world that only we could do. I can discover my mission by examining my strengths and weaknesses. What can I do well? What do I enjoy making, shaping, changing, initiating? Instead of allowing them to go on complaining that the world is so difficult, it's sensible to help young people to feel that they should not only take charge of their own lives, but also begin to tackle the problems of their own world. They can help to make the world about them more human and fit to live in. What could the confirmation group do to make some aspect of the environment in their parish more natural and acceptable to people? Is there a project they could all cooperate in? One parish might look at environmental-protection projects, another at rearranging church services, yet another at ways of helping immigrants, migrants, unintegrated families from abroad and the homeless or ex-prisoners. The kind of responsibility confirmation candidates might be encouraged to assume will depend on the social structure of the parish. One parish will concentrate on neglected old and sick people; another will focus on outcasts. One might find that helping with household tasks is appropriate, whereas another might offer to do shopping or cleaning out a flat or house. In all cases, boys and girls will need the support of adults to avoid taking on projects that are obviously beyond their capabilities, and those where they might be tempted to give in at the first hurdle.

It is just as important that each candidate is able to contemplate his or her own vision or life-project. When I was in South America, I saw how optimistically young people looked to the future. Although external conditions there generally offer fewer prospects of fulfilment than in Europe or North America, and similarly privileged regions, young people there feel that it is worth being alive, and that they want to contribute to making the world more humane. In more prosperous countries, however, you often meet with resignation and indifference: 'There's no point in trying to do anything. The world is run by big business or by a few elites or groups with all the power.' It is essential to realize that when I entered the world, something unique came in and with me, and that I can leave a mark on the cosmos and society that will have a lasting effect on the appearance of this world. Of course it will be a very small mark indeed. But if I start to think and act differently, the change will have its effects. As soon as I say what I really think echoes will be heard. I am not simply born into this world. I have also been sent into it. I have a task to perform, a mission to carry out. One of the aims of preparation for confirmation is to make each person involved more aware of his or her mission in life.

II. PENTECOST IN JOHN AND LUKE

In confirmation the candidates receive the gift of the Holy Spirit. Many people find it difficult to conjure up any image of the Holy Spirit. Of course some of them picture him as a dove. But that doesn't mean much to them. They can think of something more significant when Jesus is mentioned, but they find the Holy Spirit too abstract. It's true that we can't develop the same kind of personal relationship to the Holy Spirit as we can to Jesus or to God the

Father. Yet we can experience the Holy Spirit as the power that drives us forward, and as the love that fills and fulfils us. How are we meant to understand the Holy Spirit? The best place to look for an answer is in the gospels. I shall keep to John and Luke for my descriptions of the Spirit as seen by the evangelists.

The Holy Spirit in John's gospel

John sees the Holy Spirit as the personal Spirit of Jesus, whom he communicates to us. On Easter Eve Jesus breathes on his disciples and speaks to them: 'Receive the Holy Spirit!' (John 20.22). If a child is hurt, his or her mother blows on the wound and says: 'It'll get better; it won't take long.' When she breathes on the graze or cut, she wants to convey her love to the child physically. That is how we might understand Jesus breathing on the disciples. He wants to breathe out his love so that we can feel it physically and sense it in every exhalation.

Love, John tells us, is Jesus's gift to us. And love is the same as the Holy Spirit. And so John thinks there is no more suitable place to pour this love over us than from the open heart. When the soldier pierces Jesus's side on the cross, blood and water flow from the wound. For John, this symbolizes the Holy Spirit, who is poured out over all of us. And this Spirit is the love that flows from Jesus's heart. People – John knew this well – are scarcely capable of true love. Their love is always mixed with possessive claims, reciprocal expectations and demands. John sees the Holy Spirit as the love which Jesus breathes over us so that our closed doors give way (cf. John 20.19), and he turns our reluctance into readiness to accept others. We often live with our doors closed. We often shut ourselves off from other people. We are afraid to let people come near us. They might hurt us. And if we dare to express our love we might be deceived all over again. Young people long for a boyfriend or girlfriend to love. But when they're disappointed in love, they clam up; then their desire for love is their only company. The Holy Spirit is their assurance that they can open their doors for other people, and experience the mystery of love with them.

The Holy Spirit appears not only in love but in forgiveness. When Jesus breathes the Holy Spirit on the disciples on Easter Eve, he says: 'Receive the Holy Spirit. If you forgive anyone's sins, they are forgiven; if you pronounce them unforgiven, unforgiven they remain' (John 20.22f.). If we manage to forgive someone who has offended us, that is the work of the Holy Spirit. A deacon from Switzerland told me that he tries to make this aspect of the Holy Spirit apparent when preparing young people for confirmation. He invites the candidates to a service of reconciliation together with their parents, brothers and sisters, and sponsors. After a brief introduction, he asks each candidate to stand in a group with family and sponsors. The members of each group decide on the things for which they seek forgiveness, and those that have offended them. Then each of them lays hands on every member of the family, first the father on the candidate, then the candidate on the father, then the mother on the candidate and vice versa, and so on, and prays for God's forgiveness. This is an impressive communal rite. Initially, the deacon said, he was worried that some candidates and their families would fight shy of anything so public. But every year he is overjoyed to find that this practice actually improves family relations, and that the exercise in reciprocal forgiveness contributes enormously to the general atmosphere of the parish.

Another symbol for the Holy Spirit in John is that of the source or spring. Whoever receives the Spirit, 'as scripture says, "streams of living water shall flow from within him"' (John 7.38). The Holy Spirit flows within us like an inexhaustible spring from which we drink the power God sends us. Whoever drinks from this source will never be exhausted, for it is never-ending. The Holy Spirit is a source that can enable us to face our lives fearlessly and undertake tasks without any initial anxiety about overtaxing our capacities. Whoever drinks from this spring will enjoy life, work and commitments, and remain fresh and vitally engaged. Those who draw on the Spirit will not be controlled by exasperation and disappointment, anger or fear, by the emotions that beset so many people's minds and hearts nowadays. Instead they will see things clearly and enjoy offering this clarity to the world around them. Those who live a Spirit-centred life will find living water flowing in and through them. I am horrified nowadays to discover how often young people are already fixed and frozen so early in life. They have no vitality, imagination or creativity. There is so sign of natural effervescence. They can scarcely even communicate. The Holy Spirit urges life to flow in us when we seem forever petrified.

John uses another important symbol for the Spirit when he talks of him as the Supporter and Counsellor (also, the 'Paraclete', or Helper) who is always at our side. We are not on our own in this world when our parents neglect or abandon us, or we leave home. The Holy Spirit accompanies us, defends us, and stands up for us. He speaks to us too. We are not without good advice when we no longer agree with our parents' demands and reject them. The Spirit speaks within us and shows us what is right for us, what suits us, and what will lead us into real life. Jesus promised his disciples the Counsellor's support when they had their backs to the wall. Life is a struggle too. Young people find this out when they go through adolescence. They are not on their own in this trying period. Someone is there to back them up. This is a promise that young people can relate to.

The Holy Spirit in Luke's gospel

Luke takes the image of the Counsellor a stage further. In the Acts of the Apostles he tells us how the Holy Spirit came like a tempestuous wind among the scared disciples and gave them the courage to go out and tell people what God had done for them in Jesus Christ. The Holy Spirit drives out fear and fills the disciples with confidence. First and foremost, the Spirit is confidence. He wants to make sure that young people have the courage to trust in themselves and develop self-confidence. Those who feel the power of the Spirit within them don't have to construct a façade of assurance for the outside world. The cool front assumed by so many young people obviously conceals great insecurity and a strong sense of inferiority. The Holy Spirit liberates the disciples from their worries about what other people think of them, and whether they will make fun of them or treat them with contempt. They simply speak as the Spirit prompts them. Those who live by the Spirit are freed from the constant need to compare themselves with others. They don't say what others want them to say, but speak frankly. They say what they feel and think. They live on the basis of their own awareness and conscience and do not rely on others for affirmation.

In Luke's account of Pentecost, the Holy Spirit is apparent in the gift of a new ability to communicate. The disciples 'began to speak in different languages as the Spirit gave them power to proclaim his message' (Acts 2.4). The Holy Spirit enables young people to find their own voices. The basic meaning of the Greek word *lalein* is 'talk, speak' but in the sense of 'chat, chatter away, prattle as it comes, babble on naturally'. The disciples don't try to please their audience by considering each word they say, choosing carefully to make a good impression. They simply speak from the heart and, because they do so, their words move their listeners' hearts. The Holy Spirit can inspire young people not to copy anxiously what everyone else is saying, as is usual nowadays, but to express their own feelings and needs confidently. Then they will find that adults understand what they have to say. Language empowered by the Spirit is relational, encouraging and supportive. At times I am shocked at the inarticulacy of some young people. Others, however, can say what they feel and perceive with exceptional clarity. The language that comes from the heart is the language of the Holy Spirit. It can touch other people's hearts too, and move them to action. The Bible calls the spirit that makes us inarticulate an evil spirit, a demon in fact (cf. Mark 9.17). Those who have no language for their inner reality, who can't express their passions and emotions intelligibly, become sick. They are as if thrown to the ground, convulsed and simply worn out – as Mark describes a certain young man – by the spirit of deafness and dumbness (Mark 9.20). Therefore a primary task of preparation for confirmation should be to give young people a chance to talk about themselves and their feelings, in one-to-one discussions or in a group. When a group is nervous, even frightened, it's often difficult to create a confident atmosphere so that people's tongues are loosened and they can speak plainly (cf. Mark 7.35).

Those who are ruled by a dumb spirit are also silent when they see injustice around them. They say nothing when someone next to them in a bus or train is attacked. The Holy Spirit wants to prompt us to speak up for those who have no voice, and for those who have been made speechless. A suitable exercise for young people preparing for confirmation would be to discuss where it might be appropriate for individuals or the group to speak out. The group might see that the parish clergy are behaving unjustly, and that certain people are wrongly excluded. Or it might be helpful to speak up in the classroom for those who never say anything, who are squashed and ignored. Another useful exercise would be to assign a whole week just to speaking up on others' behalf when an inner feeling says you ought to. Too often other people or the wrong sort of inner voice stop us saying what's right: 'It's a waste of time. I don't want to make a fuss. No one listens to me anyway. There's nothing I can do about it. They'll just shout me down.'

The Spirit turned a bunch of frightened disciples into the Church of Christ. When the Spirit descends on people he produces a community with a spirit of community. He forms the Church as a community of people commissioned by Jesus who do what Jesus did. This is evident when Luke shows the apostles Peter, John and Paul working the same miracles of healing as Jesus, and when the dying deacon Stephen forgives his enemies as Jesus did. The Holy Spirit enables us to behave like Jesus. Like Jesus we can approach people, help them to stand up on their feet again, encourage them, and open their eyes so that they see things as they really are.

Confirmation is about being filled with the Spirit of Jesus, so that we can bear witness to him in this world, work miracles of healing and encouragement in the power of the Spirit, and undermine this world's evil and indifference. Perhaps that seems too far-fetched a claim. But whenever one of us describes his or her worries, troubles and injuries, and we just hear him or her out, the miracle of healing is under way. Then someone will leave us in a better state than before. One person heals through good humour, another just by listening, yet another by addressing the problem and actually helping the hurt friend to find a solution. Part of the purpose of confirmation is to make us aware that today, too, we can be the means by which signs and wonders are worked. We can't work miracles magically, just like that. But we should be thankful when a seemingly insoluble conflict is resolved, another obstacle collapses, and life prevails.

III. CONFIRMATION AS A RITE: THE MEANINGS OF THE INDIVIDUAL RITUALS

The Creed: 'I believe ...'

Confirmation generally takes place in the setting of a eucharistic celebration, and usually after the bishop's sermon or address, which follows the gospel reading. The rite calls for an assistant to summon each candidate by name before the bishop's sermon. They pass individually before the bishop and take their places in the choir stalls, or nearby. A helpful addition would be for each of them to say something like: 'I am ready.' This would make it clear that it is an active decision on each person's part to receive the sacrament and the Holy Spirit's commission. Like priests receiving Holy Orders, confirmation candidates are given a mission. As when ordaining priests, the bishop directs his address primarily to the young people before him. After the address, the candidates make a confession of faith. They will not find it very moving merely to repeat the Creed without preparation. They should have considered it carefully beforehand. One idea would be for them to write their own Creed. This would face them with the task of telling other people about their faith in their own words.

A deacon told me once that he gave all candidates the task of writing out the statement from the Creed that most appealed to them and which they intended to live by especially, and asked them to explain it in their own words. They found it a challenge to say what they believed in simple, straightforward language. But the total result was a testimony to belief that astonished and moved the parish deeply. Many adults had not thought these young people were capable of thinking seriously about their faith.

The Stretching out, or Extension, of Hands

After the Creed, the bishop stretches his hands towards the congregation and all the candidates and asks God to send down the Holy Spirit on them. The Extension of Hands is an ancient gesture. It means that God's Spirit is being asked to come down to protect and transform these people. During the eucharistic transformation the priests extends his hands over bread and wine and asks the Holy Spirit to descend so that they become the Body and Blood of Christ. The bishop calls the Spirit down on the young people so that they may be reborn and transformed as in the Eucharist, and so that they may be filled with Christ's Spirit, and with his love and power. The laying on of hands will make them the bread of heaven as nourishment for others on their way, and the wine of heaven to gladden people's hearts.

When he ordains a priest the bishop lays his hands on him to strengthen him in his office. In confirmation, too, this ritual means that these young people are sent out into the world to shape it through the power of the Holy Spirit and to bear witness for Christ. The spreading of the bishop's hands also signifies that God himself holds out his hand in protection over the young people and will go with them on their way. But the Stretching out of Hands also expresses possession. In this gesture God is saying: 'You belong to me.' If I belong to God that also means that I am free, that I am not the property of any human being, that no one has power over me, and that no monarch or ruler, but only God, can decide who I am. This gives the young people a sense of their unique dignity and value, for they are not there to satisfy the expectations of their parents or teachers or friends. They belong to God. They are unique. They are free. No one has power over them. They are to live in this world as free children of God, and make their way with heads erect, aware of their worth, for they are supported by the Holy Spirit.

The Laying on, or Imposition, of Hands

Then the candidates pass before the bishop, one by one, each accompanied by a sponsor. The bishop has spread his hands over them all in blessing; now, as when ordaining a priest, he lays his hands on the head of each boy or girl and prays for him or her. All great things are done in silence. Now the Holy Spirit descends silently on each of these people to do what is appropriate for each one. The Holy Spirit will work differently in each of them. The silent prayer to the Holy Spirit doesn't mean that each boy or girl has to behave in the same way. Each one will receive the gift of the Spirit he or she needs, together with the power needed to learn how to live and bear witness in a personal way for life and for Christ, the 'Author of life' (Acts 3.15). The silent Imposition of Hands is an impressive rite for everyone who receives it. Each boy or girl can be sure that the Holy Spirit descends on him or her personally, with all his or her weaknesses and strengths, characteristics and peculiarities. The Holy Spirit flows through the bishop's hands into the candidates' bodies, filling them with his love. He radiates the dark rooms within them and their lives. He heals their wounds, and transforms everything in them.

Anointing with Chrism

After the Laying on of Hands and silent prayer, the bishop anoints the young people with chrism, making the sign of the cross on their heads, and addresses each of them by the name he or she has given him: 'N., you are sealed with the Gift of God, the Holy Spirit.' The confirmation rite describes the Anointing with Chrism as 'sealing'. This is a biblical term. The Letter to the Ephesians says: 'In him you also, who have heard the word of truth, the gospel of your salvation, and have believed in him, were sealed with the promised Holy Spirit, which is the guarantee of our inheritance until we acquire possession of it, to the praise of his glory' (Eph. 1.13f.). In antiquity, the Greeks and Romans gave people a signet or seal to show that they belonged to God and were under his protection. The Jews also used a seal as a symbol of protection, as a kind of amulet. An ancient Hebrew text says that those who bear the seal of circumcision need never fear evil spirits and are as strong as a man girded with a sword. The early Christians used the cross as a seal or sacred sign. Some of them tattooed the sign of the cross on their foreheads, to acknowledge that they belonged to God and that no human being now had power over them. In confirmation, sealing is a sign that the newly confirmed boys and girls no longer belong to their parents, but to God, and that through the seal of the Holy Spirit God will give them the strength to withstand life's adversities, the worldly things that will so often confuse them, and the inner obstacles that threaten to cut them off from life.

The candidates are anointed with chrism, which consists of olive oil and balsam. Olive oil gives foods additional savour. Oil heals wounds. The Good Samaritan poured oil and wine into the wounds of the man who had fallen among thieves. In the ancient world sportsmen anointed their limbs with oil. This made their bodies supple and capable of greater achievements. All these meanings play a part in confirmation. Through it life receives a new savour from the Holy Spirit, the wounds of life are healed, and young people are anointed for the contest of life, so that they can issue forth with new strength and vitality, and vanquish their foes. The oil is mixed with balsam. Balsam, or balm, consists of the aromatic resin obtained from various plants and trees. In antiquity the addition of balsam turned oil into a cosmetic. Only when balsam is added does oil become 'chrism', a word that reminds us of Christ. Chrism is intended to symbolize the fragrance of Christ's love, to fill the young people with Christ's beneficence, and impart some of his loving radiance to them.

The full effect of these rites will be felt only if they are explained. It is essential to discuss the main confirmation rites, and to interpret them so that the young people can enjoy them and experience their profound significance.

The Sponsor

The candidates are not alone during the laying on of hands and anointing by the bishop. The sponsors stand behind them and put their right hand on their shoulder. A sponsor has a major role in the rite of confirmation. It is helpful for young people to know there is an adult there to back them up. The sponsor is a tangible sign of the Holy Spirit as Supporter. Sponsors support the candidates, help them to stand up for themselves and face the inevitable risks of life. Part of a sponsor's task is to place his or her left hand on the boy's or girl's shoulder. The shoulder is a centre of power. A warrior directs a spear from the shoulder. To show someone a cold shoulder means distancing yourself from that person. The sponsor's hand on the shoulder tells the boy or girl: 'I am glad you exist and are here. You have power. You are learning to take control of your life. Keep it up! Carry on!' The reassuring hand also says that a candidate's power, though it often seems insufficient, comes from the Spirit, who will strengthen his or her back so that he or she can step forward confidently with head held high.

In some parishes not only the sponsor, but parents, brothers and sisters and friends, go up with the candidate. They all lay their hands on a shoulder, or form a semicircle or circle by placing each hand on another's shoulder. This shows that the candidates are not alone, that many people they can count on are behind them and will accompany them through life. Through confirmation they are received into the circle of adults and of people who have already taken the same steps to maturity. They are received into a community of believers who are ready to share their faith with the new adults and go with them along the road of faith. They will experience the strength of the Holy Spirit in these companions, especially when they feel dejected and deserted.

The Sign of Peace

After the Anointing with Chrism, the bishop gives the young people the Sign of Peace, saying: 'Peace be with you', in order to greet and welcome them as equal members of the Church. The usual sign is an embrace. In the past it took the somewhat mysterious form of a tap on the cheek, or *alapa*. One explanation is that the recipient, once strengthened by the Holy Spirit, need never blush when called on to confess Christ's name. Another interpretation refers to the scene in which St Benedict freed a monk from an evil spirit by slapping him on the cheek. This showed that he need no longer fear evil or worldly spirits, or unknown forces within him. The power of the Holy Spirit was stronger than any alien influence that might try to take him over. Other commentators explain the tap or slap as a modified survival from the ceremony of dubbing a knight; yet others as an affirmation of maturity. As always, the multitude of theories shows that the practice gave rise to too many misconceptions and controversies. That was why the Second Vatican Council abolished it. Some rites die out only to be rediscovered. Today, of course, it would be more difficult to introduce this one than in the past. But it might be possible to preserve its significance if the bishop warmly embraced the young man or woman and held him or her firmly by the shoulders as an assurance of the Spirit's strength. Whatever gesture is used for the Sign of Peace, it must be made positively; otherwise it will look like an empty ritual. Then he would show the young people that they were adults, and empowered, and that he had confidence in them. Sometimes the Sign of Peace is only a suggestion of an embrace. The Sign of Peace should express the truth that the recipients are wholly accepted, welcomed into the community of the Church, taken seriously in all their uniqueness, and recognized as the men or women they are becoming.

Petitions

The Sign of Peace closes the confirmation rite proper. The newly confirmed boys and girls respond to reception of the sacrament with their Petitions (Intercessions, or Bidding Prayers). Their creativity can come into play here. This is an opportunity to show that they have understood the meaning of confirmation. There are various ways of arranging these prayers. The young people could express their worries and hopes about the world and the Church in their own language. This can be done in words or by choosing symbols that accord with their vision of the future. They can show them to the congregation, explain them, and lay them before the altar as signs of hope that the parish and society will be transformed by their confirmation. Another possibility would be for each of them to stand up and tell the congregation what he or she sees as a particular mission, and which task is foreseen as an expression of responsibility. Each person would have a specific time in which to carry out this practical mission. This would be an opportunity to give an example to other young people for the future.

Furthermore, these petitions offer a chance for the young people to thank the parish for their experiences there, but also to say what they expect of the parish and to offer to do something to help fulfil those wishes. Another idea would be for each young person to choose someone in the congregation, not necessarily a parent, and make the sign of the cross on his or her forehead. This could be done in silence or with a personal blessing chosen in advance, such as: 'I sign you with the cross. You belong to God. I am glad that you exist. May you live in the freedom of the Holy Spirit.' Since confirmation now contains only a few individual rituals, this is an opportunity to devise new ones that symbolically unite the newly confirmed children with the church community. Rituals allow us to express feelings that we would repress otherwise, and to enhance the quality of our relationships. Of course, certain inhibitions have to be overcome before the kind of thing I have suggested is successful. But the profound experience that results is worth the effort. Young people will remember such experiences for many years.

After the rite of confirmation, the celebration of the Eucharist continues with the Preparation of the Gifts, or Offertory. Of course the newly confirmed members of the parish should take the gifts to the altar. The offerings will be transformed just as they have been changed by the Holy Spirit. In the bread the boys and girls bear before God the concerns and labour of the parish but also all its disagreements and longing for unity. In the cup they take the world's needs and joys to the altar so that the Spirit can transform them. This simple ritual must be well rehearsed and carried out with care and reverence, so that the paten(s) with the hosts and the chalice(s) are taken slowly to the altar on behalf of the parish. This will show that the Eucharist is the continuation of confirmation, and that the offerings they bear are transformed into divine gifts to nourish and strengthen people on their way through life.

IV. LIVING ON THE BASIS OF CONFIRMATION

Many adults can still remember their confirmation. But when I think about my own confirmation, I must admit that I didn't find it so intense that it stayed in my mind indelibly. I suspect that is most people's experience. So I can't live by the memory of my confirmation. But the reality of my confirmation can enable me to see and shape my life differently. This means that I am aware that I have been anointed with the Holy Spirit, and that the Spirit is in me. For me, living by the power of confirmation is the same thing as living by the life of the Spirit. But what exactly does living by God's Spirit mean?

Living by the freedom of the Spirit

In his letters Paul often tells us what living by the Spirit and not by the flesh means. For him, living by the flesh is behaving as the standards of this world demand, living under pressure, and having to be successful and recognized. According to Paul, freedom is the most important experience of those who live by the Spirit: 'There is therefore now no condemnation for those who are in Christ Jesus. For the law of the Spirit of life in Christ Jesus has set me free from the law of sin and death' (Rom. 8.1f.) The Holy Spirit liberates us from attachment to the old psychological behaviour patterns to which we keep reverting.

We constantly re-experience the same modes of behaviour and psychological mechanisms at work in us. We react with hatred and

111

anger to those who do us harm. We allow other people to force the rules of their game on us so that they become our code of behaviour. As soon as conflicts arise, we feel guilty. Paul says that this type of behaviour is obeying the law of sin and death. It results in failure to live our lives effectively. Sin means missing the target. It means death because we are deprived of real life. But allowing the Spirit to guide us liberates our inner selves. This was certainly Paul's most intense experience when he encountered Jesus Christ: 'Now the Lord is the Spirit, and where the Spirit of the Lord is, there is freedom' (2 Cor. 3.17).

For Paul, the freedom we receive in the Spirit means first and foremost that we are no longer slaves but free sons and daughters of God. 'For all who are led by the Spirit of God are sons of God. For you did not receive the spirit of slavery to fall back into fear, but you have received the spirit of sonship. When we cry, "Abba! Father!" it is the Spirit himself bearing witness with our spirit that we are children of God' (Rom. 8.14–16). Paul thinks of those who have to model themselves on others, who are constantly afraid of not doing what other people want, as slaves. Paul says that Christians are free people. They can go through life with their heads held high. Their worth is incontestable. They don't have to pawn their dignity and value by achievement, or by trying to be liked and loved for immediately adopting the prevalent opinion. Those who feel really human only if they satisfy others' expectations are slaves. They are ruled by another power. Those who live by the Spirit deny others power over them. The Spirit in us liberates us from domination by people who want us to have a bad conscience, who make us dependent on them, who repress us and try to mould us as they would like us to be.

Living by the power of the Spirit

In the Acts of the Apostles Luke tells us how we can live by the power of the Spirit. I shall choose only a short passage from Acts to show what living by the *dynamis*, the strength of the Spirit, might be like. The disciples pray:

'Lord ... grant to your servants to speak your word with all boldness, while you stretch out your hand to heal, and signs and wonders are performed through the name of your holy servant Jesus.' And when they had prayed, the place in which they were gathered together was shaken; and they were all filled with the Holy Spirit and spoke the word of God with boldness. (Acts 4.29–31)

The disciples see the power of the Spirit in their ability to proclaim the word of God fearlessly. *Parresia* is the Greek word for 'boldness'. *Parresia* is freedom to speak, the courage to say aloud what I feel in my heart. When we speak we often tailor our words to other people's expectations. We don't say what is in us but what pleases others, whatever makes us liked and puts us in a good light. But then no power radiates from our words. Living by the power of the Spirit would mean saying freely what we feel deep down in our hearts and what God inspires us to say, without any phoney concern for what others might think.

For Luke the power of the Spirit is evident in healing and in signs and wonders. The power of the Spirit is in us. Healing can also take effect through us. Of course, we are either too self-effacing and unable to trust in ourselves, or we think we are actually great healers and helpers and that we can cure others' wounds by our own power. Living by the power of the Spirit means that we become open to the Holy Spirit. If I'm talking to someone who asks me for advice, I mustn't pressure myself, and try to devise especially slick and clever solutions, or rely on my intellect to find the way out for him or her. I have to listen to what this person has to say and trust in the Spirit. He will inspire me and show me how to react and what to say. That relieves me of any pressure to perform. The result is a number of miraculous healing acts in the people before me that fill me with admiration. They leave me with new confidence and hope. But I didn't do it. It was the power of the Spirit working through me.

The memory of confirmation can encourage us to make room for the Spirit to operate in us. Even today, more signs and wonders occur than we might think possible: when an encounter between two people has a successful outcome, when someone's heart is suddenly touched and moved, if someone mourning a loved one is comforted by a supportive friend or neighbour, and if someone filled with self-contempt and intent on self-mutilation discovers his or her dignity and value and takes pleasure in being alive again. In these cases God's Spirit takes effect not only through our strong points but equally through our weaknesses.

Even when I take part in a discussion, suddenly can't think of anything to say, and feel totally ineffectual, the Spirit of God can work through me if I trust in him and offer myself to him. That frees me from the pressure to say and achieve something. All I have to do is to be open to the Spirit.

For the disciples the power of the Spirit was something they experienced physically when the floor of their meeting-place was shaken (Acts 4.31). The Greek verb *saleuo* means not only to shake, wave, oscillate, totter and reel, but also to get moving, and to get things moving, to 'make them rock' in fact. Sometimes the power of the Holy Spirit can get things going when a heavy atmosphere makes an act of worship dull and sluggish. All of a sudden, things change and we all switch into the same enthusiasm. This sense of joint movement can have an extraordinary force. Sometimes we experience the same movement when we are all silent. We don't produce this kind of 'shaking' by all willing it to happen simultaneously. It comes to us as a gift. When we receive it, we feel as a group that we possess the power to shape this world and start something moving. When the Spirit sets us going, then the old structures and behaviour patterns in our soul begin to shift too. Something breaks through our rigidity and a new vitality is born. We are shaken up and out of our soul's doziness. We discover that we have made ourselves too comfortable sitting on the mere surface of our lives. The Spirit shakes us up so that we can contact our innermost depths again. Suddenly something moves in us, and between us. Then we start something going in the world around us. For me, living by the power of the Spirit means always being ready for the Spirit to set me in motion, and trusting that God's Spirit will fill me with his power and inspire me to effective action.

Living by the gifts of the Holy Spirit

In the First Letter to the Corinthians, Paul talks about the many gifts of the Spirit. Every human being has a particular gift. But one and the same Spirit gives us these gifts.

> People have different gifts, but it is the same Spirit who gives them. There are different ways of serving God, but it is the same Lord who is served. God works through different people in different ways, but it is the same God who achieves his purposes through them all. Each person is given his or her gift by the Spirit that he or she may use it for the common good. One person's gift by the Spirit is to speak with wisdom, another's to speak with knowledge. The same Spirit gives to another person faith, to another the ability to heal, to another the power to do great deeds. The same Spirit gives to another person the gift of preaching the word of God, to another the ability to discriminate in spiritual matters, to another speech in different tongues and to yet another the power to interpret the tongues. Behind all these gifts is the operation of the same Spirit, who distributes to each individual person, as he wills.
> (1 Cor. 12. 5–11)

Traditionally, according to Paul and the Spirit's promise in Isaiah 11.2f., there are seven gifts of the Holy Spirit: the spirits of wisdom, of insight, of counsel, of perception, of strength, of awe of God and of piety. Seven is nearly always the symbolic number of aspects of the transformation that changes the earthly into the divine. These seven gifts are characteristic of people who live a Spirit-centred life. They are people with perception, who see reality as it is and understand the inner workings of their own lives and of the cosmos. They can empathize with others, advise them, and direct them to the right path. They are people of great wisdom, who have experienced, tasted and realized the mystery of existence as a whole. They are aware that God is the source of their lives, always take him into account, and relate to him in everything they think and do.

We all have our particular gifts. When I consider my life-history to date I recognize my personal gift. My wounds can also turn into gifts. They make me sensitive to others' difficulties. My strong points can help me to detect my gifts. One person is good at listening, whereas another takes the initiative, has ideas, is creative or starts things moving. Another sees things through, is loyal, someone you can trust. Another faces up to conflicts until they're resolved. Yet another is able to reconcile opponents and mend divisions between people.

Many people don't believe they can do anything. They compare themselves with others and suppose they're never quite up to it, and have nothing to contribute to the community and to the welfare of this world. Becoming aware of the meaning of confirmation means trusting in our gifts, listening to our innermost selves and scrutinizing them to discover the gifts the Spirit has given us. At Pentecost each churchgoer in some parishes draws a slip bearing the name of a gift of the Spirit, and tries to live by its ethos for the rest of the year. When we put this into practice in my parish, the effects were very gratifying. Many people were moved to find they had drawn a particular gift. One man drew the gift of healing. It was a challenge for him to adopt a more trusting attitude to his wife's depression. One woman who thought she was pretty incapable of anything received the gift of leadership. After her initial shock and reluctance to accept it, she found she could deal more effectively than she imagined with unresolved conflicts among her relatives. We all agree to trust in the Holy Spirit who has given each of us the gift he or she pulls out of the basket. It never fails to put us in touch with undreamed-of capacities and opportunities. At the year's end we can all look back gratefully at what the Spirit has produced in us.

Following the Spirit

For Paul, living by the Spirit means directing your life as the Spirit asks: 'If the Spirit is the source of our life, let the Spirit also direct its course. We must not be conceited, inciting one another to rivalry, jealous of one another' (Gal. 5.25f.). Being centred in the Spirit has consequences for our behaviour. It is a challenge to learn how to act differently. Paul talks of the fruits of the Holy Spirit. On the one hand, they are gifts of the Spirit to us; on the other hand, they are challenges to train ourselves by the Spirit's power to act through him: 'The Spirit ... produces in human life fruits such as these: love, joy, peace, patience, kindness, generosity, fidelity, tolerance and self-control' (Gal. 5.22f.). These fruits are effective criteria for deciding whether I am living a Spirit-centred life. They show me where worldly concerns have slipped into my life. Even my religious life can be distorted by such unspiritual influences as fear, narrow-mindedness, rigour and self-righteousness. A long process of transformation is necessary before my whole existence truly radiates love, kindness, generosity and tolerance.

The Holy Spirit challenges me to work on myself. Healthy self-discipline is needed before I can feel that I am living my own life instead of my passions and needs living it for me. Self-control also means taking responsibility for my own life. Confirmation is initiation into adulthood. Recalling confirmation will prevent me from falling back into infantile attitudes and making other people responsible for my problems. It asks me to live from the source of my own life instead of feeling that I am the victim of my upbringing, education or social conditions.

To develop in the Spirit of Jesus as expressed in all these fruits, I need to meditate daily. I find that the Jesus Prayer is a very helpful way of training myself in the right attitudes. In the midst of my anger and annoyance, worries, hardness of heart and overcritical moods, I try to say the following: 'Lord Jesus Christ, Son of God, have mercy on me!' Then I often find that my unspiritual feelings are clearing, and that I can feel something of Jesus's mercy and love in myself.

The Jesus Prayer, pronounced in accordance with my breathing, transforms my indifference into love, my disruption into peace, my impatience into forbearance, my severity into kindness, my rigour into tolerance, and my infidelity into loyalty. I don't have to develop these attitudes entirely by my own efforts. When I meditate and thereby allow God's Spirit to flow into my emotions and passions, he transforms my soul, so that it becomes capable of living these attitudes and virtues. But I am also aware that I have to live in the sphere of tension between the Spirit and all that is opposed to him, and that I am always prone to let the spirit of this world rule me in some way. But the memory of confirmation enables me to trust that the Spirit is stronger than all unspiritual things. I am not merely the victim of my past. I am not condemned to relive the miseries of my childhood. The Spirit can transform me. But I must constantly put myself consciously in his presence, and hold out the unresolved aspects of my existence so that he can permeate and change me.

Recalling confirmation

Various practices serve to remind us constantly of what it means to be confirmed. Most people can't remember the date of their confirmation, so they can't celebrate or commemorate it precisely. A good idea for those who can is to light a candle on the anniversary to kindle the fire of the Spirit within them. For all of us Pentecost is a regular opportunity to remember that we are confirmed and intend to live by the reality of the Spirit. One way of celebrating Pentecost as a commemoration of our own confirmation would be to draw a gift of the Holy Spirit from a selection of suitably chosen mementoes, preferably in a family circle. This would give Pentecost a special emphasis. For many people Pentecost passes without particular notice because, unlike Christmas or Easter, it is a feast without received family rituals. Another possibility would be for everyone after parish Mass at Whitsun to draw a slip bearing the title and description of a gift of the Spirit from a basket at the church door. The slip would remind the recipient of the meaning of that gift until

Pentecost came round again. He or she would continually ask what effect it was having, how it changed his or her viewpoint, and helped to prompt or even shape hitherto neglected attitudes and ideas.

One ritual I like to practise as a reminder of the reality of the Holy Spirit is standing in the wind. According to the strength of the wind, I imagine the Spirit of God blowing all my dusty notions out of me, driving out the dead spirit of idle gossip and ineffectual conventions, and refreshing me. Or I think of the Spirit stroking me tenderly and enabling me to share in God's love. Breathing consciously and emphatically also helps me to experience the Spirit. When I am fully aware of my breathing, I imagine myself inhaling not just air but the Holy Sprit in that air, permeating me and filling me with his love. Augustine was convinced that we take the Holy Spirit in with our breath, and expressed this thought in his famous prayer: 'Holy Spirit, let me feel your breath so that I think of holy things.' This kind of breathing exercise enables me to contact myself. This self-possession also reminds me that another power, God's Spirit, is within me.

On other occasions, I stand in the sun and let its rays penetrate my whole body. The Holy Spirit is fire and ardour warming me. I am not burnt out, for there a glowing heat constantly fans the flames of love within me. For the devotional writer Henri Nouwen, spiritual life means watching over our inner fervour, making sure that the Holy Spirit is keeping it ablaze inside us. I find it helpful to place my hands on my chest at the same time and imagine the fire of the Spirit burning in me and infusing me with divine love.

In John's gospel the Holy Spirit is primarily the source flowing inside us. When I sit down by a stream or river and simply watch the water going by, I sense the ever-flowing, never-quenched spring within me. The Holy Spirit constantly refreshes me and gives me life. He cleanses me of all that is dark and troubled and clarifies my innermost self. He is water streaming within me, carrying away every obstruction, wearing down the barriers, and making my dried-up country fertile again. But my main thought is that the spring flowing in me is inexhaustible because it is divine. When I am in touch with this spring of the Holy Spirit, I can do an immense amount of work without exhaustion. Work just seems to flow out of me. It is a pleasure and I feel no need to prove myself.

For me, living on the basis of confirmation means taking the reality of the Holy Spirit seriously. If I constantly remind myself, whatever I am doing, that the Holy Spirit is there in me, in my breath, in my thoughts, in my language and in my actions, then I am liberated from the pressure to achieve, and from having to do everything myself. I feel that I am living by the power of another reality. I am not alone in the process of becoming who I am. I don't have to engage in the struggle of my life with no one to help me. I don't have to solve all my problems by myself. I don't have to throw off depressive feelings on my own. The fight to conquer my negative emotions is not unending. God's Spirit is fighting in me too. He doesn't solve all my problems. He doesn't simply dissolve my depression. But when I am depressed and then remember the Spirit of God in me, it is as if a breach had been made in the wall of my melancholy. It doesn't enclose me totally now. I am no longer obsessed with it. Yes, it's still there, like my wounds and hurt feelings. But I don't have to tackle them all at once, on my own. I know that the Holy Spirit is flowing in me and that he can transform these injuries. If I have confidence in this Spirit in me, in the very midst of all my sensitivity and instability, I stop focusing anxiously on my psyche and trust that God's Spirit will guide me through all life's uncertainties.

Faith in the Holy Spirit, whom I received irrevocably in confirmation, who anointed and sealed me, enables me to trust and rest assured that my life will be successful. It will not necessarily satisfy the expectations of my environment and meet the standards of this world. But I will succeed. For after giving my confidence to God's Spirit , I was 'so to speak, stamped with the promised Holy Spirit as a guarantee of purchase, until the day when God completes the redemption of what he has paid for as his own' (Eph. 1.13–14). He is my promise that because I belong to God he will never let me drop from his loving, kind and protective hand until I sing his glory for ever (cf. Eph. 1.14).

CONCLUSION

Part of the real nature of confirmation is reflected in the creativity with which many parishes prepare for the sacrament. Since we are anointed with the Holy Spirit in confirmation, it is only logical that the Spirit should be at work in the candidates' preparation. Experience shows that there is no single right way to make sure young people are ready to receive the sacrament. During this period, it is essential for candidates, priests and others to entrust themselves to the Spirit's guidance and to use their imagination and creative power. Then confirmation will not be a transient experience without any lasting meaning for these young people, or effect on them. It will touch their hearts and minds and enable them to live differently: as more adult, mature, courageous, creative, responsible human beings aware of their own mission in life.

Anyone who has been confirmed will find it immensely beneficial constantly to recall his or her own confirmation, or to think about the nature of the sacrament, in order to draw on the strength of the Holy Spirit in everyday life. Those who make room for God's Spirit in their lives will discover how the Spirit inspires them, infuses them with vitality, and gives them the gift of true freedom. Freedom is the most important gift of the Spirit. We are all in dire need of freedom nowadays, for we are hemmed in and conditioned by so many forms of dependence. Our confirmation has the power to remind us again and again of St Paul's words: 'The Lord ... is the Spirit of the new agreement, and wherever the Spirit of the Lord is, our souls are set free' (2 Cor. 3.17).

4

Reconciliation

INTRODUCTION

Of all the sacraments, reconciliation, or penance, popularly known as confession, would seem to be the one avoided by the greatest number of people in recent years. In the 1950s it was still customary for devout Catholics (and for Christians belonging to other denominations with a similar tradition) to go to confession about every four weeks, but at the very least at Christmas, Easter and All Saints. Nowadays, however, many people have simply dropped the practice. They no longer go at all. You scarcely ever see long queues before confessionals. At best you come across these lines of penitents in monasteries and convents, during pilgrimages and on certain feast days. The decline of this sacrament undoubtedly has something to do with the overemphasis on frequent confession in the past, but also with a deficient theology and practice of reconciliation.

It would be pretty pointless to regret the disappearance of regular confession as it was still practised half a century ago. It wasn't necessarily carried out as Jesus wanted, but as the Church required. It was a sign of the Church's power over the souls of the faithful. But people paid for frequent confession with fear and a variety of wounds.

During some thirty years of work with young people I have often spent twenty hours at a time talking to a succession of young men and women coming to confession. They realized how healing and liberating these discussions were for them. Accordingly, in this section of the book, I want to describe the sacrament of reconciliation as a healthy and restorative process offered to us by God. During a large number of conversations with people seeking help, I have learnt that guilt and guilt feelings are a really important topic for many of them. The sacrament of Reconciliation is an opportunity for people to talk about their guilt and associated emotions as they wish and need. But it's more than that. It's also a chance for people to know that their guilt is forgiven. No other sacrament comes as close to the therapeutic discussion as practised in counselling or in some analytical or psychiatric consultations. Yet many therapists feel a certain envy about this sacrament, which is more than two people talking about guilt, for in it a special rite penetrates the depths of the unconscious and effectively conveys a firm conviction that guilt has been forgiven.

I see my task as drawing on the riches of Christian tradition to help people in our own time. The healing and liberating effect of reconciliation will become clear when we consider the theology and practice of the sacrament and inquire into its meaning for us today.

I. UNDERSTANDING THE SACRAMENT

Words and meanings

Popular Catholic usage generally uses the term 'Confession'. Theologians often describe it as the 'sacrament of Penance'. But the attitudes and procedures of confessing and 'doing penance' comprise only one, admittedly essential, aspect of reconciliation. The acknowledgement of your sins is not a Christian invention. In almost all religions it is usual for those who have burdened their relationship with God with sin to bring this situation 'back to normal' by some form of confession. Open confession is practised in many religions. When the due order of life has been disturbed, people have to restore it by acknowledging their sins publicly. Monastic confession to keep the way to redemption pure has been a feature of Buddhism since the second century AD. The New Testament describes the admission of sins before God (1 John 1.9) and before one another: 'You should get into the habit of admitting your sins to each other, and praying for each other, so that if sickness comes to you, you may be healed' (Jas. 5.16). This does not refer to confession before a priest but to a mutual admission of sins which also involves prayer.

In confession, people try to restore their relationship to God and to other people. Every individual has an inborn need to confess, for everyone realizes that he or she is constantly inclined to deviate from the right way of life. To confess effectively, a resolve to begin afresh is necessary. In many religions this new beginning is expressed in the form of a ritual. This may be personal or public. In ages past, when bad weather had destroyed the crops, or too many misfortunes had befallen a tribe, confessional rites were celebrated in common to appease God. Confession can be expressed through the adoption of a new pattern of behaviour or in a more intense union with God. But it can also take the form of the actual destruction of sinners, or of their symbolic representatives, by sacrifice. Animals are often sacrificed instead of human beings. The Hebrews practised the expulsion into the desert of a 'scapegoat,' a goat symbolically laden with the national guilt.

The Bible, especially the New Testament, does not mention 'penance' as such, but uses the terms 'atonement', 'conversion' or 'repentance' (modern English translations ring the changes on these time-honoured synonyms and more colloquial phrases which come to the same thing). The Greek word is *metanoia*, or 'after-thought'. In the Old Testament period there were days of atonement, when the people publicly repented of their sins with fasting and loud cries or wails, and promised Yahweh to turn back to him wholeheartedly. The prophets criticized these practices as often no more than external symbols of repentance with no inward change of disposition. They asserted the need for a change of heart, and maintained that true conversion and an inner 'turning', or adoption of a new attitude to Yahweh, occurred in the innermost depths of the soul. John the Baptist is wholly in the tradition of the Old Testament when he calls on people to repent if they wish to escape God's judgement, for his kingdom is at hand.

Like John the Baptist, Jesus of Nazareth proclaims the need for repentance, a change of heart. Yet he does not preach the law but the imminent arrival of God's kingdom. People ought to repent because God comes to humankind in Jesus himself. Jesus's first words recorded in Mark's gospel are: 'The time has come at last – the kingdom of God has arrived. You must change your hearts and minds and believe the good news' (Mark 1.15). *Metanoia* in the sense of 'after-thought', means 'thinking differently, rethinking, looking behind things'. The improvement and alteration of behaviour start with a new way of thinking. Only if minds and hearts change, can behaviour be different. Among the New Testament writers, the author of Luke's gospel uses the term *metanoia* most frequently. In the Acts of the Apostles, which he also wrote, he tells us that when Peter's Pentecostal address deeply moved the hearts of those Jews who had come from all the nations of the earth to assemble in Jerusalem, they asked him and the rest of the apostles: ' "Brethren, what shall we do?" Peter answered: "Repent and be baptized every one of you in the name of Jesus Christ for the forgiveness of your sins; and you shall receive the gift of the Holy Spirit." ' (Acts 2.7f.). Peter is not issuing some kind of ascetic summons to do penance, but a heartfelt invitation to all Israelites to convert, to change their hearts. This conversion is expressed in the rite of baptism.

Baptism is an acknowledgement, or 'confession', that Jesus Christ is the Lord and Messiah. In baptism the penitent receives the gift of forgiveness and the gift of the Holy Spirit. The past is effaced at the same time, so that he or she can begin again by the power of the Holy Spirit.

The baptized person is also filled with the Spirit of Jesus Christ. Then, like Jesus, who also preached and healed by the Spirit's power, he or she can follow a new road, one that leads to true life. For Jews and Gentiles, or 'pagans', *metanoia* is a gift of God. Non-Jews are not compelled to accept circumcision; all they have to do is to see the world differently, turn away from their previous state of 'not knowing what they were doing' (Acts 3.17), and turn to God and Jesus Christ the Lord. They must abandon false paths, repent, and follow the new way, which Jesus Christ not only proclaimed but took before them.

The reconciliation of humans and God will be brought about through confession or repentance. Reconciliation is a central concept in the New Testament. The word 'reconciliation' comes (though Old French) from the Latin *reconciliare* (to bring together again, to reunite, to re-establish or restore). To reconcile means to restore to full membership, to make friendly after an estrangement, and to heal, settle, harmonize and make compatible, but also to purify something sacred after it has been desecrated.

Reconciliation ensures peace and restores community. Most of the foregoing meanings apply to the experience of division and dissension between individuals and groups of people. But the term 'reconciliation' can also apply to our relationship with God. By sinning, people alienate themselves from God. They forgo their relationship with him. For the Bible, reconciliation, the restoration of community or communion, is always a free offer which God makes to us. People don't have to carry out some kind of penitential act to achieve reconciliation. They have to accept it thankfully. For Paul, this is the good news which he is to proclaim in Jesus's name: 'In Christ God was reconciling the world to himself . . . We beseech you on behalf of Christ, be reconciled to God' (2 Cor. 5.19f.).

The Latin word for 'penance' is *poenitentia*, which comes from *poena* (punishment). If we keep to the etymology, penance is associated with doing penance, engaging in an act of penitence. Whoever has sinned receives a punishment and must give satisfaction by paying up and carrying out some penitential act in reparation for the sin committed. The main emphasis is on actually doing penance. For too many people today the Roman principle of performing something in reparation is still predominant and more decisive than the biblical message of reconciliation. They still think that they have to discharge their debt of sinfulness. In this interpretation penance would be something akin to imprisonment and carrying out a statutory assignment until satisfaction has been given.

A brief history

There were penitential rites in the Christian Church from the start. Whenever they said the Lord's Prayer, Christians prayed: 'Forgive us our trespasses as we forgive those who trespass against us.' This is how Jesus taught them to pray. In the early Church the Our Father closed morning and evening prayer. People began the day with a request for forgiveness and ended it in the same way. The Our Father was repeated before communion during every eucharistic celebration. If Christians wished to become one with Jesus Christ at his Meal, and with their brothers and sisters through him, they had to be prepared to repent and to forgive those who had offended them. Therefore the celebration of the Eucharist was associated with a penitential rite from the start. If people wish to draw close to God, they must not boast of their virtuous deeds, like the Pharisee, but act humbly like the tax-collector. For Luke, the tax-collector's modest request, 'God, have mercy on a sinner like me!' (Luke 18.13), is a prerequisite of a truly Christian attitude of prayer. Readiness to repent forms part of every prayer and every act of worship.

A special penitential service was developed from some point at the end of the second or at the beginning of the third century AD. It was intended for sinners who had fallen away from the church community because, for example, they had lost their faith or had committed a public sin such as murder or adultery. The development of penitential rites for the reincorporation of such Christians was the beginning of the sacrament of penance or reconciliation. Its history has developed from two sources: the act of reconciliation, which derived from the confessional practice of urban Christian communities, and the act of spiritual direction, as practised in early monastic communities.

a) Confession and reconciliation

Reconciliatory confession was the means used by the early Church to receive back into the community those Christians who had fallen into grave sin after baptism. This meant that they had jettisoned their faith, or committed adultery or murder. For a long time there was debate in the Church about whether it was actually permissible to accept someone back into the Christian community if he or she had made a total decision for Christ in baptism, but had then rejected that option by committing a crime. Eventually the more compassionate viewpoint won the day. If a sinner acknowledged his or her guilt before the bishop, he or she was granted the status of a penitent. But penitents were excluded from the Eucharist.

The Eastern Church divided penitence into different stages. There were the weepers, who were wholly shut out from the Eucharist; the listeners, who attended it only in an ante-room; and the kneelers, who were allowed to stay in the church during the celebration but, like those standing, were excluded from the offertory and communion. Penitents were assigned specific penances, which they had to carry out. They had to prove themselves by leading a Christian life and, in order to heal the wounds which they had opened by their sins, were required to fast, pray and give alms.

The Eastern Church stressed the healing effect of penances, whereas the Western Church laid more emphasis on the aspect of reparation for the injustice done. When the penitential period had been completed, the penitents were restored to a standing position in the Christian community.

This so-called 'Reconciliation' was celebrated in a special rite which included the prayers of the community, a laying on of hands by the bishop, and reception of Holy Communion. In some places the laying on of hands was supplemented by anointing. The prayers stressed reconciliation with the Church. In the West the liturgy of reconciliation was associated primarily with Lent. The penitential period began on Ash Wednesday and the reconciliation with the Church was celebrated on Holy Thursday. Initially these rites were intended only for public sinners, but were gradually extended to all Christians. The sign of the cross made with ashes on the foreheads of the faithful on Ash Wednesday expressed the fact that all Christians were sinners, and in need of penitence in order to re-experience the mystery of the eucharistic community on Holy Thursday.

b) Confession and devotion

From the early Middle Ages onwards, general confession in public was gradually suppressed in favour of private oral, or 'auricular', confession, which spread from Ireland to continental Europe. In the early Church sinners had to do penance before receiving absolution. In private confessions absolution was given before the penance, so that the latter became more of a symbolic act no longer associated with the original public sacrament. Private confessions could be repeated frequently. In the nineteenth century a plethora of missions to parishes and sections of the population led to people confessing as often as possible. Special devotions or 'devotional confessions' became a popular practice. The general attitude was that the more often you went to confession, the more grace you earned. Grace was thought of almost quantitatively, as if it were possible to make sure of having a large amount of it marked up to your credit if you carried out specific actions, such as going to confession or saying prayers with indulgences attached.

Twentieth-century Catholic piety was closely associated with the Eucharist. The rigorous religious practice recommended by Jansenism, a school or trend of Catholic theology and religious life that spread from seventeenth- and eighteenth-century France, held that Christians were worthy of receiving communion only if they had been to confession beforehand. This led to infrequent communion, which had to be prepared for by confession. The eventual outcome of the official reaction against Jansenism was that in the first half of the twentieth century people went to confession more than at any other time in the history of the Church. But this conception of the sacrament no longer accorded with the theology of reconciliation in the early Church. It is not surprising that the way the sacrament was used until about the end of the 1950s has gone for ever.

c) Confession and spiritual direction

The second source of our present-day sacrament of reconciliation is spiritual direction as practised in early monasticism. The roots of this kind of confession are already apparent in the thinking of Clement of Alexandria (d. *c.* 215) and of Origen (d. *c.* 254). Clement advises Christians to seek out an experienced director of conscience to whom they should confess their sins. Then he will pray on their behalf and support them sympathetically. Origen speaks of spiritually endowed men with the power to forgive sins. If they possess the Spirit, then they too are priests, even if they hold no confirmed office in the Church. Origen thinks of a spiritual director as a physician. When Christians confess their sins to him, he administers the medicine of the divine Word, making confession a quasi-medical procedure. In such cases, a physician needs not only a proficient knowledge of the human heart but the gifts of empathy, supportive advice and prayer. He prays for sinners, asking God to forgive them their sins, and sustains them in their efforts so that they do not falter. But he does not give sacramental absolution. This was unknown in the early history of confession. Forgiveness was always God's concern. The spiritual director merely asked God to forgive sinners. And the penitents, so to speak, incorporated their petitions in his prayer.

Monks were the main practitioners of confession to a spiritual director. Every monk had a spiritual father (*abbas*) or mother (*amma*) to whom he revealed his thoughts. This was a question not only of guilt but of all movements of the heart, thoughts and feelings, passions and needs. He talked to his spiritual father about his dreams and his body, about sickness and difficulties. All this was considered to be vital information about the inner condition of the soul. The spiritual adviser contributed the gift of discernment of spirits and knowledge of the heart to this joint effort of assisting the young monk on his spiritual journey.

Spiritual direction was thought of not as a sacrament but as the spiritual aid which every monk needed to advance along the spiritual path. This spiritual direction was comparable to a therapeutic discussion or analysis. Although it was a matter of honest self-knowledge, of progress on the way to God, the procedure did not avoid dark aspects of the soul, or 'evil thoughts', for these were to be disclosed to the spiritual father in order to render them ineffectual.

Thus Benedict of Nursia advised his monks: 'If any evil thoughts enter your heart, crush them directly on Christ by revealing them to your spiritual father' (*Rule of St Benedict*, 4).

As monastic communities received an increasing number of priests into their ranks, the directional form of confession became a sacrament. But this involved a levelling of distinctions and a neglect of the actual intention of monastic spiritual direction. Because sacramental confession was concerned with the remission of sins, the varied matters disclosed in the course of spiritual direction now had to be presented as sins. This was the origin of 'devotional' confession, in which any inconvenient lack of current sin was redressed by 'elevating' all possible imperfections to the status of sins, or by absolving all over again sins already forgiven a long time before.

d) Is confession necessary?

The history of the sacrament of reconciliation shows that what remains the general form of confession nowadays, an acknowledgement of sins in a confessional and a brief exhortation or a few encouraging words, does not reflect its real purpose as the Church originally conceived it. We have to return to the sources in order to make the sacrament the really helpful spiritual aid people actually need in today's world.

Unfortunately, even today there are some Christians who have been deeply injured by confession. Sometimes a form of spiritual abuse entered into confession. Penitents were interrogated unmercifully and quite often condemned. Their inclination to obedience was misused to make them do things that overtaxed and harmed them. They encountered a rigorous, uncharitable attitude, instead of understanding and compassion. This behaviour on the part of confessors made many people afraid of confession or persuaded them to reject it altogether.

Many people think that, as Catholic Christians, they 'have to' confess. But there's no 'must' about confession. We can confess if we need to do so, and should experience God's loving kindness and forgiveness in the sacrament. From a theological viewpoint, mortal sins are the only ones we have to confess. But mortal sins are committed only when we make a conscious decision to oppose God in a grave matter and on the basis of a totally free conscience and awareness. Most sins are not sins involving a conscious decision against God but sins of weakness, sins in which we are ruled by our emotions and passions. Psychology also tells us that an absolutely free decision is a very infrequent phenomenon. Most of the sins and mistakes which we confess do not require absolution but a process of purposeful clarification. Much of the former practice of confession in order to receive spiritual direction now takes place in spiritual counselling. This is a process by which we get to know the depths of our own heart, and develop strategies not only to change our behaviour but to retune the psychological mechanisms that constantly produce the same mistakes.

Although most of the confessions we experience as priests nowadays, whether in the confessional or in a relaxed discussion, are also occasions for spiritual direction, reconciliatory confession is still practised today. When people incur guilt which they can't forgive themselves, they need the experience of being accepted by God and restored to the human community. When they are guilty they feel excluded from human fellowship. They need the rite of confession and reconciliation in order to feel that they are restored to membership of the community and to be reconciled with and to themselves.

Reconciliation is part of every confession. For we constantly approach God as people who find themselves unacceptable, are dissatisfied with themselves, and therefore wish to experience God's acceptance in the sacrament in a visible and tangible form. Nevertheless, we have to distinguish between the two aspects of reconciliation and direction of conscience, lest we treat everything as sin and spy out sin in all our thoughts and actions. To understand and use the sacrament properly we must be sure what sin and guilt actually are and how we ought to deal with them.

e) Lay confession and confession to a priest

In the early Church, the priest in confession was primarily a petitioner who bore the sinner's guilt before God in an act of solidarity with him or her. It was not absolutely necessary to confess your sins to a priest. A layperson could also give absolution. This conception of the sacrament was still present even in the Middle Ages, when lay confession was a widespread practice. The English monk and historian, the Venerable Bede (d. 735), interpreted the injunction in James 5.16 ('You should get into the habit of admitting your sins to each other, and praying for each other, so that if sickness comes to you you may be healed'), as meaning that Christians, if not burdened by grave guilt to be admitted before a priest, can confess to their neighbours, to obtain absolution. Lay confession was still practised well into the sixteenth century. Before the Battle of Pamplona (1521), St Ignatius Loyola confessed to an ordinary soldier. Albert the Great also calls confession to a layperson a sacrament. Thomas Aquinas classifies it as at least 'quasi-sacramental'.

The ascription to priests alone of the authority to hear confessions was first raised by Scholastic theologians. In his sacramental theology, St Thomas Aquinas bases this ascription on the fact that in the sacrament the priest is the sole representative of Christ and of his healing action. According to Aquinas, the priest is the instrument of Christ. He pronounces the penitent forgiven by God through Christ's authority. Until well into the Middle Ages, the priest pronounced the penitent forgiven in the petition he made on his behalf, but from Aquinas's time the indicative formula of absolution, 'I absolve you from your sins', became the usual practice. Aquinas bases this on the claim that the priest is acting by Christ's authority and that the statement made to the penitent in the indicative mood offers him or her greater assurance of forgiveness. In 1439, in the 'Armenian decree' of the Council of Florence, the magisterium, or teaching office, of the Church made St Thomas's view binding on Western Christians.

This brief survey of the history of the sacrament of reconciliation shows that a one-sided fixation on the priest's authority does not correspond to the original intention. The original aim of confession was to reintegrate sinners fully into the community of the Church. Sin separated them from that community. Therefore, in conversation with a brother or sister they were to experience his or her prayer on their behalf, and know that God wished to show them his mercy and grace, and forgive all their sins. This petitionary prayer on behalf of sinners helped them to believe in God's forgiveness and to feel that they were restored to fellowship as members of the Church.

The history of the sacrament convinces me that it would be helpful to devise new forms of lay confession today. Many priests and pastoral workers think that as soon as guilt is in question, those in search of help must unconditionally confess to a priest. That is the only way for their guilt to be forgiven. But this view does not accord with the meaning of the sacrament. Therapists, counsellors, pastoral workers and spiritual directors can all offer to pray for forgiveness of the guilt felt by those who look to them for advice and help. This will help to assure their 'clients' that God really forgives sinners.

The teaching of the Church is that absolution is reserved to the priest alone. In the case of grave sin, penitents must go to a priest to experience forgiveness. This is quite cogent. A grave sin is a conscious turning away from God with regard to an utterly serious matter, committed with full knowledge of the implications of the act and with complete freedom of choice. Those who commit grave sins consciously exclude themselves from the Church. Then they need the priest as the official representative of the Church to receive them once again into the community of the Church in the rite of confession or reconciliation. The Church offers this as the reason for confessing to a priest. A psychological reason for doing so would be that those who have sinned gravely need the church rite, reserved to the priest alone, if they are to go away convinced that their guilt has been forgiven. The rite dissolves the unconscious obstacles which they have put in the way of forgiveness and allows forgiveness to penetrate into the depths of their unconscious minds. Then they can feel truly liberated and know that they have been entirely restored to fellowship as members of the Church.

Dealing with guilt

We often hear the complaint that people nowadays no longer have any sense of guilt and sin, and that the drop in the numbers of those going to confession has much to do with this deficient awareness of sin. Undoubtedly people today no longer accept the traditional notion of sin as a failure to observe commandments. Today we can't understand the commandments so unambiguously as people did in past centuries. Furthermore, our knowledge of psychology tells us that the perfectly correct façade of a Christian who keeps to the commandments can conceal immense aggression and deceit.

People nowadays no longer feel any guilt about areas of behaviour covered by some of the sin catalogues which the Church has proposed in the past, and sometimes still offers, for the 'examination of conscience'. Yet a reading of many important modern authors shows us that they are very concerned with the question of the guilt in which people are enmeshed. Modern literature relentlessly exposes the occasions of human guilt. People are guilty when they refuse to recognize reality as it is, and when they accept everything that happens with equanimity or indifference. People incur guilt when they fail to change social conditions out of laziness, inertia, intellectual indolence and cowardice. The whole world of business and the contemporary insistence on achievement and success drive people to the point of guilt so surely that they scarcely even notice what is happening to them.

a) Guilt and guilt feelings

Contemporary psychologists confirm the existence both of a deficient awareness of incurring guilt, and of a simultaneously rampant spread of guilt feelings. Here we have to make a distinction between real guilt and feeling guilty. Many guilt feelings are not indicators of actual guilt but signs of a lack of clarity and of inadequate self-confidence.

Many people feel guilty when they become aware of the accusations directed at them by their own superego, or internalized conscience. They have internalized their parents' commandments and values to such a degree that indulging in guilt feelings seems the only way to be free of them. A young woman who as a child was always forced to work by her mother feels guilty if she takes even a few minutes off and awards herself a short rest. Others feel guilty if they can't satisfy the expectations of other people: marriage partners, friends, colleagues at work and so on. Yet others condemn themselves because of the feelings of hate and envy that suddenly grip them. They punish themselves by means of guilt feelings when they perceive their own aggression. Instead of analyzing the aggression and integrating it into their understanding of life, they turn it against themselves. Then therapeutic psychologists and clinicians as well as proficient pastoral workers have to help them to distinguish their guilt feelings from authentic guilt.

Because guilt feelings are always unpleasant, human beings have developed a large number of mechanisms to palliate or escape them. One way to suppress guilt feelings is to project them onto other people and phenomena: individuals and groups or impersonal structures. People defend themselves from guilt feelings because these destroy their ideal self-images and cut them off from the human community. To acknowledge their own guilt would take the ground from under their feet and radically threaten their humanity. In that case, guilt suppression is understandable. Yet it leads to the freezing of life in what are known as 'repetition-compulsions', or blind impulses to repeat experiences without any pleasurable or painful advantage, and in apathy and insensitivity. Suppressed guilt feelings also emerge in the form of anger, fear, irritability, obduracy and impenitence.

Ultimately, the loss of any sense of real guilt signifies a loss of humanity. 'When people no longer recognize the possibility that they are guilty, then they no longer acknowledge their real existential depth, their characteristic uniqueness, freedom and responsibility' (Albert Görres, *Das Böse* [Evil], 1984, p. 77). When people have lost all awareness of guilt, evil no longer appears in them as 'a bad conscience, but only as diffuse fear or depression, as a state of abnormal tension' (A. Görres, *ibid.*, p. 78). Such individuals are no longer plagued by guilt feelings but by fear of failure and by depressions.

But analytical psychology is concerned not only with guilt feelings but with authentic guilt. Jung sees guilt as a 'psychic split'. I refuse to see and accept myself as I am. I repress what is unpleasant and 'split it off'. For Jung, guilt is not something necessary, something which inevitably happens to people. It is associated entirely with a free decision, when I consciously close my eyes to what contradicts my ideal self-image.

Human beings are always trying to evade the truth about themselves. Some just avoid their own reality by minimizing their guilt, whereas others do so by exaggerating it. Instead of looking guilt straight in the eye and 'converting' (conversion = repentance), they exaggerate their remorse, 'because it is so nice to have such a wonderful remorseful feeling, to enjoy it like a warm eiderdown on a cold winter's morning, when one should be getting up. This dishonesty, this refusal to see, ensures that there will be no confrontation with the shadow [the repressed dark side of the self]' (C.J. Jung, *Civilization in Transition* [1964], p. 468).

b) Guilt as an opportunity

Jung tells us that people are guilty when they refuse to face their own truth. But Jung also recognizes an almost necessary form of guilt, which is an ineluctable human experience:

> Only an exceedingly naïve and unconscious person could imagine that he is in a position to avoid sin. Psychology can no longer afford childish illusions of this kind; it must [obey] the truth and declare that unconsciousness is not only no excuse but is actually one of the most heinous sins. Human law may exempt it from punishment, but Nature avenges herself the more mercilessly, for it is nothing to her whether a man is conscious of his sin or not. (*Civilization in Transition*, p. 357)

Guilt is an opportunity to get down to the bedrock of reality and reach deeper self-knowledge, to search the innermost depths of the heart and find God himself.

Our task is to accept our own shadow and, in full humility, our own guilt. People constantly incur guilt on their way to full self-possession. Jung does not exonerate us from this, let alone say that we ought to be guilty, but simply confirms what happens over and over again in life. If people face up to their guilt, it will be powerless to harm them as they advance towards greater self-awareness. But dealing with guilt demands a moral effort. Becoming aware of our guilt also requires us to change and improve specific aspects of ourselves. If something is left to fester in the unconscious, it will just stick there, and that aspect of our being will never change. Psychological adjustments can be carried out only in the conscious mind. Full consciousness of guilt can become the most powerful of moral suasions for and instruments of change. It has even been said that, however unfortunate guilt may be in itself, no spiritual maturation and no extension of our mental and spiritual scope are possible without it, for experience of our own guilt can be a vital sign that our inner transformation is beginning to take effect.

c) Evil

A proficient acquaintance with analytical psychology prevents us from adopting a one-sided concept of sin as straightforward disobedience, simply not obeying commandments. Guilt is closely related to and mixed up with mismanaged drives and instincts, maladjustments of experience and failed attempts to internalize it beneficially. It is not always possible to discover the exact proportion of individual guilt in behaviour that we might confidently assess as objectively evil. But analytical psychologists also admit that we can be guilty if we allow the evil in us enough space in which to take effect, refuse to work through our past, and just let evil determine the course of our lives without putting up any struggle against it.

Albert Görres has described some of the ways in which analytical psychology interprets evil, especially in accordance with the theories of Sigmund Freud. For Freud, evil is whatever is inappropriate to happiness and well-being. Evil is what society forbids and punishes because it is detrimental to community life. Evil arises when, because of excessive deprivation or demands, instinctual needs (the demands made by fundamental drives, and arising from the organism itself and not from the outside world) assume forms threatening to communal life. 'Transfer' is a constant source of evil. For instance, on becoming an adult, a formerly unloved and unjustly treated child will 'transfer the desire for revenge against the parent to other people, who will be treated as if they were the parent who deserved this act of vengeance. Many examples of evil in adults are attempts in later life to compensate for old wrongdoing by taking it out on innocent parties'. Freud, therefore, sees evil as a form of maladjustment, or 'maldevelopment', because of unsuccessful processing, or inadequate mobilization and discharge, of psychic wounds. In this view evil takes control if someone is denied the appropriate satisfaction of his or her drives and desires for too long a time. In most cases of this kind negative childhood experiences lead to a vicious circle of evil acts and agonizing guilt feelings. Görres rejects the view proposed by some 'virtuous' people that anyone might commit evil acts for sheer pleasure: 'For the most part evil is not a pleasurably malign act committed with a buoyant heart and soul, for the sake of sheer unrepentant pleasure, but a tormented, compulsive and obsessive or neurotically and instinctually driven emotional reaction to unbearable injuries and deprivation' (A. Görres, *Das Böse* [Evil], 1984, pp. 78, 134–6).

Analytical psychologists warn us against unilaterally condemning people who commit evil acts. But they also tell us that forgiveness is a decisive prerequisite for the healthy development of the human psyche. Only if I can forgive people who have wounded and tormented me can this solid block of frozen hatred melt, and at least some part of evil be transformed and vanquished. We owe this not only to ourselves but to society. Without forgiveness evil proliferates like a cancerous growth.

d) Neither accuse nor excuse

The question is how to deal with our guilt. We have to beware of two tendencies: to accuse and to excuse. When we accuse ourselves, we tear ourselves apart with guilt feelings and use them to punish ourselves. We dramatize our guilt. Then we have failed to distance ourselves adequately from our own guilt. We do not really deal with it but let it rule us and drag us down. This self-devaluation is often unrealistic, and ignores things as they really are. That makes it an obstacle to genuine self-criticism and responsibility. Then people condemn themselves totally while avoiding any real analysis of the certain facts. But often self-accusation is no more than pride in reverse. Essentially it means that people want to be better than others and elevate themselves above the mass. Then, all of a sudden, they hear the forbidding voice of their own superego. This, according to psychoanalytical psychology, represents social morality or conscience and our own ideal aspirations in the psyche (consisting of the three functional divisions of id, ego and superego). Such people often describe themselves as the worst sinners on earth. They must be the worst because they can't be the best. Refusing to recognize that they are just average human beings, they are determined to outdo others at any cost, if not in being and doing good, then at least in being and doing evil. They desperately need humility: the courage to realize and stand up for their humanity.

The other danger is that of excusing ourselves. This is also a way of evading guilt. I search for a thousand reasons why I am not guilty and try to justify myself in every possible way. But the more I try, the greater doubt I feel. The only recourse I have is to go on looking for new grounds for self-justification. My refusal to face my guilt makes me all bustle and push. I can't stand being quiet and peaceful, for then my feelings of guilt would seize me and I would realize that all my attempts at self-justification are pointless.

e) Liberating talk

Facing up to our own guilt is an essential aspect of human dignity and an expression of our freedom. If I minimize my guilt by shifting the blame onto others or by looking for excuses, I diminish this dignity and surrender my freedom. But if I take responsibility for my failures, I have to avoid all attempts at justification and any attribution of guilt to others. This is the condition for continuing to live inwardly as a human being. I have to break out of the prison of ongoing self-punishment and self-humiliation and find my true self.

Admission of guilt to another person often leads to an experience of greater closeness and deeper understanding between two people. The chance of such an outcome makes talking to someone else an appropriate way to deal with guilt. In this discussion I admit my guilt but also enjoy the benefit of a certain distance from myself. I show my readiness to accept the basic rules of human fellowship. This kind of conversation can help me to see that nothing now separates me from others because I have nothing to hide. The other person knows my guilt, and is neither shocked nor repelled nor impelled to take revenge. It is an occasion for an exchange of fully human responses between two people aware of their humanity.

The other person has to take my guilt feelings seriously, even if they derive not from authentic guilt but from an excessively strict superego. Each guilt feeling has a reason. The cause often lies in childhood conflicts. Even if the guilt feeling seems extraordinarily abstruse, the adviser must take it seriously and act as if it were justified. The skill of the confessor lies in neither strengthening nor making light of these feelings. If I play down a penitent's self-accusations I am not taking him or her seriously in his or her state of need. I am not taking the trouble to empathize with this person. It is better to encourage penitents to examine their guilt feelings more proficiently. What feelings are associated with them? How is the guilt manifested physically? What thoughts are associated with it? What exactly are penitents accusing themselves of? What does the sense of guilt remind them of? Do they connect this guilt with similar experiences in the past? I encourage penitents to look at these guilt feelings without evaluating them. Unflinching confrontation with them will make them more accurate signposts to the real truth about their souls.

There is always a reason for guilt feelings. The problem with neurotic guilt, however, is that such penitents do not know the true sources of these feelings, but attach them to secondary experiences. What they cite as the cause is not the underlying conflict situation but a coded image of the actual problems, which can be deduced from it only indirectly. The confessor's task is to search for the actual sources of the guilt feelings and to direct penitents to the original guilt, which they have probably never named directly. A discussion of guilt feelings will often disclose repressed aggression, taboo instincts, suppressed sexual desires and self-mutilatory or self-destructive tendencies. Then the purpose of the sacrament would be for penitents to face the truth about themselves and become reconciled to it. As a result of a carefully managed discussion, it might be hoped, they would see that any blame is to be attached not to anything confessed but to a refusal to face the truth about themselves.

II. FORM AND CONTENT

When I sit in the confessional in our church and 'hear confessions', most of them last only a few minutes. People very often just go through a few formal paces, then it's over. That makes it difficult for me to administer the sacrament effectively. But I realize that some people find it very difficult to talk about themselves in private. So at least I ask which aspect of what they've said they most regret or what troubles them most. Some people are thankful for this invitation and start to give a very personal account of what really moves them. Others act as if they haven't heard what I said. Then I go no further. I respect the fact that they can confess only in the time-honoured way. All I can do is to encourage them, sympathetically, to forgive themselves. I try not to give them, say, an Our Father as penance but ask them to spend a few minutes considering which aspects of their lives they should be thankful for, or what they would like to change in them. I hope then that this confession will mean more to them than the usual formula.

In the following pages I am concerned not so much with the sacrament of reconciliation in the confessional, but with the kind of reconciliatory conversation that can take place in a special room set aside for the purpose. This will give more time to celebrate the sacrament as the effective rite it is intended to be.

Greeting

The sacrament begins with a brief greeting. The priest and the penitent make the sign of the cross and thus place themselves within God's merciful love, which shone forth most visibly on the cross. Then the priest can say a short prayer. Depending on the country or region, the official rite prescribes something like: 'May God who illuminates our hearts make you truly aware of your sins and of his mercy.' I prefer to use my own words, and to say something like the following:

> Merciful and loving Lord, N. has come here to hold out his (her) life to you with all its ups and downs. Make it possible for him (her) to see the obstacles on his (her) way to you and to real life. Send him (her) your Holy Spirit and free him (her) from everything that weighs him (her) down. May he (she) have faith in your forgiveness and may your Holy Spirit enable him (her) to forgive him(her)self, so that he (she) can continue on his (her) way strengthened and liberated by this sacrament. I ask this through Christ our Lord.

The rite then calls for the priest to read a passage from the Bible. The following are prescribed or recommended texts: the Letter to the Romans (Rom. 3.22–6; 5.6–11; 6.2–13; 12.1f.; 9.19; 13.8–14); the first Letter of John (1 John 1.5–10; 3.1–24; 4.16–21); and the gospels, for instance Matthew (Matt. 3.1–12; Matt. 4.12–7; Matt. 9.9–13), or Luke (Luke 15.1–10; Luke 15.11–32; Luke 17.1–4; Luke 18.9–14). Personally, I find a text from the first Letter of John most effective:

> This is the message that we have heard from him and proclaim to you, that God is light and in him is no darkness at all. If we

say we have fellowship with him while we walk in darkness, we
lie and do not live according to the truth ... If we say we have
no sin, we deceive ourselves, and the truth is not in us. If we
confess our sins, he is faithful and just, and will forgive our sins
and cleanse us from all unrighteousness. (1 John 1.5–9)

This passage invites the penitents to look more searchingly into their
darkness. God's light will help them to show God their truth. The
words of the Bible have their own power and create an atmosphere in
which we find it easier to admit our guilt and express it openly.

Self-examination

Many people don't know what they ought to confess. They are
dissatisfied with the usual examination of conscience which lays out
various categories for a thorough self-examination. Some people go
through the commandments one after the other and accuse
themselves of disobeying this or that injunction. Many people,
however, find that superficial and far too schematic. A proven
method is to confess from three viewpoints: my relationship to God,
my relationship to myself, and my relationship to my neighbour. The
penitent can take them one by one and say what each means to him
or her, in what respects he is dissatisfied with himself or herself, and
where he or she feels guilty.

Many people say they haven't much to confess. Their primary
complaint is there is nothing to repent of, to feel sorry about. But it's
not only a matter of admitting guilt. It's quite an achievement in
itself to consider our lives and express what we feel in words. Of
course there are areas where we aren't so pleased with ourselves. And
of course it's often difficult to decide precisely whether a particular
thing is sin or merely weakness, inattentiveness, or an everyday error.
That's not very important. The main thing is to consider our lives
and to face at least what is worrying us. If someone describes a
disagreement with his or her father or mother, or with the head of
department or a colleague, all that needs to be said is how it affects
him or her, how he or she feels about it, how he or she has behaved as

a result. Then discussion will bring out the proportion of guilt involved and how the penitent can change things. There is no point in evading the conflict or trying to solve it by oneself. Discussion could point to a helpful approach or resolution. In any case, the confessional discussion should make it clear that guilt is never the responsibility of one party, but that both people are involved, indeed entangled in it. This entanglement has to be worked through so that the other person can be seen more objectively.

Some people approach the sacrament of reconciliation with a specific instance of guilt, with something they feel is a burden here and now. Then they confine themselves to this subject. That is sensible. They only confess what is troubling them at the moment. But they have to focus appropriately on this single problem. When they describe the whole situation, the priest can ask how they see it, what exactly is worrying them, what else they could do, what action they feel confident of, and what outcome they want or expect. He can ask them if they are prepared to forgive themselves too. It's not much use if penitents only complain and accuse, but aren't ready to believe in God's mercy and be merciful to themselves. The confessor's questions must never be motivated by curiosity but should help a penitent to see more clearly what the particular problem is. Talking them out helps him or her to express relevant feelings and interpret them.

Because a lot of people find it difficult to decide what to confess and how to talk about themselves, a few suggestions may be helpful here. With regard to the relationship to God, we can ask ourselves: What role does God play in my life? Do I take him into account? Do I look for him? Or do I pass him by? How do I begin and close my day? Do I have any minor rituals to remind me of God's presence? Do I sign myself with the cross every morning to place myself under his blessing? Do I set aside time to pray, for quiet, to read? Has my relationship to God become empty? What do I yearn for? Do I use God for my own purposes or present myself to God exactly as I am? Is God really the goal of my life and the source from which I live? None of these questions is primarily concerned with the question of guilt, but with the quality of my relationship. Talking about them will enable me to sense in what respects I am closed to God. This kind of closure has a lot to do with guilt, even if it involves no offence against any of the commandments. It's a matter of where my heart is directed and who or what determines it.

In respect to my relationship to myself, I can consider essential aspects of my existence. Do I live my own life, or is it lived for me? Am I inwardly free, or do I make myself dependent on people, things and habits? Do I eat and drink appropriately? Am I satisfied with my health? Do I lead a healthy life? How do I organize my life? Do I have a set of procedures for the day, or do I just let it happen? Am I too self-critical? Do I devalue myself? What do I think about? What kind of fantasies and feelings do I have? What prompts them? How do I deal with them? How do I see and treat my body? How do I deal with my sexuality? Do I give way to depressive feelings? Do I indulge in self-pity? Do I depress myself by constantly putting myself down?

With regard to my relationship to my neighbour, I can begin with the aspects I find especially tiresome or troubling. How do I see the disagreement from my side? How do I think the other person sees it? What is the background to the conflict? What does this person remind me of? Why do I find him or her so difficult to accept? How has he or she hurt me? What are my sensitive points? It is important to describe the conflict without immediately accusing or excusing myself or the other person. Describing it can reveal exactly where my share of the guilt lies and how I can improve myself in that respect. When I consider my relations with other people, I can find out who I think of most often, how I talk about others, whether I respect or despise my fellow human beings, whether I am continually standing in judgement over them and condemning them, and whether I think I'm better than they are. Do I treat other people with sympathy? Do I care how they are, or am I concerned only with my own welfare?

Encouragement and discussion

During the actual confession the priest can ask the penitent how he or she feels about this or that area of life and deals with the problems and guilt involved. These questions should be designed only to elicit information that will help the penitent to see and describe his or her own situation more plainly. I sometimes ask penitents what portion of the guilt for what they have related they would attribute to themselves, and to what extent they have ignored themselves and their own hearts. This question is designed to lead them to their innermost layer of truth, and to ask about the central point where their lives are out of joint and they are actually rejecting the life God offers them.

After the penitent's confession the priest should say what he thinks about the points raised and any special issue that has moved him. He should listen to the voice, as it were, of his own sensibility and provide a kind of feedback that will help penitents to see their situation in a new way, as reflected by the priest. This is a good basis for a real discussion which, however, should be brief and mainly concern the results of the sacrament.

Agenda for the future

In Irish confessional practice of centuries past it was usual to assign a particular penance to each sin which corresponded to the degree of guilt involved. This was often related to the notion that sin had to be 'paid for' by penance. This does not fit our present-day understanding of reconciliation. It is not a question of the satisfaction of guilt but of what might help penitents to progress in their inner lives. The priest can ask them what they would like to do themselves, which aspects of the problem they could improve. This isn't a matter of resolutions, which won't be kept to, but of practical steps that will help people to go forward. Many people undertake something which is condemned to failure from the start. I can't resolve to be more friendly and not to react aggressively from now on. I can't compel my feelings so precisely. Instead of 'resolutions,' I would rather talk about a 'training programme' which penitents can prepare themselves. I can only undertake something specific. For instance, I can undertake to pray, on leaving the house, for people whom I'm going to meet today. But I shan't be able to decide whether I actually run across anyone. I must just remember the specific intention. Whether I am able to realize it depends on many other factors.

A training programme is not classifiable according to the strictness of the penance, as was often the case in the Middle Ages. It is more a question of our optimism about not living as mere victims of our weaknesses. Some people think they are always doomed to go on confessing the same things, and that there's little point in that. Of course we can't change our skin but we can train ourselves to be different in some ways, and to try new approaches to life. The priest has to motivate penitents to discover by themselves what they can do to make inward progress. If they can't think of anything, the priest can make suggestions. But these mustn't be purely external, possibly irrelevant proposals. I always ask penitents whether they think the suggestion is a realistic choice for them.

Taking responsibility for your own mistakes

The rite calls for a short prayer of contrition or penitence after confessing. One verse of a once-popular nineteenth-century hymn began: 'O great Absolver, grant my soul may wear / The lowliest garb of penitence and prayer.' Many people today find not only such statements but the whole complex of ideas associated with 'penitence' difficult to accept. They say: 'I can't be penitent or contrite for what I've done. It wasn't right. I can see that. But I can't go around wearing the lowliest garb of penitence because of that!' In the past, penitence was often overdone, as though you had to make yourself feel really bad, keep saying you were the greatest sinner of all time, and run yourself down in order to prepare for the moment of uplift in absolution. That conception of penitence is contrary to human dignity. Often enough all it does is to stabilize wrong behaviour. One man who entered into a seemingly never-ending series of sexual relationships with different women was also very devout. He was very contrite about his lapses and felt he was a shocking sinner. He went to confession regularly. But his behaviour never altered. Devaluing myself doesn't motivate me to change myself. All I do then is to humiliate myself until I have no power to abandon my way of life.

The Council of Trent defined contrition as 'sorrow of heart and detestation for sin committed, with the resolution not to sin again'. We find this kind of language unappealing nowadays. Karl Rahner says it is necessary to formulate the concept carefully so that modern people can understand it. Penitence 'has nothing to do with a psychological, emotional shock (melancholy, depression), which may often, though not necessarily, follow from the bad action for psychological and physiological or social reasons'. It is much more a question of reacting to the moral worthlessness of the past action and to the attitude which gave rise to it. That doesn't mean repressing my past, but facing it, acknowledging it, and assuming responsibility for it. A much better method of contrition than intricate analysis of the past is 'unconditional turning to the merciful God in love' (Rahner, *Encyclopaedia of Theology*, pp. 288–9).

Penitence is sometimes understood in the sense of agonizing sorrow, eating your heart away, which overstresses the emotional element of the process of rejecting sin, and has made the concept problematical for many people. They find it very difficult to force themselves to the point of agonizing sorrow when they remember a past act. But that isn't necessary anyway. The decisive factor is my insight. I have to see that I didn't act as required by the will of God, the welfare of my fellow humans, and my own truth.

In confession I sometimes hear people say: 'I can't feel contrition for a sexual lapse. I had a fantastic experience with that woman.' But there's no point in condemning sexual experience. It's more important to think about its consequences. I injured my wife, and if I continue the relationship I shall be leading a dual inner life which will tear me apart. It won't do me any good in the long run. If I think along those lines I shan't be condemning myself. I understand that I have a lot of needs which my own wife can't satisfy. But because I know that my behaviour offends my wife, I set boundaries for myself. I can't fulfil all my needs. I don't have to satisfy all my wishes. I can also live a fulfilled life even if certain desires remain unsatisfied. I have no guarantee that I won't fall in love with another woman later on. But I know that I must always answer for my behaviour with regard to my own partner. In the long run it can only be good for my soul if I live a quite straightforward life in spite of all the feelings which sometimes threaten to tear me apart.

One danger of penitence is that we remain fixated on our past. We focus on our guilt and keep getting depressed as a result. Fixation on guilt doesn't liberate us so that we can start behaving in a new way.

The abbot Pambo asked the abbot Antony: 'What shall I do?' The old man replied: 'Don't be confident of your own righteousness. Don't grieve over something that is past. And restrain both your tongue and your belly' (*Vitae Patrum* [Sayings of the Fathers, 1628]). Antony doesn't advise Pambo to justify everything that is past. It doesn't help to wallow in memories of the past. What is gone, is gone. Whatever happened, happened. There's no point in constantly reproaching yourself because of it. The reason why some people can never let go of their past guilt is often their belief in their own righteousness. When they are guilty of something, they can't forgive themselves for not measuring up to an ideal they have set themselves. Antony wants to teach us humility. We are never righteous. We shall always make mistakes. We shouldn't be satisfied with the situation, but we should let go of the mistakes, treat them as the past. Then our psychic energy won't be focused on the past and we shall be able to look to the future.

Antony advises Pambo to practise continence of the tongue and of the belly. If he heeds this advice and says nothing when he is injured, this will also change his inner attitude to people and to himself. If he practises asceticism and due restraint, he will create order within himself. This saying of the Fathers helps us to understand contrition today. We can hold our past out to God without lacerating ourselves.

We should ask God to help us so that we proceed along a path that leads to him, and to direct us in the ways of love, freedom and vitality. This might well be expressed in a very brief 'act' or prayer of contrition, something like this: 'Jesus have mercy.' Or: 'May everything that was in me and is still at work in me be held in God's mercy. May he bless me on my way forward in life.'

Forgiveness

After the penitent's confession and discussion with the priest, the priest absolves him or her. Absolution means dissolving, releasing, acquittal. In Jesus's name, the priest releases penitents from their guilt, and assures them that God has forgiven them. The rite provides for the laying on of hands at this point. When I as a priest lay my hands on penitents' heads, they can experience physically their unconditional acceptance by God and his inclusion of their guilt in his love. The prescribed absolution is approximately as follows:

> God, the merciful Father, has reconciled the world to himself through the Death and Resurrection of his Son and has sent the Holy Spirit for the forgiveness of sins. He grants you forgiveness and peace through the service of the Church. Therefore I absolve you from your sins in the name of the Father and of the Son and of the Holy Spirit. Amen.

It is advisable to precede this official absolution with a personal prayer summarizing the previous conversation with the penitent. It might go something like this:

> Merciful and loving God, thank you for all you have given N. and for everything you have done in him (her). Forgive him (her) anything of which he (she) was guilty, and any injury he (she) may have done to himself (herself) or to others. Fill him (her) with your Holy Spirit so as to transform everything in him (her) and bring him (her) into contact with the inner source of your love. May your forgiving love penetrate to the

uttermost regions of his (her) soul so that he (she) can now forgive himself (herself) and know that you accept him (her) unconditionally. I now pronounce the following in the name of the Church: 'God, the merciful Father ...'

The rite of absolution helps penitents fully to accept the truth that God has forgiven them. Jung stresses the fact that people in situations in which they are really guilty not only feel excluded from the human community, but inwardly torn, and in a condition from which they can't free themselves by their own power. The rite of absolution, Jung says, can surmount the obstacles in our soul which make it difficult for us to believe in God's forgiving love. Our unconscious contains blocks which prevent us from believing in forgiveness, and archaic ideas that all guilt must be paid for. The rite is necessary in order to dissolve these archaic images in our unconscious. It tells not only our intellect or feelings but the depths of our unconscious that we are unconditionally accepted by God, and that we no longer have to blame ourselves for our guilt. The rite is supra-personal. It amounts to more than a personal request by the priest. In the rite the priest shares in the healing power of the ultimate Source. This is the conviction of all religions, and similarly of the psychologist and thinker Jung: 'Quite apart from its purely personal significance, the rite does justice to the collective and numinous aspect of the occasion' (*Briefe* [Letters], Vol. II, p. 440).

Trusting in God's mercy

The sacrament closes with a 'dismissal'. The official recommendation is something like: 'The Lord has forgiven your sins. Go in peace.' If it seems appropriate, the priest can give the newly reconciled person a sign of peace to show that he or she is totally accepted by God and to symbolize acceptance by the church community.

I think it is really important to invoke God's blessing on people after confession, to encourage them not to stop trying but to go on their way trusting in God's mercy. They won't succeed in everything along the route, but they will know that wherever they are they will always be enclosed in God's healing and loving presence.

III. LIVING ON THE BASIS OF RECONCILIATION

Reconciled with yourself

Some Christians go to confession constantly, but never succeed in being reconciled with and to themselves. Yet the most important task of being a Christian is to be able to say 'Yes' to ourselves. We can make a start by becoming reconciled with our own lives to date. Many people spend their lives railing against their childhood, because it was a time when they felt no one understood them and they were often hurt. Now, however, they use their damaged life-history as an excuse for not having to live their own lives effectively, or turn it into a permanent complaint that their parents were responsible for their child's past and present misery. No matter how many spiritual resources they call on, people as unreconciled as that with their own past lives will get no further.

Being reconciled with myself also means being on the right terms with my own body. Many penitents confess to a deep self-hatred. They just can't accept themselves as they are. Often enough, it's their bodies they reject. They imagine that they don't measure up to the ideal image of a handsome man or an attractive woman. They can't forgive themselves for being so fat. They don't like their faces. Their hands aren't the right shape. They're furious that their bodies always give them away when they're nervous, and that they blush or start to sweat. They try to fight these tendencies, but that only makes things worse. For them, reconciling themselves to their own bodies, being at ease in them, is a lifelong task.

Many people get angry when they're confronted with the dark side of their personality, the 'shadow' in the depths of their unconscious selves. They long to be just right, perfect in fact. But something irritates their sensitive areas, and then whatever wells up from below foils the attempt to be perfect. Sometimes they feel a deep hatred of other people. Merely meeting certain individuals puts them in a rage. They can't accept the fact that they're continually subject to depressive moods. When they feel envious they criticize themselves harshly. When they're obsessed by fear they complain that as Christians they shouldn't be subject to anxiety. The more they object to themselves and the dark side of their nature the stronger it becomes. What they actually need is humility.

Humility is the courage to descend into our own darkness, into what Jung calls the 'shadow' area of our personal unconscious, which consists of repressed drives or instincts and part-instincts, those inner aspects of our outwardly well-functioning ego that we experience as 'dark', or negative. Becoming reconciled with these instincts doesn't mean gratifying them. But we have to realize that there is no guarantee that we shall be able to make our spiritual journey on perfectly firm ground. Some people try to use the spiritual path as a means of evading their own 'shadow'. They want nothing whatsoever to do with such banal things as their sexual fantasies and angry emotions. They believe that in spiritual practice they have found a way to exist in harmony with their own nature. But all they have done is to repress a vast array of dangerous impulses. Humility means always taking into account the possibility of long-forgotten and supposedly vanquished needs and passions rising to the surface of our egos. Humility doesn't mean humiliating ourselves but allowing ourselves the inner calm and composure needed to proceed carefully and trustingly, and to see everything we encounter on our journey as a sign from God that we have to reconcile ourselves to all that lies within us.

Reconciled with the community

When I direct courses and ask those taking part in them who they are still on bad terms with and can't forgive, they always come up with a long list of people. More often than not, they become very agitated as they reel off the names, because some relationships are very emotionally charged and wearing. Yes, they attempted some kind of reconciliation, but it didn't work. Or perhaps they were so hurt by these people that in spite of the sacrament of reconciliation they just couldn't forgive them from the bottom of their hearts. They sense how these individuals still affect them, and know how much effort it costs to remain unreconciled with them.

I can be reconciled if I simply put to one side all the wounds and pains I have suffered, together with my angry feelings about the people who have injured me. First of all, I have to abandon my anger, and distance myself from these individuals as I do so. Only when I have put a healthy space between us will I be free from the destructive forces that emanate from them. I let them be, just as they are, but I refuse to let them have any power over me. Forgiving them doesn't mean embracing them warmly.

The first step towards reconciliation with other people is to let them be, to stop judging or condemning them. I just let them exist as they are. What they've done is their problem. They've wounded me, but I refuse this injury house-room. I transform my rage about this hurt into the satisfaction of living my own life instead of being determined by these people.

The second step is to re-establish a relationship with them. But this is not always possible. It always depends on the other persons being ready to clear things up by talking about them. If they refuse to take this step, I can still be reconciled by no longer complaining about them and by putting them out of my mind for the present. I just leave them alone and wait. I try to be reconciled inwardly with myself and with the past. As soon as they make it possible, I shall be ready to approach them, or to react positively to any favourable moves they make.

If people live together in a community without resolving their quarrels, their whole society can collapse. The members of a group can only get along with each other if there is some readiness to repair the situation, and if there are repeated attempts at reconciliation. We find ourselves drawn towards mutual forgiveness in the interwoven lives of a family or a monastic community or even an office or factory. The evangelist Matthew sensed this in the communities of his day. Consequently, in chapter 18 of his gospel he summarized the part of Jesus's message that focused on forgiveness as a basic rule for living in community with others. When Peter asks how often another person can wrong him and he must forgive him or her: 'Would seven times be enough?', Jesus replies: 'No, not seven times, but seventy times seven!' Seventy times seven really means again and again, without any limit. But Matthew doesn't see forgiveness as just brushing discord under the carpet. If someone sins and disturbs life in the community, one of its members has to approach the offender and talk to him or her about it. The aim of the discussion is to win the offending individual over. Of course, he or she has to be prepared to listen to what is said to him or her. A conflict can be cleared up and reconciliation can occur if we listen to each other and talk things over. But if the offender doesn't listen, then – says Matthew – two or three people should talk to him or her. If that produces no result, the whole community should try to win this recalcitrant person over (cf. Matt. 18.15–17). This doesn't mean setting up a court but creating a situation in which people listen to what everyone has to say, in order to discover the cause of dissension. The community must always be ready to forgive, but the individual has to be prepared to listen, to realize what his or her behaviour does to others. If people listen to each other, they will find a way to resolve the conflict, or at least to deal with each other fairly. Then the disagreement will no longer be an excuse for division. Reconciliation removes the divisive power of insoluble conflicts.

The sacrament of reconciliation must not be used as a way of repressing antagonism just at the level of a private discussion with a priest. Instead it requires us to look for ways of solving conflicts together. It sends us home aware of our duty to be reconciled with people whom we have harmed or who have done us harm.

Conversion

Jesus's first words in Mark's gospel are: 'The time has come at last – the kingdom of God has arrived. You must change your hearts and minds and believe the good news' (Mark 1.15). Conversion, a change of heart, or repentance, is not only an aspect of confession but something essential to our lives as a whole. It is necessary because the kingdom of God is at hand. We must repent because God is close to us and, in his mercy and loving kindness, has approached us in Jesus Christ. We have to turn away from ourselves and focus on God.

The fundamental threat to our life is to focus excessively on ourselves and keep asking what we are going to get out of life. Then we shall always be concerned with ourselves and our own welfare. Jesus sees this attitude as taking a wrong turning, and more than that: one that leads to a dead end. When Jesus asks me to repent, he questions me and my existence. He asks: Does your existence lead to life or to death, to vitality or to rigidity, to fruitfulness or to emptiness? If you go on like this will you reach your true self, the real you, or will you actually leave yourself behind?

Conversion, or repentance, means turning to God. By turning to him, by approaching him, I find my true nature, my real self. Jesus sees conversion as faith in the gospel, in the good news of God's healing and loving closeness, which he proclaims. If we trust in what Jesus has to say, we shall be freed from the oppressive multitude of opinions that assail us and falsely promise us life. Belief in his word liberates us from anxiety about losing our way. Conversion is an invitation to live properly. Some preachers calling for repentance offer us bad rather than good news, threats rather than good promises. They menace us with judgement and hell-fire. They want to force us to follow them and their frightening notions of God. But that is not the good news of Jesus, who proclaims the closeness of a loving and merciful Father. The actual meaning of *metanoia*, the Greek word for conversion or repentance, is: 'after-thought', 'perceiving subsequently', 'changing one's view', 'thinking differently'. *Meta* can also mean 'behind'. Then repentance would signify: 'seeing behind things', 'seeing God himself in all people and in creation', and 'recognizing the God who speaks to us in our everyday experiences'. In that line of thought, repentance means perceiving the uniqueness concealed in everything. Jesus spoke of God as shining forth from the reality of this world. In his parables he made the world transparent so that we could see God through it. Conversion or repentance means trying to see things with Jesus's eyes, so that I can discern the presence of God in everything I come across, and acknowledge him as he speaks to me through a meeting with another person, through a fortunate event, through misfortune, through success and failure, through my thoughts, and through what I hear other people say. Repentance means being aware of the closeness of God talking to me and acting on me in every object, occurrence and human being.

Jesus's new image of God

In the past, sermons about penance or revivalist addresses during retreats concentrated on the image of God as a judge and as a kind of supreme celestial accountant. We were told that God could see exactly what we were up to, and was watching us all the time. He put it all on his scales and decided whether it was good or bad. Then he passed judgement on us.

Of course this picture of God is quite different from Jesus's description of him. Yes, the God of the Old Testament is the only one that Jesus preaches, and he stresses aspects of God already announced in the Old Testament, but the result is a new interpretation of God. Jesus proclaims God's merciful love, patience, and loving kindness towards sinners.

The God Jesus tells us about always helps us to begin again. He doesn't delete us from his file when we've sinned, but raises us up and supports us. When we condemn others, God doesn't condemn us. John's first Letter says it perfectly: 'We are children of the truth and can reassure ourselves in the sight of God, even if our own hearts make us feel guilty. For God is infinitely greater than our hearts, and he knows everything' (1 John 3.19–20). God isn't the judge. The judge we fear is often within us, and quite unmerciful. It is our own superego, which is always trying to humiliate us: 'You can't do anything. You're nobody. You make a mess of everything. You're evil. You're putrid and corrupt.' The God Jesus wants us to know enables us to forgive ourselves over and over again, to distance ourselves from the court inside us, and to reject its authority.

Jesus was especially concerned for sinners. He could see they were prepared to change. When he looked at the Pharisees he recognized the danger of devout people feeling so self-satisfied that they thought there was no need to repent. There are people who have grown rigidly devout like that and never open themselves to God's merciful love. Jesus never condemned sinners or threatened them with hell-fire. Instead he told them that their failures were opportunities to change and begin all over again, and that they could understand God's merciful love more profoundly than self-righteous people.

The God and Father of Jesus Christ doesn't impose arbitrary rules and laws on us. He gave us commandments to help us to live effectively. Jesus reinterpreted God's will and the meaning of these commandments: 'The Sabbath was made for man, not man for the Sabbath' (Mark 2.27). He reminded us that commandments are intended to help people to live in accordance with their dignity and value, and to deal with each other justly.

But God never lets us lie fallow. We can't say: 'We've done everything we should do. Now God will reward us.' Jesus makes us aware that we have to ask what the will of God is again and again, in every situation we find ourselves in. And God always wants us to be alive, to be healthy and whole, and to exist in accordance with our true nature. The God preached by Jesus is the guarantor of our development as authentic human beings. We shall never find the way to our true selves by our own power. God enables us to become truly human.

CONCLUSION

The sacrament of reconciliation offers us a practical way of ensuring that we are reconciled with ourselves and with each other, constantly repent, and experience God as the One who loves us unconditionally. We must not isolate the act of confession and separate it from all that Jesus preached and taught. It is meaningful only within the context of Jesus's call to lead a life that is appropriate to God's will and to our own human existence. In the sacrament of reconciliation we meet the Jesus Christ who forgave sinners their guilt. We also meet the God of Jesus Christ, who frees us from our guilt and our guilt feelings, and allows us to experience his merciful love in this form.

As for my personal experience, I can't say that I exactly enjoy going to confession. But I know that it's good for me. From time to time, I need the opportunity to pause for a while, look at my life, assess it, and ask: 'Is the way I live the right way?' I have to struggle to overcome powerful inhibitions when I ask another monk if he will hear my confession. But, after confessing, I realize that it was a good thing to do. Of course I'm not going to change my skin. And I have to go on living with my problems and everyday faults. But confessing is a stimulus to begin again and live more thoughtfully and responsibly. Sometimes confessing makes me aware of tendencies which I'm liable to. Facing them makes me more wary of them, and being forgiven assures me that now I don't have to go on delving into the past. It's buried and I can leave it like that.

During a recent Easter course, the group leaders chose the theme 'Guilt and Guilt Feelings.' I thought it was quite brave of them to tackle this subject with young people. But the actual sessions showed how very important this topic is for the young. They need some occasion when they can speak quite openly about their guilty feelings. Moreover, they long to be rid of them and to be absolved of their guilt. The sacrament of reconciliation is not the only place where the subjects of guilt, guilt feelings and forgiveness come up and can be dealt with. But it is certainly a major chance to experience therapeutic healing for many people not merely distraught but quite torn apart by all sorts of scruples. It is especially important for those who continually reproach themselves for their failures. In reconciliation Jesus gave us a sacrament in which we can know that we are loved unconditionally.

When I gave a talk on the subject 'Everyone has an Angel', a ten-year-old girl asked me: 'Do you really think that my angel will never leave me?' When I said Yes, she asked: 'Even if I'm naughty?' I replied: 'Yes, your angel is very, very patient.' But she wouldn't let it go: 'All right, but what if I'm naughty over and over again?' So I said: 'I'm absolutely sure that your angel will never leave you, but stay with you always. Even if you can't stand yourself, your angel can take it, that's certain.' She was quite satisfied and comforted to learn this. It was essential for someone to tell her that she would never be abandoned and that the angel who looked after her would stick it out.

The sacrament of reconciliation is our chance to experience the truth that the God of all-forgiving love never abandons us, that his forgiveness can deal with all our guilt, and that God accepts us without imposing any condition on us. As a confessor, I always find it miraculous to see people oppressed by guilt straighten up, as it were, and go home liberated. They have experienced what Jesus really intended when he gave us a sacrament in which we can feel we are truly reconciled.

5

Marriage: the blessing of life together

I. THE SACRAMENT OF MARRIAGE

a) Words and meanings

Marriage

The bride and groom are the actual ministers of marriage. They administer the sacrament to each other. They marry each other.

This fact about the ministry of marriage is central to any discussion of its mystery. I shall approach it by way of, first, a brief look at the language of marriage, and, second, an examination of the theology of the sacrament.

The marriage language used by us, our ancestors, the Church, the State and the law, then and now, expresses various aspects of the history of marriage, our experience of it, and the wisdom distilled from this recorded and practical knowledge. The etymologies and associations of these words betray the basic legal and formal contexts of marriage over thousands of years.

There are various terms for and associated with marriage, some of which are roughly equivalent, such as 'marriage' and 'matrimony', whereas others, such as 'betrothal', 'espousals', and 'nuptials', usually emphasize certain stages or aspects of it. Although the last three have gone out of general use they can be useful for purposes of exact definition.

Other terms, such as 'wedlock' (from the Old English *wedlac*, a pledge), 'marital alliance', 'matrimonial union', and even 'matrimony', are dated in other ways; they are generally considered to be too formal or narrowly ecclesiastical, or are favoured only by certain social groups in some English-speaking countries. 'Matrimony', however, is still used by theologians and in legal, anthropological and similar contexts. The term 'wedding' refers more to the actual ceremony and the accompanying festivities, and is used in a multitude of compounds, such as 'wedding-breakfast', 'wedding-cake', 'wedding-ring', 'wedding-dress', 'wedding-cards', 'wedding-flowers', 'wedding-anniversary', 'wedding-bells'.

The English word 'marriage' is derived through the Old French *mariage* from the Latin *maritare*, to marry, to give a husband to, or to give in marriage to a man; *maritus*, a husband or married man, and *marita*, a woman provided with a husband. 'Matrimony' comes through the Old French *matrimoine* from the Latin *matrimonium*, the action of marrying or state of being married. 'Wedding', from 'wed', descends through the Old English *weddian*, from Germanic, Old Norse and other verbs meaning 'to pledge', 'to wager', 'to espouse'.

The background to all these terms is fascinating, but far too complex for me to do more than touch on here. It is clear, however, that the ways in which we refer to marriage, and especially the terms we favour, reflect our views of it, and have not lost deep meanings going far back into history. For most people, the word 'marriage' itself immediately evokes a number of vital yet diverse associations with special feeling-tones.

Marriage, however, is not only an emotional phenomenon but remains an institution with a specific structure intended to help the partners to live together appropriately. They make an openly declared agreement to do so. People who are really in love evidently have a basic need to demonstrate this publicly. Their contract is not only binding but binds them together. Sociologists say that people today feel the need to belong – to someone, to something – more intensely than people in the past. The sense of belonging makes us feel safe and secure.

Marriage is also associated with honesty and authenticity. A marriage will succeed only if the partners are honest, and don't try to fool each other.

Marriage also suggests belonging in the sense of home and home-making. In order to provide a real home for a family, a marriage needs not merely the external equipment for setting up home together, but the right kind of behaviour, attitudes and ideas that will make the marriage not only a place of partnership but home in the sense of somewhere that attracts other people. When people are in love their home becomes a loving location where friends and relatives know they are liked and welcome.

Wedding

A church wedding is a liturgical act of marriage, but also a social occasion for festivity and congratulation. Since times immemorial people have recognized it as a time for rejoicing when two people are so much in love that they decide to spend the rest of their lives together. A wedding can have a magical effect on other people too, and brighten their daily lives with a reminder of the promise for the future that comes from God's love. When we celebrate a wedding we express the fact that the married couple's lives, but also our own, are fulfilled by the mystery of divine love. The future partners and their parents certainly feel this when they invite other people to share the celebration. If two people are reluctant to celebrate their partnership by getting married, we might feel that this betrays a certain inadequacy in their joint venture. They can't trust one another, so it seems, to contract a marriage, celebrate it, and invite others to witness and share their marriage feast. How stale their love must have become if they never feel the need to express it in the form we know as a wedding.

Betrothal

'Betrothal' originally meant the same as 'engagement', the promise to marry which precedes the public celebration. In many countries in centuries past this was the actual marriage, which was merely blessed in church or at the church door. But marriage itself is a betrothal, and an engagement is also made, or ratified, in the marriage ceremony. If you are betrothed, you plight your troth to one another, offer your trust to one another, and express your confidence that God will bless your commitment to one another. You trust yourself and you trust that your partner is loyal. 'Troth' is very close to 'truth' and 'true'; and 'true' carries the associations of 'strong', 'strong as a tree', 'solid as a rock', 'loyal and trustworthy'. If you trust yourself and entrust yourself to this other person, you hope that the loyalty and truth that emerge from plighting this troth will be firm enough to hold on to. Trust must grow like a tree and become all the stronger and more secure. If you celebrate this betrothal in marriage you affirm your belief that your trust in this other person and in God's blessing is sufficiently robust to bind you together for life, and to make your marriage and home secure – a stronghold in fact.

Saying Yes

Some people still talk of bride and groom 'saying Yes' to each other, although not so long ago it referred only to the future bride accepting a proposal from her suitor. This once-popular expression has a deep significance, for if you say Yes to someone in respect of something so important, you accept him or her whole and entire. But you can do that only if you can say Yes to yourself, if you can accept yourself unconditionally. When two people accept each other as they are, and when they say Yes to everything in and about the other person, they create a space where each of them can increasingly conform to God's intended image of him or her. Another person's acceptance of me is like a wholly beneficial clamp or weld holding together everything in me that is various and contrary. It makes it possible for me to develop as the person I am intended to be. The mutual Yes also makes the married couple an inspiration for other people, who feel affirmed and accepted in the presence of those who affirm and accept each other unconditionally. A wedding is a feast of affirmation and joy because God accepts us all unconditionally, and therefore we can accept each other.

Marriage bond and marital union

In various parts of the English-speaking world some more formal marriage announcements and reports still occasionally refer to the 'marital union' or 'union in marriage' of the couple, or even the 'marriage bond' they enter into. The newly-wed man and woman are indeed bound to each other. But of course their mutual union should not turn into a bond in the sense of fetters or shackles. It is intended to hold together something good that might always threaten to crack or even break apart. We all sense a certain potential for upset and disruption within us. Our feelings often threaten us in this way. Our various duties and tasks can disturb and even shake us up. We are always in need of a secure bond for these inevitable strains before they widen to announce a crack-up. The Bible says that love binds us together in perfect harmony (earlier translations spoke of the 'bond of perfectness') (cf., e.g., Col. 3.14). To bind yourself to another person expresses your unconditional love for him or her, and your trust that this union will not only ensure that you both remain vital and enlivening individuals, but banish any threat of an inner split.

Marriage customs

Language is not the only thing that offers clues to the mystery of marriage. There are countless marriage customs among all the tribes and nations of the world, some of them reaching back into antiquity. Many marriage customs are associated with the theme of the bride's release from her parents' control and her entry into a new way of life. One such practice is to present the newly married couple with bread and salt, to make sure that they are equipped for their journey together. In some areas of Europe, bride and groom have to saw through a log or cut down a tree to show that old bonds have been dissolved and a new stage of life is beginning. In Israel the bridegroom leads his bride in a festive midnight procession from her house and into his own, where the marriage is celebrated. This expresses the truth that the marriage will succeed only if the bride allows herself to be freed from her parents' influence and to be taken into the new home which she is starting together with her groom.

b) The sacrament

Meeting Christ

Language and usage give us some important clues to the nature of marriage. But the Church also celebrates marriage as a sacrament. 'Sacrament' means 'religious mystery, consecration, commitment'. The Latin verb *sacrare* means 'to consecrate, dedicate to God, sanctify, make holy, make inviolable and unbreakable, strengthen and seal'. The Church sees marriage as a sacrament because it wants to show that this occasion when two people say Yes to each other has something to do with God. When the Church blesses this marriage, it declares it to be holy and whole, for it has placed it under God's blessing. This secures the couple's hope and trust that their marriage bond will remain inviolable and unbreakable. This divine blessing also declares that in their mutual celebration of the sacrament this man and this woman receive a new vitality. Under God's blessing they will embark on the experience of mutual openness, understanding and love.

From a theological viewpoint, a 'sacrament' is something which Jesus brought about two thousand years ago, which is enacted in our present-day world, and which flows into human activities and achievements now. With regard to marriage, it means that the love which Jesus showed us to the point of death and beyond flows into and transforms the love of this man and this woman. Marriage as a sacrament means that it sanctifies and makes whole and completes the love between two people, which is always fragile and endangered by possessive claims, projections and misunderstanding. It also reminds us that the Church sees marriage as one of the main places where we meet Christ. The mutual love of husband and wife enables them to sense what Christ's love actually means for them. Through married love they constantly grow into the mystery of Christ's love, which he completed in utter devotion on the cross. In their daily efforts to love one another they realize the deep significance of Jesus's words: 'There is no greater love than this – that a man should lay down his life for his friends' (John 15.13).

Touch

Medieval theology took a different view of a sacrament, seeing it as the visible sign of something invisible. The outward sign in many sacraments is an imposition of hands or anointing associated with effective words. Sacraments always use touch. The Fathers of the Church say that in a sacrament we are touched by the hand of the historical Jesus as he conveys his love to us. In marriage God's love is transmitted in the tender touch of the married couple, culminating in sexual union. The sacrament confirms the dignity and value of married love. Sacramental theology sees sexuality in a much more positive light than Catholic moral theology, which still tends to be hostile to the body. Husband and wife can experience God most intensely in physical love. This sacramental concept of sexual love accords with the insights of present-day psychology. Marriage counsellors with a background in Jungian psychology remind us of the transcendent potential of sex, for the sexual act always points beyond itself to the mystery of transcendence, to the mystery of God's infinite, inexhaustible love. The Jewish philosopher Walter Schubart stresses the close connection between God's Spirit, which unites opposites, and married love, where some part of the Oneness of God enters our world: 'The divine Oneness becomes visible in this twofold human experience ... Every act of love is an approach to perfection, a prelude to the re-blending of God and the world ... When two lovers discover each other, the wound of isolation closes at that point in the universe' (Walter Schubart, *Religion und Eros* [Religion and Eros], 1941, pp. 83ff.).

Love

If the invisible is conveyed through the visible, this also means that the visible is not all there is. It's only a hint and taste of the invisible, of the Divine. If the sacrament is seen in this way, it can be a great help for married people, who often overtask themselves by obedience to ideal images and impossibly demanding stereotypes. Many marriages fail because one partner expects something absolute, even divine perfection, from the other. He or she wants perfect love, perfect understanding, and perfect loyalty, which are obviously beyond the other's capacities. Only God can grant us something absolute. If I expect perfection from a human being, I shall be perpetually disappointed. Eventually I shall realize that the other's love is always limited, for it must be confined within the bounds of his or her moods, foibles and projections, and of the wounds suffered under the slings and arrows of a separate life-history. What this other person can give me will never be enough for me. But if I see his or her love not as absolute but as a pointer to God's love, I shall be able to appreciate its worth. Then I shall respect and enjoy it. I know that this love is fragile, too, and that perhaps in the very next moment he or she will be ruled not by affection for me but by some sensitive reaction determined by the past. I know that I can't compel this love, and that I can't force more and more of it from him or her. But I can receive and enjoy it, and as I do so sense something of God's perfect love, which is never exhausted. If married love is open to God's love, it will never be seriously threatened by to-and-fro claims that 'You just don't love me enough!' Husband and wife can rejoice in each other's love, not clinging to it for increased self-assurance but assured that their mutual love will keep each of them closer to God. God, not the feeling that I at least am loving even if he or she isn't, is the real ground on which they can build.

If love is the couple's way to God's love, it will never prove boring. Many married people worry because their love has become so very ordinary and the sensation of love as an overpowering force seems to fade more and more. They both know each other so well. Love just doesn't have the same thrill. It's losing its magic. But if love is always a way to the mystery of God's love it never fails. I am very familiar with this body, but if it announces the mystery of ultimate Love and I sense God's own loving gaze in my partner's eyes, love will remain vital, because it draws on the immortality and infinity of the Divine. Then I shall always experience my partner's love as an undeserved gift, and my own loving as a mystery, for as I love I shall touch the everlasting mystery we call God.

c) Biblical references

Created man and woman

The Church has drawn its theology of marriage from statements in the Bible. One is the important passage in Matthew 19.3–12, which is primarily concerned with the question of divorce. At the same time, when talking to the Pharisees, Jesus says what he sees as the essence of marriage. He refers his audience to Scripture: 'Have not you read that he who made them from the beginning made them male and female, and said, "For this reason a man shall leave his father and mother and be joined to his wife, and the two shall become one flesh?" So they are no longer two but one flesh. What therefore God has joined together, let not man put asunder' (Matt. 19.4–6). This text contains three important statements about the nature of marriage. The first concerns the precondition and basis of marriage. God made human beings male and female, so marriage is part of the Creator's will for humankind. Man and woman are made for each other, and in their inclination to each other comprise a single image of God. Essentially, God is love; in himself he is pure relationship; and in this world he is most clearly reflected in the relationship of husband and wife. The second statement is about the success of marriage.

Leaving parents

If a marriage is to succeed, the man has to leave his father and mother. Many marriages fail because the husband remains his mother's son. He can't leave her inwardly or outwardly. But this means that he can't give his undivided attention to his wife. He continually asks his mother for her opinion of this or that. Or he keeps comparing his wife with his mother. His wife can never be herself. She is always seen as his mother's rival. Then she becomes a substitute mother, and not a partner. A wife, of course, can behave in much the same way. If she hasn't said goodbye to her father, as it were, she is not ready to be her husband's partner. Or if she lives in too great a state of symbiosis with her mother, the man doesn't marry his wife, but his wife and her mother. Marriage presupposes an end to dependence on parents and their patterns of life.

Being one flesh

The third statement is about the purpose of marriage: husband and wife become one flesh, which terminates any kind of dualism. Our longing for unity is fulfilled in marriage. Human beings suffer from division. There are many myths and legends about the splitting of a single person into male and female. The topic is associated historically with aspects of the 'war between the sexes'. Fear of women has often made men attack and humiliate women. And women have developed strategies to make men submissive. But this conflict leads only to feeling wounded, and to actual wounds and reciprocal fears. The real purpose of the male–female polarity is mutual fertilization and the experience of unity. The highest form of unity is sexual union, in which the human longing for oneness is satisfied. The love between man and woman is 'emergence from a solitary existence and return to divine wholeness' (Schubart, p. 84). Walter Schubart helps us to elucidate the meaning of our biblical passage when he says:

> We can hear the distant roar of the ocean's power in a tiny shell, and in the sound of our beloved breathing we sense nature as a whole. You are made to be freed from this loneliness, it says. Now you can leave yourself and meet the one person to whom you can say You with utter tenderness. He or she is your helpmate, and leads you to God. Ultimately, love between the sexes takes a human being into the arms of the Deity and removes the gulf between me and you, me and the world, the world and God. (Schubart, p. 86)

Catholic theology derives its view of marriage as a sacrament from Jesus's statement that man and woman become one flesh and thus bear witness to the union of God and humanity. Marriage calls people to God, who is One, and in whom human beings find true Oneness: 'When lovers embrace the beloved's body they embrace the One who embraces everything. The beloved offers the lover the security of the loving Ground of all that is. The beloved is the lover's testimony that God exists' (Schubart, p. 85).

Indissolubility

Because husband and wife become one flesh in sexual union, marriage is indissoluble: 'What therefore God has joined together, let not man put asunder' (Matt. 19.6). Jesus's statement scares many people contemplating marriage nowadays. The indissolubility of marriage seems frighteningly unrelenting. People entering into marriage have to promise their partners to stay loyal to them forever. Yet at the same time they know they can't guarantee this perpetual loyalty. They're afraid that they might develop differently, and, indeed, grow away from each other, or that hitherto unsuspected psychological problems will come to the surface and make it impossible for them to stay together. For Jesus, the indissolubility of marriage corresponds to God's original will and therefore to the nature of the marital relationship between husband and wife. But at the same time Jesus is aware that people aren't always able to fulfil this ideal. He takes exceptions into account, as in the 'unfaithfulness' clause in Matthew 19.9. If you bind yourself to another person, you shouldn't make a mental reservation, saying: Yes, all right, but we'll part as soon as there are difficulties. At the same time, people who want to get married have to realize that they can't guarantee that they will remain faithful. They can make this binding commitment only if they trust that God will bless this marriage and enable the two partners to remain loyal to each other. Marriage doesn't derive from human intentions alone but, as a sacrament, calls on the grace of God, who alone makes a lasting union possible.

The Marriage at Cana

John outlines Jesus's theology of marriage in his account of the Marriage at Cana (John 2.1–11). It is a symbolic story. John wants to show that there is a close connection between God's Incarnation in Jesus and the union between husband and wife. When God becomes human he celebrates his wedding with humanity, and becomes one with them as a man and a woman do when they are married. By becoming a human being God unites with us in married love. That transforms our lives. From now on, they aren't influenced by the six stone water pots, which symbolize Jewish purification rites. It's no longer a question of any meticulous fulfilment of the law. Mere obedience to the commandments can easily make you numb and torpid. Your life will become rigid, shallow and spiritless: without vitality, in fact. Through the Incarnation God turns our water into wine. Our life tastes different and becomes more vital. Now we can celebrate a wedding with God. That was why the early Church thought of the Eucharist as a marriage feast, as a festive meal of union with God.

Probably John intended his story of the Marriage at Cana as a response to the Greeks' pursuit of ecstasy and change. The cult of Dionysus expressed this longing for intoxication. Dionysus stood for the experience of inebriated love by which humans are as if enchanted. He was also the god of wine. On the night before his feast day his priests placed three pots of water in the temple. By the next morning the water had changed into wine. Many married people are afraid that their love will dwindle, that the experience of everyday life will take all the intensity out of it, and that it will become as flat as water. The initial enchantment that completely carried them away has lost its power. The wine has run out. Now it's just routine. John counters this fear by saying (for this is what the story tells us): 'Because God has become human the wine of his love never runs out. You don't have to keep relying on your own strength of purpose to be loving. You have the undying Source of divine love within you. You're not like members of the Greek cult of Dionysus. You don't have to take part in orgiastic feasts to keep love alive. If you are in touch with God's love inside you, its transforming power will work its enchantment on you ever and again, making so many moments and occasions as captivating as your wedding day.'

Marriage – a sacrament of daily life

Another text, Ephesians 5.21–33, is important for understanding the Church's theology of marriage. It compares marriage to the relationship between Christ and the Church. Husband and wife should love one another as Christ loves the Church: 'Husbands should love their wives as their own bodies. He who loves his wife loves himself. For no man ever hates his own flesh, but nourishes and cherishes it, as Christ does the church' (Eph. 5.28f.). The Letter to the Ephesians applies what Jesus says about marriage to the relationship between Christ and the Church: 'For this reason a man shall leave his father and mother and be joined to his wife, and the two shall become one flesh. This mystery is a profound one, and I am saying that it refers to Christ and the church' (Eph. 5.31f.). Marriage symbolizes not the union between God and humankind but that between Christ and the Church. In the Vulgate, which for centuries was not only the standard Latin but the standard Catholic version of the Bible, the word used for 'mystery' in this context is *sacramentum*. Accordingly, the Catholic Church has always cited this passage to support its view that marriage is a sacrament. But it is not a question merely of the word used. The decisive point here is that married love between a man and a woman symbolizes Christ's love for his Church. By loving each other, husband and wife experience how Christ loves them.

The mystery in you

Paul says that Christ offered himself up to make his Church holy. Consequently a man should love his wife like his own body. The sacramental understanding of marriage also involves a specific kind of behaviour between a man and a woman. Just as each of them nourishes and cares for his or her body, so the husband should nourish and care for his wife. This is not a reference to any kind of claim by a husband to own his wife, or to marital duties which a partner has to fulfil, but to a respectful and attentive treatment of one by the other. Both Greek words in the original mean to nourish, foster, cherish and care for. The husband must not repress and rule his wife but cherish and support her, so that she recognizes her divine dignity and value, advances through life with head erect, and becomes herself wholly and entirely. He must care for her so that she feels comfortable as the person she is. But this demands a great deal of attentiveness and sensitivity to the other person. We are told that the wife should honour her husband. The Greek word can even mean 'fear'. What is intended is 'respect', in the sense of realizing that the other person is a mystery. Precisely because husband and wife come to know each other better in marriage, they have to respect and heed each other, or their love will grow stale. It is continually renewed by a sense of the other person's special mystery, and by a realization that some part of God's infinite mystery shines out from him or her. Paul means that a wife (or husband) should respect the other partner, and thus sense in him (or her) something of the mystery of Jesus Christ, who devoted himself utterly to his Church.

If we forget the time-bound associations of Paul's' comparison of love between Christ and the Church to marriage, we shall see that it says something vital about the mystery of married love. The partners not only meet in an experience of mutual love, but are in touch with the mystery of Christ's love. Marriage is an initiation into the mystery of Jesus Christ's love as shown in his total devotion on the cross. Through their everyday love married people can experience Christ and feel his love just as they do in worship. Therefore marriage is a sacrament of daily life. It is enacted not only in the ceremony before the altar but in the everyday exchange of loyalty and love.

II. CELEBRATING MARRIAGE

Even many Christians who have lost any close association with the Church feel the need to get married in church. Some critics say that such people are making use of the Church as a kind of service access point. They just want to give their wedding a touch of class. But I am not all that pessimistic about this. I think in most cases it's a healthy sign that people believe living together isn't all that simple, and it's a good thing to begin married life with God's blessing. And at the very least it means that not a few people are aware that no secular institution can provide so impressive a celebration as the Church. Even when people make fun of outdated church rituals, they are pleased to take advantage of them for their own weddings. Celebrating a festive occasion is an expression of an important desire for your life together to be right and successful. If you haven't enough confidence to do that, perhaps your relationship is lacking in other respects too, and your joint venture will be tedious and uninspired. We must remember, too, that all religions have special ceremonies for the changeover to a married state. Rites of transition are intended to assuage our fear of a new way of life and to release the energy we need to live through this new stage in our existence.

a) The marriage rite

Greeting and questions

The rite of marriage in church is very simple. There are only a few steps, which may be supplemented with a Eucharist (making it a nuptial Mass) and certain other touches. The actual rite begins when the celebrant greets the couple with a brief address or homily and may put formal questions to them about their willingness to obey the obligations of marriage and their freedom to marry. These are suggested in the official service, but the prescribed questions about the pair's actual will and desire to conclude this marriage can make it sound like a legal interrogation. This will have been discussed already with the parish priest when preparing for the wedding. I always advise the couple to decide in advance what they would like to say in front of everyone about their future life: what's important to them about getting married, say, and why they've chosen a church wedding. They have to exchange ideas to do this, and talking it over will often help them to express their deepest convictions and feelings for the first time.

When he addresses the congregation, the bridegroom might say how happy he is to have met his bride. She has shown him new aspects of himself. She has helped him to see how extraordinary being in love with someone can be. He wants to share his life with her and hopes that this joint experience will bring them even greater love, vitality and inspiration. The bride might say that she wanted a church wedding because she knew that this kind of sharing needed God's blessing, and that if you know God has blessed your union it isn't such a frightening prospect. She chose this particular church because it is associated with major events in her life. It has been a source of energy and inspiration for her which she wants her husband to share. She loves the architecture and the roof shaped like a rainbow, the sign of peace, and she hopes that God will make theirs a marriage in which they will always be able to overcome any conflicts in the spirit of love and cooperation.

Neither of these brief addresses should make any attempt to be theological. Of course the couple can restrict what they say to a few personal remarks, something about their memories of the church, and of religious occasions, or just to a few words about what they hope for and their trust in God's blessing on their life together. If they like, the couple can introduce the best man and chief bridesmaid, or their formal witnesses, to the guests, and say why they have chosen them. Witnesses are not there just to testify to due process but as people who will always help the couple and be loyal to them in crises.

The form here differs from country to country. In England, for instance, the civil declaration of freedom and matrimonial consent has been incorporated into the church rite, and much the same formula is used in the United Kingdom, in Ireland, in the United States and elsewhere in the English-speaking world, although the exact words and practice may differ. The consent spoken in turn by bridegroom and bride, as they take each other by the appropriate hand, is based on the ancient English formula from the pre-Reformation Sarum rite used for centuries by Catholics and other Christians, for a similar form of words still appears in the service-books of churches of the Anglican Communion and of other denominations. The time-honoured statement was: 'I, N., take you, N., to be my wife (husband) to have and to hold from this day forward, for better, for worse, for richer, for poorer, in sickness and in health, to love and to cherish, till death do us part' ('wedded' may appear before 'wife (husband)'; 'to love and to cherish' may be omitted; and additional words, such as 'and thereto I plight thee my troth' or 'according to God's holy law; and this is my solemn vow' may be added, depending on the place). Whatever form it takes, the consent may be spoken instead when the rings are exchanged.

Blessing the rings

After the consent, the priest blesses the rings (or ring, since practice is not consistent in the English-speaking world). A circle of precious metal is an ancient symbol. Its roundness signifies the unity of humankind. It polishes to smoothness whatever is rough and recalcitrant. Because it leads back into itself, a ring is a symbol of oneness and perfection. Since it is unending, it also stands for eternity. Wedding-rings symbolize the hope that both partners will achieve the unity that offers perfection and that their love will extend into eternity. The ring is also a sign of protection against evil forces. It is intended to defend the couple from threats to their love. Rings are also signs of commitment, faithfulness and membership of a community.

The rings are blessed. Nowadays, of course, very few people know anything about the profound symbolism of wedding-rings, so the priest should say something about this before or after the blessing. God's love and fidelity should flow into the rings so that the couple see them as signs that they belong to each other for the future, that love will smooth away any imperfection in them, that they wish to be loyal to each other, that they commit themselves to each other, and that their love should be protected from all threats. Their rings also show the world that they love each other and belong together.

Placing the rings

When the priest has blessed the rings (or ring), the bridegroom takes the bride's ring and promises to take her as his wife in the sight of God, to be loyal to her, and to love, care for and honour her always. He places the ring on the appropriate finger of the bride's left hand, saying a modern version of the time-honoured words: 'With this ring I you wed, with my body I you worship, and with all my worldly goods I you endow. In the name of the Father, and of the Son, and of the Holy Spirit. Amen.' The revised words are basically these : 'In the name of the Father, and of the Son, and of the Holy Spirit, take and wear this ring as a pledge of our love and fidelity.' If she is to give a ring, the bride then takes it, and does and says the same. The reference to the Trinity is most fitting, for the Trinity is love in itself, and just as love flows between the three Persons in a perpetual circuit, so the ring symbolizes love flowing endlessly to and fro between bride and groom, so that no one can tell the difference between divine and human love.

'I place myself in your hand'

The priest now invites bride and groom to take each other by the right hand, tells them of God's faithfulness to them, lays his stole about their joined hands, confirms the union they have celebrated, and reminds everyone of Jesus's words: 'That which God has joined together let no man divide.' Since the fourth century AD the stole has been a sign of office worn in different ways by deacons, priests and bishops. When the priest puts his stole around the couple's hands he confirms their commitment in the name of the Church. They hold hands to indicate that they have entered into a legal engagement to each other but also to indicate openness, devotion and forgiveness. They also show that they are committing themselves into each other's hands so that they can protect each other, follow a common road, and be united physically. In the past, the stole was also thought of as symbolizing the robe of immortality. With it the celebrant now expresses his hope that the love between husband and wife is undying, and will flow beyond death into eternal life. The priest wraps the bridal couple in the unending and indestructible love of God. He also lays his hand on them to stand for God protecting and blessing them with his own loving hand, so that they are both held there and whatever they undertake will be touched and blessed by God.

The marriage blessing

Then the priest pronounces the marriage blessing. He should place his hand on the couple while giving the blessing to show that God's love is flowing into their love. These words touch not only head and heart, for God's healing and transforming power moves through them into their entire bodies. God's loving kindness blesses and permeates all parts of the body and the soul. The celebrant can speak or chant the prescribed blessing, or bless them in his own words, expressing his personal hopes for their life together as a continuation of his remarks in the homily. Alternatively he might take up a special theme of this marriage raised by the couple when they came to him to prepare for it.

The bridal candle

A custom well worth preserving or introducing is that of blessing a bridal candle at this point. Before the ceremony I ask the couple to find an attractive candle. Some people decorate it with appropriate symbols, or ask friends with artistic or handicraft skills to do so. Others buy one or order it from a candle-maker. After the blessing of the couple, a witness or a bridesmaid brings the candle to the altar. If she made it, I ask her to say why she has chosen this design and those particular symbols. Otherwise I try to explain the pictures on the candle myself. I tell the congregation about a ritual one married couple reported to me. Whenever they quarrel and aren't talking to each other, one of them lights the wedding candle, which means he or she wants to end the dissension. Even if one of them is too hurt or upset to say anything, the lighting of the candle will show that they both trust in their mutual love and want light to shine again in the darkness.

Then I light the bridal candle at the Paschal Candle. It shares the power of the light of Easter, which has vanquished all the darkeness and coldness of death. I bless the burning candle with these words:

> Loving and merciful Lord, bless this bridal candle. May it stand for the fire of your love always burning in N. and N. May your love always illuminate this world. May love bring warmth to the coldness of this world. May the light of the candle radiate from their house, so that it becomes a place where others can feel accepted and at home in the tender light of love. Stay close to N. and N. in this candle and show them that your love consumes any threat to their love. May it give warmth when love seems to grow cold and may it banish the darkness of anger. Be with N. and N. and let your love shine out to give hope to all who enter their home seeking warmth in the light of their love. May this candle make their house a home for the lonely. May your love enlighten and warm the hearts of everyone here.

The intercessions

After this blessing a brief silence is called for, so that everyone can sense the mystery of married love. This is also a good point to ask friends or other musicians to play a suitable piece or to sing a song expressing their wishes for the couple. Then the guests can let all their goodwill and prayers flow into the music. The rite also prescribes a few intercessions, or bidding prayers. Now friends of the couple can take an active part in the celebration. Sometimes, before the wedding the couple ask friends to compose a petition and to recite or read it out. They could also bring along a symbol that illustrates the point of the prayer. This often inspires great creativity. Friends bring their symbol to the altar, explain its intention, and end with a wish for the bride and groom. The congregation can follow each presentation with a 'Lord, grant our prayer.' Sometimes I ask the guests to light small candles or night lights from the bridal candle and to say what they wish at the same time: 'I light this candle to wish N. and N. . . .' Or: 'I light this candle for all married people who . . .'. Lighting a candle is a wonderful symbol of prayer and a prayer in itself. As long as it burns a prayer is rising to heaven. If the petitioners place their candles on the altar, they will burn throughout the rest of the service and show that the whole congregation wish to enclose the couple in their prayers.

b) Marriage service and Eucharist

This brings the actual marriage rite to a close. It may be incorporated in a Eucharist or a service of the word. This will depend on how close the couple and guests are to the Church. As a symbolic meal, of course, the Eucharist itself contains many apposite signs that supplement and deepen the meaning of the marriage rite.

I shall now say something about a wedding celebrated in the context of the Eucharist – a nuptial Mass – or of the ministry of the word. The service begins with a procession by the priest, any other celebrants and servers and the bridal couple. The greeting is followed by a prayer of penitence, or confession. Life together is possible only on the basis of forgiveness. Then come the reading and the gospel.

The reading

When preparing for the wedding the priest should ask the couple which readings they would prefer. Some already have very firm ideas about this and have chosen texts they have found inspiring or that speak to actual experiences they have had together. The following are favourite readings: Genesis 1.26–8 (God made us male and female); Genesis 2.18–24 (inner union between husband and wife); Tobit 8.4–8 (the nature of mutual love); Ruth 1.15–17 (following the same path);

or passages from the Song of Solomon: Song of Solomon 2.10–12; Song of Solomon 4.9–15; Song of Solomon 8.6f. Other Old Testament texts would also fit the occasion, such as Sirach 26.1–4, 13–16 (conditions for a happy marriage), or Jeremiah 31.31–4 (the New Covenant). Suitable New Testament readings are: Romans 8.31–5, 37–9 (God's boundless love for us); Romans 12.1–2, 9–18 (straightforward love); 1 Corinthians 6.13–15, 17–20 (the worth of the body). The best-known text is Paul's celebration of love in Colossians 3.12–17 or that in 1 John 3.18–24. The account of Noah's Ark, the dove of peace and the olive branch is most suitable for a couple who have already undergone certain difficulties before their wedding. At this point they could offer olive leaves to the congregation.

The gospel

The liturgy proposes the following as gospel readings: Matthew 5.1–12 (the Beatitudes); Matthew 19.3–6 or John 1.1–12 or John 15.9–17. Couples who want to emphasize the importance of security in marriage might choose the house on a rock passage in Matthew 7.24–7. Others might choose an account of healing, such as Luke 13.10–17, if they want to stress the curative and cooperative aspects of their union. Another suitable image in the same line would be the healing of the leper in Mark 1.40–45, which stands for unconditional acceptance of one by the other, and even of characteristics which the possessor can't accept. Their mutual love heals the other's difficulty. The light of love enables both to feel clean and entirely accepted. The healing of the man who was deaf and unable to speak intelligibly (Mark 7.31–7) describes the possibilities of a marriage when one partner enables the other to hear his or her desires properly in every word, paying attention even to the most subtle notes, so that the longing for love and cooperation can be sensed even in the most contentious statements. The passage also brings home the importance of one partner helping the other to speak effectively, so that every word helps to secure the relationship, and his or her own truth is conveyed as a message of love.

183

The choice of a gospel reading is a good opportunity for the couple to understand even more clearly how each of them sees their life together and how Scripture can help to pinpoint this vision more accurately. The priest should never choose the texts himself but always ask the future husband and wife to look for them in the Bible. Of course, he should give them some help, especially if they don't know the New Testament well.

The homily

After the gospel the priest expounds the texts. A personal address is possible here only if he has discussed it with the couple beforehand, and knows something about their convictions and what they expect from marriage. The homily should not enunciate general principles of married life. It should be a personal address to the couple, but also one in which the guests feel included. The marriage rite needs both prescribed ritual and the personal element of words that address the actual situation of this man and this woman. People will always know if the priest is merely using a familiar homily for all such occasions, or is truly addressing these particular people with their unique life-histories and wishes.

The offertory

The homily is followed by the marriage rite as already described. Then the Eucharist proceeds with the offertory, or preparation of the gifts. If the couple wish to take a more active part in the Eucharist, I ask them to bring the gifts of bread and wine to the altar. If she agrees, the bride can carry her own home-baked loaf to the altar. The bridegroom can take the wine and pour it into the chalice. This is a powerful sign that husband and wife are bringing the offerings of their own love, which is expressed in the bread and wine. God's Spirit transforms their gifts into the Body and Blood of Jesus Christ, which are then offered to all present. In the actual rite of marriage, the couple's love was permeated with the transforming power of divine love. Now all those who are guests at the feast can drink from the Source of divine love, so that their human love can flow all the more strongly.

A meal together

The Eucharist continues with the eucharistic prayer, or canon, and the transformation of the gifts into Christ's Body and Blood. Then everyone says the Lord's Prayer. If appropriate, I ask them all to join hands and form a great circle or a long chain, so that as we pray God's Spirit of love will flow through us and unite us. After the prayer of peace I give the bride and groom the sign of peace and ask them to offer it to all their relatives and friends. Then comes the high point of the Eucharist, our Meal together. First, I give husband and wife communion under both kinds and receive with them. Then everyone is invited to eat and drink the love of God in the forms of bread and wine. If bride and groom are willing, I ask them to offer the chalice with the Blood of Christ. They brought bread and wine to the feast as signs of their own love. Now this love has been transformed. There is enough for everyone. All those present can drink and be filled with God's love. The resulting spirit of community is more profound than any produced by external rejoicing. The Eucharist closes with the prayer after communion and the blessing. Then priest, bride and groom and guests process out of the church. Outside the church it is time to congratulate the newly-wed couple.

If the rite of marriage takes place with a service of the word, the first part is the same as in a Eucharist. But the celebration closes with the general Our Father, the sign of peace, final prayer and blessing. To ensure that this part of the service includes some appropriate symbolism, the sign of peace can be made more festive. The bride and groom can offer it to each person there and wish him or her the peace of the Lord, or they can give everyone a symbol, such as a small olive branch. (Of course they or the priest should explain its meaning). Then every guest will have a memento of the wedding.

It is essential for the bride and groom to devote enough time to preparing for a church wedding. If the service has to be as short as possible to accommodate the caterers, it won't be a real celebration. Sometimes the future husband and wife also make some very opinionated demands which have nothing to do with the celebration in church. It isn't always easy for the priest to take them seriously and not appear too harsh. At the same time his own viewpoint has to be taken into account, or the celebration will lack dignity, unity and significance. If the priest feels used, it won't do him or the parish any good. Achieving the right degree of flexibility and clarity is often something of a precipice-walk. If the couple try to insist on pop music with no relation whatsoever to the service, it's extremely difficult to talk them out of it politely. To make sure that the preparatory discussion doesn't turn into an unseemly row, a priest is well advised to ask later what the desired song or ritual means for the couple. Then everyone can sit down together to work out whether it might not be played at a more suitable point, during the wedding party for instance. The priest must never appear to be the only person deciding what happens during a marriage. It is a joint celebration and must be appropriate for everyone, without compromising the nature of the religious service. A real discussion is the only way to strike the right balance. Then the priest must explain quietly but surely what has to be done, while paying full attention to the couple's own wishes.

III. THE ART OF LIVING TOGETHER

Some couples have only superficial memories of their wedding. It would be unrealistic to suppose that they live their everyday lives on the basis of the sacrament. Others will have recorded the ceremony on a tape or video and sometimes listen to the readings and hymns and the homily, or watch the whole event. Then the rite can affect the way they are from day to day.

The following pages are not designed to offer a systematic description of everything you have to do or watch out for if you want a successful marriage: for example, how to learn and practise the right ways to communicate, and how to deal with every aspect of each kind of conflict. Marriage counsellors have much more experience of those aspects of a married relationship, and plenty of strictly psychological or spiritual introductions to marriage are available. I shall just look at a few texts from the Bible that are read out at weddings, and interpret their relevance to the joint experience of being married.

a) Building on solid ground (Matt. 7.24–7)

Jesus closes the Sermon on the Mount with these words: 'Everyone then who hears these words of mine and puts them into practice is like a sensible man who builds his house on the rock' (Matt. 7.24). Jesus's words are a solid foundation on which to build the house of marriage. Many people, however, find mere references to what Jesus said rather abstract and difficult to apply to real life. I shall add another quotation from the Sermon on the Mount that helps to provide a firm basis for a life together: 'Judge not, that you be not judged. For with the judgement you pronounce you will be judged, and the measure you give will be the measure you get' (Matt. 7.1f.).

Constant criticism is a continual threat to reciprocal love. If my partner isn't good-humoured, I immediately interpret this as a lack of love. I reproach him or her for ruining my good mood: 'I was so looking forward to this evening. And then you go and make a face like that. You've spoiled everything!' Criticism turns to judgement. I establish a norm which has to be obeyed and won't allow the other person to be as he or she is. I won't even let him or her feel down or off-colour from time to time. As a result, my partner feels devalued and begins to feel it's impossible to live up to the critical partner's ideals. The reproaches and judgements evoke either justifications or counter-accusations. Then I am constantly under the pressure of having to justify myself and explain why exactly I feel as I do, or I try to defend myself by attacking the other person and criticizing his or her behaviour. If he's a real husband he should appreciate my needs. If she's a real wife she should make sure I feel all right. These criticisms and reproaches hem us in and take us down. They make us feel we're never right, that we're an incompetent marriage partner, and that we don't deserve to be the husband or wife of Mr or Mrs Perfect.

Building on weaknesses

The rock on which we can build the house of marriage is a level-headed view of reality. We mustn't see the other person through the rosy or dark spectacles of our own value-judgements, or those of our own projected images and stereotypes. Often enough we don't see the other person as he or she is, but as we'd like him or her to be. And we see ourselves unrealistically too. We don't seem to notice that we aren't measuring up to our own ideals. We have to take our weaknesses as well as our strengths into account. But we have to see them plain. Then, strange to say, we shall find that our weak points actually make the rock strong enough to bear the weight of our house. Seeing our reality for what it is means knowing our limits. We mustn't overtax ourselves by excessive demands on our life together. Devout people run the risk of letting their religious ideals set their sights too high. They seem to ignore the fact that they just can't reach up there. Excessively high ideals make weak foundations. The house can't sit firmly in its rocky niche, but floats in the higher atmosphere where it is mercilessly buffeted by even a minor storm.

Nowadays there is less danger of failing because of lofty religious ideals. Today, of course, they have been replaced by neo-romantic ideals that blind couples to their own reality. People who obey these romantic notions build their house on illusions. No wonder then if it collapses under any onslaught.

One such illusion is that marriage always makes you happy. Some people misinterpret marriage as a kind of reciprocal happiness machine guaranteed to run for ever. But it isn't an everlasting happiness system. It's a way of training that needs lifelong dedication. If both of you are prepared to keep up your practice and constantly adapt and learn, you'll find happiness along the way.

But happiness isn't something you can find and impose on the way you live once and for all. It consists of a series of fortunate happy moments and occasions that spur you ahead through the rest of this life to the next.

Another illusion is that the other person has to be close to us all the time in marriage. But life together can succeed only if we get the relation between closeness and distance right. One problem here is that the ways in which partners want to be close and distant are often very diverse, and depend on different cycles, body clocks and temperament clocks. One may want to snuggle up close when the other just wants space. Examining this tension together and finding a viable way out of it is an art that has to be learned before it's acquired.

Another neo-romantic notion is that you will always feel your love, that marriage must always be an intense sensual experience, and there's something wrong if it isn't. But feelings change. There are times when the only way love can be expressed is by loyalty to the other person or by trust.

Love makes us vulnerable

St John Chrysostom offers another interpretation of the house built on a rock. He sees it as a demonstration of the truth of the idea he took from the Stoic philosophers: 'All wounds are self-inflicted.' If you have built your house on a rock, no matter how many storms and floods batter it, they cannot harm it. Chrysostom says: 'People can't hurt you. Only the *dogmata*, or "dogmatic" images, you have made of people can wound you.' Many marriages fail because they end up in a state of ongoing reciprocal insults and wounds. Warring couples who come for marriage guidance have often worn themselves down and out by mutual savagery. They just feel wounded. Love makes us vulnerable. If you love another person you can't escape being hurt. But it depends on the type of wound, and its appearance.

Those who come close to the other person in genuine love will always recognize that they themselves feel wounded, and acknowledge their shadow, the sensitive spots that make up the dark side of their personality. This will help them to advance in self-awareness. The experience can also deepen the partners' mutual loving. If they admit their hurt and discuss it with the other person without any kind of reproach, they will get to know themselves better, and progress in that awareness. This will bring husband and wife closer together. The hurt will open them up to each other more effectively.

But some wounds are directed at the partner, for they seem to carry their own malevolent desire to replicate in that person too. This always happens when I infect the partner with my own unconscious injuries. This means that I can't see myself clearly. I'm subject to the illusion that I'm perfectly all right, and in the right. And if my partner allows himself or herself to be continually wounded by me, he or she too must ask whether that isn't due to entertaining a false image of me. Possibly some archetypal image has been substituted for the real me. Perhaps I have been typecast as the healer, the liberator or redeemer. If this other person unconsciously expects me to exude healing, I shall just carry on hurting him or her, even when I don't want to. My partner will feel hurt all the time because I just can't satisfy all these unconscious expectations of healing and salvation. Then I'm not inflicting the wounds. Instead they are self-inflicted results of illusory ideas of me. Then a woman doesn't see her husband as he really is, but imprints on him the image of the father who never took her seriously. She interprets everything her husband says as instance after instance of not taking her at her true worth. Even if he makes a joke, she thinks he isn't taking her seriously. Or a man doesn't see his wife as the person she actually is, but sees his mother in her. Because he expects her to react as a mother to him, she can't help but disappoint him. But his wife isn't wounding him. The fault lies with the ideal image of her that he has manufactured.

A major task in marriage is to see the other person as she or he really is, and to work hard continually at the task of freeing him or her from the images we have unconsciously imprinted on that person, so that the real individual is allowed to emerge.

Married people will only build their house on firm ground if they are always prepared to remain aware of reality – their own and the other person's – and to accept it for what it is. Part of the reality they have to accept is that their way passes through storms and floods. On our road together we shall encounter our tempestuous passions, our whims and tantrums, and our wild emotions, fierce arguments and conflicts. We shall constantly experience the ways in which the flotsam and jetsam of the unconscious come to the surface, collect and threaten to overwhelm us. Then it is essential to let unconscious needs and expectations out and to look at them together to prevent them flooding our house and carrying it away. Then this marriage will become a house built on rock, a house besieged by breaking waves yet one where people can take refuge when their own lives are menaced by the waters. It becomes a house where other people also feel at home.

b) Sign of peace after the flood (Gen. 8.1–12)

I find that the narrative of the deluge and Noah's ark offers a very appropriate description of how married people can deal with their conflicts. In every marriage a great deal of repressed material surfaces from the unconscious, where all psychic material – both mental functions and contents – not in the immediate field of awareness dwells. ('Whatever appears in the light of perception is conscious; what lies in the darkness beyond is unconscious, although none the less living and effective' [C.G. Jung, *Contributions to Analytical Psychology*,1928, p. 90]). The contents of the unconscious will keep coming to the surface if the partners never talk about what they feel and how each feels hurt by the other, and if they refuse to face up to their disagreements and conflicts, hoping that it isn't really that bad. Then a mere pinprick can make the unconscious flood the whole landscape of their life together. The dams they have constructed to protect them from the deluge break. They seem to find no foothold, nothing to cling to. They are in an emotional whirlpool. The more they strike out, the deeper it takes them. Reciprocal accusations

191

make the situation worse by summoning up new floods, until an absolute deluge becomes a real possibility.

A protective space within

The story of Noah's ark shows a way out of this deluge. First we have to have an ark into which we can withdraw when the flood waters threaten to overwhelm us. This ark might be the inner protective space each person needs if he or she is not to be equally rent by the partner's unconscious. Everyone needs a place that offers peace and quiet in which to recollect himself or herself. This is the place in all of us where God himself dwells. There, neither person can be wounded by the other. There, neither individual can be reached by the unconscious matter which the other one drags along with him or her. When everything round about one person is flooded by the contents of the unconscious rising from the depths of the soul, he or she must withdraw into the quiet of that inner space. There I can contact myself and there I shall find God, who dwells within me. In God I shall slowly become able to see what is going on around me, and to make some kind of judgement without being overwhelmed by it all. The ark can also be the protective space into which both partners withdraw from the conflicts of their environment. They are both in constant need of time for each other, or they will drown in the deluge of daily life.

Clear structures

But the ark also stands for the structure a marriage needs in crisis situations. Noah has taken his wife, his three sons and their wives and all kinds of animals of both sexes into the ark. The ark provides an ordered structure even amidst the chaos of the deluge. An unyielding outer framework is important when a relationship is in a crisis, and no one can find solid ground to stand on. The couple must wait in the ark until the waters subside. They carry on living in the reliable structure they have chosen until they can open the ark and inspect the water.

First of all the ark reaches Mount Ararat and finds somewhere secure to rest. Then the first mountain-tops are sighted. The land that has borne the marriage can be seen again. Not everything has been ruined by the deluge. But Noah has to wait forty days until the water subsides further. Then he releases a raven from the ark. The raven stands for intelligence. Reason has to emerge and let the soul know where the secure dry land is. The mind has to work out what has happened. At this stage it doesn't assess it minutely but just tries to understand. If I understand what welled up in me and what released this inner deluge, I shall have come a long way. If the partners carry on accusing each other, more emotions will flood from their reciprocal wounds and make it impossible to resolve anything. Reason has to risk an initial description and modest analysis of what has happened, without trying to evaluate it.

The dove of love

After the raven, Noah releases a dove. The dove is a symbol of love. In ancient Greece the dove of Aphrodite, the goddess of love, was a sacred creature. In the Middle East it was associated with Ishtar, the goddess of fertility. Both partners have to get in touch with their love again. No sign of love appeared during the deluge of overflowing emotions. But when the waters have subsided it is possible to test the level of the love that is still there, and its capacity.

The first dove returns to the ark because it finds no dry land on the earth. One partner sends out his or her love. But if there is no receptive place in the other person, he or she must take it back into the ark so that it can rest and grow stronger. Noah waits another seven days until he lets the second dove fly away. Seven is the magical number of transformation. Change occurs when the divine is joined to the human. In any conflict we must remember that God can transform everything in us that is unresolved and unfinished, and turn the waters of the unconscious into a fertile source.

The olive branch of reconciliation

The dove returns towards evening bearing an olive branch (some translations say 'a freshly plucked olive leaf') (cf. Gen. 8.11). The olive branch is a symbol of spiritual strength and of light. Oil burns in oil lamps to illuminate people and their dwellings. Oil cleanses and is a symbol of purification. Because the olive tree is tough and resistant, the olive branch also stands for fruitfulness and vitality. And because oil has a soothing effect, the olive branch also symbolizes peace and reconciliation. The symbolism of the olive branch shows how, ultimately, the crisis is transformed.

If I let my love flow out again to my partner, it will illuminate the darkness of raging emotions. If I allow anger or jealousy to remain too long inside me, darkness will reign within me and I shall be unable to see in or out. This other person's love lightens my darkness, and also has the power to purge and cleanse. In the course of an argument negative emotions spin up out of me. I even feel that I hate another person and want to hurt him or her more and more. But when my hateful remarks hit home I wound myself too. Yet when another person's love flies to me like a dove, it washes my grubby soul clean of all the negativity.

But love doesn't just restore the former state of things. The crisis has brought all kinds of inner debris to the surface, so love has to purge my innermost depths. The more room I allow love, the more effectively I shall be purged. Those recurrent conflicts in a marriage are not signs of the absence of love. Husband and wife mustn't reproach themselves for a lack of love on that account. It is good to bring conflicts out into the open. Every disagreement will bring more unpurged matter to the surface to be cleansed by love.

Conflicts don't burden the soul but help to make it more pure and clear. Then both partners will know themselves better and learn greater humility. The euphoria, or over-optimism, of the first stages will have disappeared but crises will have produced an inner clarity and composure, a certain humility from which love can flow fresh and clean, as if from a pure spring.

The power of love

The olive branch is a symbol of the resilience of love. Love is not overcome by fierce conflicts. True love is stronger than death, as the Song of Solomon tells us: 'Love is as strong as death ... Many waters cannot quench love, neither can the floods drown it' (S. of S. 8.6f.). Just as storms make trees put down their roots even more securely, love is not weakened but strengthened by dissension. The husband and wife who have survived many arguments are confident that love will always be more capable of resistance. They no longer fear that their love will fade away. They know they have no guarantee that they will be protected from any further strife, but the power of their love has already proved so strong that they can face the future with confidence. Nowadays I meet with many couples who try to cover up their disagreements because they are afraid their love would suffer if they let them into the open. But they confuse love with the feeling of being loved. They think it would be disastrous actually to quarrel with each other, to air their feelings of hate and vengeance. They are wrong. The important thing is to come safely through this flood of emotions. The relationship will be transformed into an ark that will carry this couple safely through the tempests and over the troubled waters of life.

Oil in your wounds

Oil has a soothing effect. Every conflict wounds people. The words hurled at me by another person injure me. Sometimes, after a quarrel, the hurtful words come back to me and make my wound deeper. There is no point scratching old wounds. No relationship is without a degree of hurt. The decisive thing is to allow my and my partner's love to flow into my wounds. That will heal them. If I keep worrying my hurt it will go on annoying me. The irritation of my already wounded feelings will affect the relationship. Because I am wounded I shall wound this other person too. But love soothes my distress and has the power to heal it. The scar will remain but the spot where it appears is still sensitive.

Strange to say, the tender skin covering the old wound prompts me to treat myself and my partner gently. If I let love flow into my injury then it will become a pearl for me and others. Hildegard of Bingen knew this. She was well aware that we can't avoid wounds but saw the mystery of a successful life in the way our wounds are transformed into pearls. Love is the power that changes our injuries into something precious. My wound constantly reminds me that my deepest longing is to be able to love and be loved.

The wound shows me that I am directed to God's healing love. Without divine love, human love will always hurt me. Human love is fragile. It is mixed with possessive claims, desires to own, envy, jealousy and expectations. Only if our love is permeated with God's love will it possess the power to cure and change us.

The second dove brings an olive branch as a sign of reconciliation and peace. The third dove that Noah despatches after another seven days never returns. It finds enough nourishment on the earth, and dry land on which to alight. The love we send out to another person in a crisis pauses to heal his or her wounds, then flies on freely. Once again it finds sufficient nourishment on the earth of our everyday lives. Our life continues as before, but now it is suffused with the love that flies to and fro. Love has become like a dove borne on currents of air yet alighting where we work and live. Love makes our daily life flow and lends us wings to rise ever and again above the difficulties and harsh realities that threaten to keep us close to the ground.

The story of the Deluge is a symbolic account of how we can withstand and transform crises and conflicts. It shows us that we ought to enter married life realistically, not euphorically. But it also gives us grounds to hope that disagreement won't tear us apart, and that we won't be overwhelmed by what each of us brings along from our previous life-history. Conflicts are perhaps inevitable, but leftover fragments of our past wounds which we haven't worked through certainly have to be dealt with. We don't enter our life together as people who have already dealt with every possible problem and devised a civilized warning system to defuse any conflict automatically at the first whiff of gunpowder. We enter it as people marked by our environment and infected by the evil around us. But we do so full of hope that when we make our commitment to each other God will give us an ark to bear us safely through the storms and over the floods of our lives.

c) Finding the source of love and joy (Phil. 4.4–9; John 15.9–17)

One couple I know chose two texts from the Letter to the Philippians and John's gospel as readings for their marriage service. They offer excellent hints for a successful married life. Both texts are concerned with joy and love.

Paul tells the Philippians that they should rejoice. But joy is also a question of opting for it. There are plenty of people who rejoice outwardly but celebrate their inner frustration. They're not even in a good humour. It's all show. In fact they are borne down by depression and frustration. They are not living their own lives, but are being lived. Married people must constantly opt effectively for joy and love. These are not feelings you can simply produce to order. But if you opt for these emotions, which are already there waiting to be chosen in the depths of your soul, they will grow stronger and gradually determine your attitude.

A partner's closeness

Paul says we should rejoice because the Lord is near. The closeness of Christ is always a reason to rejoice, but so is the closeness of a partner. If we know that he or she is inwardly close to us, even when we happen to be a long way off physically, we can rejoice at that nearness. We are not alone. Love overcomes boundaries and assures us of a partner's presence wherever we are. Another reason for rejoicing is the absence of anxiety. 'Do not be anxious . . .'. In other words: Don't worry about anything at all. The Greek word in the original means anxious self-concern. Worrying about yourself destroys joy and lets love fade away. If I keep wondering whether my partner respects me, is loyal to me, still loves me, I make room for fear and melancholy, uneasiness and mistrust. Love means I trust him or her, and fills me with thankfulness and joy.

Our truth

Paul offers another reason for rejoicing, and uses words that never recur elsewhere in his letters. They are terms taken from the Stoic philosophy that was dominant in Greece at the time: 'And now, my friends, all that is true, all that is noble, all that is just and pure, all that is lovable and attractive, whatever is excellent and admirable – fill your thoughts with these things' (Phil. 4.8). Paul clearly intended these remarks for people in Philippi who thought they could solve every difficulty by prayer and piety. You can't base a marriage only on piety. It also calls for the human values enumerated by Paul. Living together also needs clear rules of communication for success. A precondition for mutual joy is to be truthful, to hold out our own truth and entrust it to the other person. We don't have to pretend. Everything that we conceal from him or her makes our relationship less vital. The same is true of our weaknesses. Only if we hold out our mistakes and weak points without concealment, is there room for growth of a fearless relationship that makes room for joy.

Our dignity and value

'Noble' is the adjective for 'nobility', for human worth, or dignity and value. In our life together, in all disputes and conflicts, it is essential to know our own worth and the divine worth of our partner. Those who cannot see their own value constantly devalue others in order to raise their own worth. That's not a good basis for living together. Only people who are conscious of their own dignity and value can rejoice in those of another person. We have to be aware of what is right for us. If we don't attend to our own inner harmony, our relationship will be dissonant. We often ignore our own feelings, just to avoid any conflict. But then we shall be increasingly out of tune and upset the melody of our whole relationship. We have to tell each other what is right for us. Ultimately, the reconciliation of what is right for each of us will be our joint harmony.

Worthy of love

We should also fix our thoughts on 'all that is just and pure, all that is lovable and attractive'. 'Just and pure' means being open and clear for our partner, not holding anything back, not pretending, making what is seen and heard what you are. It also means loving the other person without hidden motives, not using him or her for yourself, not making sure there's something in it for yourself.

We must also think about what is lovable and attractive. Each of us contains a sufficient number of lovable and attractive character-istics. We can love each other only if we are aware of what is lovable in our own selves. I know people who are always excusing themselves for existing, for being who and as they are. They dare not entrust themselves to others. But I can only love another person if I believe that there are enough lovable qualities in him or her, and in myself. We need positive spectacles to discover what is lovable and attractive in ourselves and in other people.

A joy to be alive

'Whatever is excellent and admirable ...'. The older translations used the word 'virtue' here, and that is exactly what Paul says: '... if there be any virtue, and there be any praise, think on these things.' We find 'virtue' a somewhat off-putting term nowadays. But the Greeks thought of it as a decisive aid to living. For them, virtue meant the experience of being able to shape and mould our lives by our own efforts. For the Romans *virtus* was the power we have within us. If we are virtuous we enjoy living our own lives, and shaping them well. We are not the victims of our emotions. Nowadays, however, you see so many people who are just sorry for themselves. They can't do anything and admit it. That's how it is, they say. If we are virtuous we are confident that we can take our life into our own hands, and enjoy making something out of it. Virtue in the sense of wanting to be alive is the final precondition for joy, as Paul understands it.

Everyday loving

Jesus talks constantly of love (cf. John 15.9–17). The precondition for our capacity to love is that Jesus loved us first. Husband and wife do not start loving when they are married. They love because they have already known love from their parents and from their brothers and sisters. They can offer love because they were accepted by their parents. And they can love because God loves them. We remain in love because we keep the commandments. The love Jesus talks of is very real. It has to prove itself in the trustworthiness, regularity and naturalness of a married couple's day-to-day life.

I know a couple who are always saying 'I love you', yet the husband simply never comes home at the agreed time and thinks nothing of letting his wife wait two hours with a lovingly prepared meal. Love has to be practical or it's just make-believe. Everyday loving is needed so that the partners can trust each other, and each can show the other his or her love by actually doing what the practical occasions of life together demand.

Devotion

Jesus shows another aspect of his love when he says: 'There is no greater love than this, that someone should lay down his life for his friends' (John 15.13). At first, this seems to be going too far. Self-sacrifice runs contrary to our drive to live our own lives, be ourselves, realize ourselves. It isn't only a matter of actually dying to save someone else's life. Some married people feel and act like genuine sacrificial lambs. They do everything possible for their partners, and feel and suffer on their behalf. Yet the resulting atmosphere isn't liberating – or in the least 'redemptive'. At best it might be called 'bad conscience'. You can't live properly in the company of anyone permanently intent on neurotic self-sacrifice. It arouses dismal guilt feelings in husband or wife about the partner's constant suffering.

Real love, of course, demands devotion from both partners and never putting up a personal security screen that decides how far you can go on the other's behalf. That kind of devotion culminates in fusion with the other person in sexual love. But what happens in sex must also occur in daily living as complete mutual acceptance.

Openness

Jesus mentions another precondition for the love which he lived before us. He calls us his friends, because he has revealed everything to us which he heard from his Father. Genuine love includes this readiness to tell the other person about everything in me: my strengths, my abilities, but also my weak points, the very aspects I so dislike because they don't fit my ideal self-image. This absolute openness creates an area of trust and freedom which is essential for lasting love. It doesn't matter what I have inside me: even fear, doubts or aggression. If I reveal them to him or to her, they can change, and something new can emerge from them. An especially important result of this disclosure is the assurance that each of us is accepted as we are. Of course, this openness will destroy some illusions that I entertain about myself and about him or her. But it will also create the free and relaxed atmosphere love demands if it is to prosper. Naturally, you have to carry on being open with each other, and that needs occasional prompting. One way to do this is to take time out every week to talk openly and freely along these lines. A number of people I know use what they call a 'let's-talk stone', which might be a beautifully rounded pebble from the beach. While one partner has this stone in his or her hand, the other is not allowed to interrupt whatever he or she says. Husband or wife has the right to come out with what he or she feels. But then, as soon as the agreed time comes to an end, he or she must hand the stone over and listen to whatever is said in return.

IV. FUTURE PROSPECTS

Thinking about the real meaning of marriage, meditating on the marriage service, and seeking the deeper meaning of the relevant biblical texts are certainly appropriate ways for a future bride and groom to prepare for their wedding and their life together. They are also worthwhile resources for married couples who have been together for many years. We have to keep our experiences in mind and reflect on their meaning, in case they should grow tired and stale. It is good for married people to recall the power and enthusiasm of their wedding day, when they felt so in love, and how attractive they found each other. Their wedding photographs will bring back memories of the actual day and ceremony. Perhaps they still have or remember the texts from the Bible which they chose then, and even some words or phrases from the sermon or homily. These will prompt them to ask whether the way they live now is a fitting sequel to all that promise, or anything that detracts from it has crept into their relationship, and there is need for renewal.

A Silver or Golden Wedding anniversary is a good opportunity to re-examine your married life to date and to draw on the very Source of love, which never dries up because it is divine. Preparing for an anniversary could be a suitable occasion for husband and wife to tell each other what unites them, what they still find difficult, in what respects they feel hurt, but also why they feel thankful and glad. They could also discuss their special anniversary service, and how they would like to arrange the renewal of their marriage vows. I know some married couples who have developed something approaching such a rite quite apart from more formal or public celebrations of Silver, Gold and Diamond anniversaries. When they sense that their love is somehow slackening, they switch off the lights, light a bridal candle and once again slip their marriage rings onto each other's finger. Each prepares a declaration in his or her own words, or just says spontaneously what is important to him or her at that moment. Some people do this on each anniversary. Each couple should work out their own private ritual for this occasion.

I hope that this section contains a number of thoughts that will inspire married people to remember when they first fell in love and to vow to continue on their way with something approaching the same enthusiasm. Commemorations undoubtedly help us to get in touch with the power of love and to renew it. Yet not only the beginning and memories of it are important. Constant rediscovery of the one true Source of love is essential. It is divine and therefore inexhaustible. The wellspring of God's undying love can refresh our own love, which is easily affected by life's various problems and by our daily grind. As our love flows freely again, we can thank God for its mystery, which has withstood all the storms and crises of life together.

6

Ordination: living as a priest

INTRODUCTION

When writing about ordination, I have to ask myself what it means to be a priest. How do I see myself as a priest? What is the most important thing about my life as a priest? I remember endless discussions in the 1970s about what it really meant to be a priest: whether he was a leader of a parish or church community, or a dispenser of the sacraments, or a pastor. In many dioceses nowadays laypeople have already been appointed to preside over parishes. Not only priests but pastoral workers, who may be men or women, do the work of pastors. Dispensing the sacraments, however, is reserved to priests. But is that all the priesthood means? I don't think so. It would be an intolerable restriction.

I'm glad I'm a priest. An important aspect of my experience of the priestly life is celebrating the Eucharist. And when I baptize children as one of my priestly functions, it's a real joy to carry out this service for people. But is service the be-all and end-all of the priesthood? What exactly does it mean and involve? When I ask myself these questions, I find that I can't answer them clearly and straight forwardly. I find being a priest so many-sided that it can't be defined satisfactorily in terms of tasks and duties. My existence as a priest has to be assessed much more qualitatively.

When theologians discuss the priesthood, they constantly return to the relation of the priesthood of all believers, which embraces all Christians, to the office of a priest conferred on those whom the bishop ordains and sends into the world to carry out their mission. This commission is certainly an essential aspect of the priesthood. We are not ordained priests to make us feel better, and to raise our self-esteem – to make us special. Priests are sent to help people.

Accordingly, I want to examine the sacrament of ordination against the background of the vocation and mission that are peculiar to the priesthood but also, in a certain sense, apply to all Christians. After all, every Christian has a particular vocation and mission. Consequently, a clear understanding of the priesthood and of ordination might help all Christians to discover not only their mission in this world but the sources they should draw on to fulfil this mission appropriately.

The Catholic Church counts ordination as one of the seven sacraments. Martin Luther protested against the special status of the priest and emphasized instead the general priesthood of all believers. The Second Vatican Council also took up the concept of the universal priesthood of Christians. But neither Luther nor the Council has very much to say about the actual meaning of the term.

For Luther, the priesthood of believers consists primarily in the free access which everyone has to God. You don't need the special function of a priest to reach God. Luther sees the priestly task of believers as residing especially in praise of God. Recent Catholic theology takes a similar view of it, but adds the point that all believers offer God a pure sacrifice in the Eucharist. Furthermore, contemporary Catholic theologians follow the tradition of the early Fathers of the Church in referring to the spiritual offering made by Christians, to the pure offering of a clear conscience, and to the offering of self-denial and love of our neighbour. In this case the image of the priest becomes that of a devout Christian as such. Yet if you search the statements of Luther and the Second Vatican Council for definitions and descriptions of the specific or essential character of the priesthood, you will find scarcely anything pertinent.

I think it's important to examine what being a priest actually is and means before looking at the notion of the priesthood in its particular and universal aspects.

For me, the priest is an archetypal image or symbol. Indeed, we can't avoid talking about the priestly life of ordained priests and of laypeople in terms of imagery and symbolism. I find the use of images of this kind the only effective way to meditate on my life as a priest. Thinking about them and their profound implications shows me who I am as a priest. Then I find that that the precise theological distinction between the particular and general priesthood fades into near-insignificance.

I. THE THEOLOGY OF THE PRIEST

a) The archetype of the priest

The history of the religions that preceded Christianity shows us that priests perform important functions in all religions. One commentator in a major work of reference defines priests as 'religious leaders who are primarily distinguished from the general mass of followers of a religion both by a special power ("charisma", "grace", or "mana") and by their function of presiding over the worship of the cult as mediators between the divinity and human beings' (Wassilios Klein, *Theologische Realenzyklopädie*, vol. 27 [1997], p. 379). A vital point here is that the priest is endowed with a special power either from birth or by means of a special consecration. He has a numinous quality. He is the locus of a power to which we ourselves have no access.

Driving out demons

A priest is close to the divinity and uses certain rites in an attempt to make the divine healing power accessible to humans. In the history of religion, priests are the special practitioners of rites. By celebrating rites correctly, they protect the life of the human community from demonic powers that could be dangerous to people. We might suppose any such service to be a totally outdated phenomenon of ancient times. But it is not difficult to imagine the comforting effect of priestly activity for people long ago. If we were to translate the magical thinking of earlier ages into terms proper to our own concept of the priest, we might say that a priest was a person who warded off demons by being himself. Monks in past centuries thought the only person capable of sending demons flying was someone who was well acquainted with them: someone, in other words, who knew his or her own soul. Those who won't let themselves be controlled by demons, projections and fixed ideas, but whose souls are determined by God, are a blessing for those round about them. They radiate a protective influence, for they have succeeded in transforming a demonic power into spiritual strength.

Teacher, interpreter of dreams, soothsayer and prophet

Another important task of priests in the ancient world was the transmission of knowledge. They had been instructed in secrets concerning not merely the nature of the gods but the successful pursuit of life. Therefore people saw priests as guarantors of achievement in their lives. They not only conveyed knowledge but deciphered dreams. Priests were the first interpreters of dreams. Dreams were seen as sacred, for they emanated from God. But many people were unable to intrerpret dreams by themselves. They consulted priests for this purpose. Moreover, in some religions it was the task of priests at shrines devoted to oracles to discover and announce the specific will of God for individuals. Other priests were soothsayers, or prophets, whom people credited with the ability to foretell the future.

Clearly, priests had to have a gift for sensing how the divinity operated spiritually. In other words, they had to discern God's Spirit in the human mind or soul. They had to discover the ways of God for the individual. For this they needed the gift of discernment of spirits.

Physician and therapist

One of the priest's duties was to undertake the ritual washing of individuals, in order to cleanse them of guilt or of the ideas that evil people had instilled in them by projection. Accordingly, the priest was there to help people find their true, essential nature. He wasn't a medicine man, yet one of his tasks was also to heal illness and to care for supplicants' souls by listening to their problems and bringing them before God through prayer in order to discover his will for each of them.

When I try to interpret these ancient tasks in present-day terms, I think especially of their cleansing effect. The priest is there to wipe out the projections others have cast on those under his care, and the self-induced notions which they use to cloud their true image. He cleanses them from the guilt that obscures their real nature. The priest discerns the original beauty of God in human beings and is not misled by prejudices. He helps people to trust these original, unadulterated marks of God in their own lives, and thus to express and assert the fundamental divine image within them.

Mediator between God and humans

Essentially the priest is a mediator between God and human beings. He stands between them and transmits God's closeness, love and healing power to humans. All religions recognize the function of the priest as a mediator between God and humans. He mediates between them by bringing their offerings before God, or by receiving their concerns and passing them on to God in petitionary prayer. The Romans expressed this mediatory function of the priest in the symbolic figure of the *pontifex*, or builder of bridges. They called the high priest the *pontifex maximus*, or greatest bridge-builder. In fact, the priest helps to build the bridge between God and humanity, but also bridges between people. He unites the two separated aspects of a dualism: light and dark, God and humanity, need and salvation, or sin and forgiveness. The priest's task is one of union. In a world where humans feel divided and too often experience that division in their society, the priest acts as a guarantor that neither individuals in themselves nor society as a whole will collapse.

For me, the priest conceived as a mediator means that he is in touch with the centre of his own being; and that at that centre he is in touch with God. I see the priest as offering up the people's gifts as an agent of transformation and transubstantiation. When a priest in some cults and countries nowadays, as in certain nations in antiquity, sacrifices the tribe's or people's gift-offerings, he burns them. This action transforms the gifts. They are raised from the earthly domain and lodged in the realm of the divine. The priest joins the earthly and the divine by transforming mundane matter so that it radiates the splendour of God. This is a symbol of the process of human self-development. People can find themselves only if they, along with their impulses, passions, emotions and abilities, are continually and increasingly encompassed and permeated by God's Spirit.

Lamentation, singing and invocation

Another group of priests carried out the work of lamentation, singing and invocation. They complained to God on behalf of suffering humanity. They brought their petitions before God and pleaded with him to help those in need of succour. The basic symbolic figure of the priest as singer is the mythical Orpheus, whom God had graced with a voice that moved human hearts, opened them for and to God, and healed their wounds. Divine worship was an essential part of the priestly office. The priest would sing on the people's behalf. He was a representative. He did not pray for himself but to ensure that a particular place would resound with divine praise as the people wished. If God were praised there, then the world itself would be transformed and grow brighter and more wholesome.

Guardian of sacred places

Many religions see priests as guardians and protectors of holy places. In antiquity many priests were appointed to care for the consecrated place of worship and to defend it from pollution. They had to ensure that the rites were celebrated regularly on this spot, and that it remained a sacred location. People clearly believed that their vital welfare depended on the sacred place. Only that which is holy can heal. People were convinced of this. One of a priest's most gratifying tasks is still to maintain the sense of the sacred in the midst of this secularized world, and to guard the holiness of the place where he is located.

For the Romans, guardianship of the sacred spot also meant watching over the holy fire. This was the task of the Vestal Virgins, who had to keep the flame burning. This is also an impressive image of all those priests and priestesses who have guarded the holy fire in human beings, in case it should fade away. Such people still make sure that others don't burn out and that what they keep alive in their innermost selves is not dissipated. They protect the fire in their own hearts, but also the flame that burns in a community and is always threatened with extinction. The Romans saw a priestess as a guarantor that the fire of divine love would not vanish from society and the State. The condition of the Roman commonwealth was thought to depend on the Vestal Virgins.

Priestesses

Many religions had priestesses as well as priests. In ancient Greece priestesses were usually assigned to goddesses, and male priests to gods. The cult of Dionysus was an exception. Dionysus was the god of love, sexuality and intoxication, and women priests dedicated to him had charge of his cult. Greek cities also had both men and women priests. The priestesses who served the divine mother Demeter had a special significance, for only women had access to Demeter's sanctuary. Priestesses also played an important part in the mystery cults, and the priestesses of Isis had a major function in ancient Egypt.

History shows that priests and priestesses did not have the same tasks, but had their own special areas of responsibility. Priestesses were closer to the cult of the sacred mother, and to the cults of earth and nature. They were the guardians of fruitfulness, growth and the hearth. In the mystery cults they inducted people into the mystery of coming into existence and of development as humans. They were responsible for birth and dying, for people's rebirth in the divinity. They were also intimately associated with the theme of love and sex, as is evident in the Dionysian cult. Priestesses initiated adepts into the mysteries of love and sex, for these are prime experiences in which people realize their union with creation and with God.

Initiation rites

Before priests or priestesses could exercise their office, they themselves had to be initiated into their duties through an initiation rite, or act of consecration or ordination.

This ordination elevated the priest above other members of society and placed him or her in the realm of the sacred. But before they were admitted to the initiation rite, priests and priestesses had to complete long courses of training. They were instructed in the correct celebration of rites and the practice of an ascetic lifestyle. Their training included a comprehensive course in traditional divine lore, but also in the art of healing and the science of divining the weather. Priests had to learn and understand everything necessary for the success of human life. Some cultures also insisted that priests and priestesses led celibate lives, so that they could approach deities as suitably pure individuals.

The foregoing shows that you can't become a priest at will. You have to undergo a long training to prepare for the tasks of the priesthood. The archetype of the priest always includes a challenge to lead a spiritual life and a constant need to learn more about your own soul and the human soul in general and particular.

Many people think that the Catholic Church's adoption of pagan elements in its image of the priest is false and improper. They say that it should reflect the viewpoint of the New Testament writings, and nothing more. Otherwise it must contravene or debase the divine commission portrayed in Scripture. But part of the Church's wisdom throughout its two thousand years of existence has been to ensure that its proclamation takes up and carries forward the profound longings expressed in all religions. It was quite legitimate to adopt the human yearning contained in the archetypal priestly image and to integrate it in the Christian notion of a priest. The Church's references to the universal priesthood of all believers would be void of meaning if it did not take the archetypal elements of priesthood into consideration. That is why I have summarized the components of the priestly life evident in the history of religion, before turning to the Bible and asking, against that background, what precisely Christianity has taken over from the figure of the priest in other religions, and what it has transformed and seen in a different light. In fact, the biblical pronouncements on the subject can be understood only when seen as comprising a reaction to existing images of priesthood.

b) Priests according to the Bible

Priests in the Old Testament

Only men from the tribe of Levi were allowed to become priests in Old Testament times. One of the duties of Old Testament priests was to deliver oracular responses. They were seers who accompanied the king and supported his political decisions by drawing on superhuman knowledge and speaking oracularly. Another of their tasks was to pass on what was known about God. Priests had to ensure that people were instructed in the knowledge of God and in belief. Another important function was to clarify questions of purity. Priests had to decide whether and when someone was clean or unclean. They instructed people in the law and often took part in legal processes. In sanctuaries, and in the Temple from the time of its construction under Solomon, they were the custodians of the sacred traditions of the cult, and offered sacrifice in accordance with its rules. The offering of diverse sacrifices was the main duty of priests in ancient Israel. Their task was also to bless the people, and to transmit God's blessing to everyone.

Priests in the New Testament

Priests appear but play no essential role in certain scenes reported in the New Testament. Jesus asks the healed leper to show himself to the priests (Mark 1.44; Luke 17.14). A priest passes by on the other side when a man is waylaid by robbers (Luke 10.31). Priests are more active in the Passion narrative. When Jesus drove the money-changers from the Temple, he attacked contemporary religious practice. This aroused the opposition of certain priests, who felt that Jesus was calling them into question. Indeed, we might deduce from the narrative that conflict with the priestly aristocracy of the Sadducees was a factor in his execution. The hearing of Jesus before the Sanhedrin and high priests Annas and Caiaphas took place in the latter's house, and we are told that the high priests and their followers handed Jesus over to the Romans.

Jesus the true High Priest

In the Acts of the Apostles, Luke tells us that priests were among the opponents of the young Christian community (Acts 4.1). But many priests also belonged to the original Jerusalem church (Acts 6.7). The concept of the priest plays an important part in the Letter to Jewish Christians (the Letter to the Hebrews), which calls Jesus the true High Priest. Jesus has made the all-sufficient sacrifice that had redeemed us, and has thus terminated the Old Testament cult of sacrifices and the Levitic priesthood for ever. The term 'priest' is used to describe Jesus's healing and saving effect. Jesus has redeemed us from our sins. Therefore we no longer need priests to purify us of our sins.

The first Letter of Peter calls believers holy priests, who 'can offer those spiritual sacrifices which are acceptable to God by Jesus Christ' (1 Pet. 2.5). The unknown author of this letter ascribed to Peter sees spiritual sacrifice as leading a holy life in a world inimical to Christians, and as offering yourself for guidance by Jesus's Spirit. The idea that they are holy priests enables Christians (who lived then as an excluded group in the Roman world) to feel that they are specially chosen. It assures them that they are at home in the sacred space of God's presence, where they may experience the closeness of God. Here the biblical author refers not so much to the duties of a priest as to the qualities that mark Christians out from others. These are selection by God, holiness, or exclusion from a corrupt world, and the royal and priestly dignity and value of the Christian community. The image of holy priesthood is intended to give the oppressed community a new sense of self-esteem, and accordingly confidence and hope.

Bishop, presbyter, deacon

The early Church did not use the older priestly terms for its offices, but drew on a range of social designations: *episkopos* ('overseer', 'supervisor'), *presbyteros* ('elder', 'president') and *diakonos* ('servant', 'minister'). The concept of a 'presbyter' derives from the Jewish synagogue and from Hellenistic urban culture. All these terms avoid the sacral dimension predominant in the image of the priest in the history of religion. They refer to functions in the Christian community: leading, presiding and serving or ministering. Leadership (the office of the *episkopos*) comprised the organization of the Christian community and the celebration of services. The 'presbyter' presided over the Eucharist. The deacon's main duty was to care for the poor. He was assigned to the *episkopos*, who allocated his duties.

These terms were applied to the archetypal concepts of the priesthood only from the third century AD onwards. Some commentators see this as a form of tampering with the typically Christian significance of these roles. But it certainly satisfied a fundamental need of the human soul. Today, however, the tension between the origins of the Christian community and the various interpretations of its offices has to be scrutinized responsibly. We have to admit, not pass over, the tension between the sacral and more functional dimensions of the Christian idea of the priesthood.

In this context we also have to inquire into the part played by women in the early communities mentioned in the New Testament. It is evident from Paul's letters that women also presided over the eucharistic meal in the early Church. They had the same entitlement as men when sharing the leadership of local churches. In the Letter to the Romans, Paul recommends 'Phoebe, our sister, a deaconess of the church at Cenchreae' (Rom. 16.1). He uses the same words to describe his own service to the community. Paul says Prisca and

Aquila 'have worked with me for Christ Jesus's (Rom. 16.3), in terms that always refer to ecclesiastical service in other contexts. He also says that Mary 'has worked so hard' for the church (Rom. 16.6), using phrases that he often applies to his own apostolic activity. He calls Andronicus and Junia (now generally interpreted as a woman, and disregarding the male reading 'Junias') respected apostles (Rom. 16.7). Paul's list in the Letter to the Romans shows that women undertook responsible posts in the service of the Church. Paul did not appoint them. They held their offices before him. But Paul acknowledges their service. This presumably included preaching Jesus's good news but also presiding over the Eucharist, which was generally celebrated in a domestic setting at that time.

Therefore the historical evidence shows that there is no reason to exclude women from the priesthood. Some theologians who think they should be excluded from priestly office argue that only a man can represent Christ as a priest. But it depends on which theology of priestly office is used to support this line of argument. Jesus's behaviour towards women certainly doesn't lend any weight to theological assertions of this kind. Jesus accepted both women and men as his disciples. And women were the first witnesses of the Resurrection. Several commentators share the view that it is out of order to use the biblical texts as evidence for excluding women from priestly office. Undoubtedly a long process of rethinking will be necessary in the Church before women can be admitted to Holy Orders. But at the Second Vatican Council many bishops were already in favour of ordaining women as deacon(esse)s.

c) Priests in the tradition of the Church

The early Church constantly referred to Jesus as the 'true Priest'. In this it based its judgement primarily on the statement in the Letter to the Hebrews, which was a favourite text in the first centuries of Christianity. According to Justin, Christians comprised 'the true high-priestly people of God'. Their task was to offer their own lives to God. Their priesthood was mainly a matter of leading lives in which they conformed themselves to Christ, took part in the celebration of the Eucharist, and through it offered themselves to God.

Bishops and priests were not described in terms peculiar to priests until the beginning of the third century AD. Since Tertullian and Cyprian, the bishop has been referred to regularly as *sacerdos* (a priest). In the Eastern Church, too, Origen described the bishop as a priest. Presbyters were also termed priests. According to Origen, however, they were priests to a lesser degree. Bishops were full priests. Presbyters shared in the bishop's priestly office. Deacons were not considered to participate in the priesthood.

The increasing significance of priests in the history of the Church

The image of those who held an office in the Church changed in the course of time. Bishops and priests were no longer seen as presiding over a priestly people but became a priesthood acting for and on behalf of the laity. Ordination was the means of entry to the status of priest. Ecclesiastical historians disagree about the reasons why the Church tended increasingly to describe its office-holders in priestly terms. Some experts think that this development was the result of social pressure on the Church, since religions in the ancient world needed a priesthood. Others believe that the pressures of fighting heresy and schism were behind the growing emphasis on priests.

Priests in the early Church did more than preside over the Eucharist. They had to dispense all the sacraments and were called on especially to proclaim the word of God in sermons and to instruct Christians in the teachings of the Christian faith. Cyprian speaks of the sacred work of proclaiming the word and uses the Greek word for 'priestly activity' (*hierourgein*) in this context. Cyprian sees the preaching of the good news as priestly activity on the same level as administering the sacraments.

Interpreting the concept of the Church's office-bearers on the basis of the Old Testament priesthood led to the increasing importance of ordination and to the gradual imposition of celibacy, since cultic ministers were required to exhibit a greater degree of ritual purity. The first Letter of Timothy requires a bishop to have been married only once (1 Tim. 3.2). In the time of the Fathers of the Church, celibacy did not mean the unmarried state, but only continence. Married priests, too, were advised to prepare for reception of the office of priest by a specific period of abstinence from marital relations. The imposition of celibacy was not confirmed until the Middle Ages, by Pope Innocent III (1198–1216). The Council of Trent (1545–1563) defended it against the Reformers' objections.

Ordination was thought of increasingly as inducing an inner transformation of the ordained man which elevated him above the mass of the faithful. Gregory of Nyssa described this inward change through ordination as the result of the power of the Word, which also

> makes the priest worthy and worthy of respect, separated by this new blessing from the ordinary mass. For he who until now was still one of the mass of the people suddenly appears as leader, director, teacher of piety and mystagogue in hidden mysteries, and does so without any change in body or form. Outwardly, he remains who he was, but in his invisible soul an unseen power and grace transform him into something better.

The image of the priest which developed gradually in the Church was heavily influenced by the Old Testament image of the sacrificing priest. In that acceptation, the priest is primarily the celebrant of the sacred eucharistic sacrifice who performs Christ's sacrifice in the liturgy. Less consideration was given to all the other archetypal images associated with the priest throughout the history of religions, thus producing a very one-sided image of the priest. This biased image still affects our thinking today. Our view of a priest is primarily one of a man who celebrates the Eucharist, administers the sacraments and possibly instructs people in the tenets of their faith, which was also one of the tasks of a priest in the Old Testament period. But only if we understand the mystery of the priesthood in the sense of the powerful archetypes I have mentioned can a priest's life be fully authentic and happy.

The Reformation and the Second Vatican Council

In the Middle Ages priests were seen increasingly in their cultic aspect. They were men entrusted primarily with the administration of the sacraments, and especially the power to celebrate the Eucharist and the faculty of remitting sins. Martin Luther protested against this. For him, the priest's main task was to proclaim the word of God. The Council of Trent, however, maintained that there was a special priesthood in the Church which had taken over the tradition of the Old Testament priesthood. The Second Vatican Council took some of the Reformers' concerns into account and its documents have much to say on the universal priesthood of all believers. They also interpret the priestly office more on the basis of biblical images, and the image of Jesus Christ as Prophet, Priest and Shepherd (or King). Bishops and priests share in Christ's threefold office as Prophet, Priest and Shepherd. The Second Vatican Council also redefined the relation between bishop and priest. The episcopate is a true sacrament, a sacrament of orders, the '*fullness* of the priesthood', and the priest *shares in* the priestly service of the bishop.

In ecumenical discussions since the Second Vatican Council, the churches have come closer to one another in their understanding of the priesthood. Catholic theologians have addressed the concerns of theologians in the Reformed tradition and have interpreted the priesthood more on the basis of Scriptural sources. Reformed churches (the situation is somewhat different in the Anglican and Episcopal[ian] traditions) have paid more attention to the specific meaning of the priestly office. Most Reformers avoided the use of the term 'priest', and were more inclined to speak of 'preachers' or 'pastors'. In 1982, however, the World Council of Churches declared that it was justifiable to call holders of offices in the Church 'priests' because they fulfilled a particular priestly service, and because they strengthened and edified the prophetic priesthood of the faithful by the word and by the sacraments, by their petitions, and by their pastoral guidance of the community. Ecumenical dialogue has brought the concepts of office of the separated churches within Christianity closer together.

II. THE ORDINATION RITE

From the Acts of the Apostles we learn that the apostles chose seven men of good reputation to see to the daily distribution of food, and laid their hands on them and prayed for them (cf. Acts 6.6). This was the origin of ordination for the early Church. The bishop and priests laid their hands on those chosen to perform a service in the Church, prayed to the Holy Spirit for them, and in their prayer gave an account of the things they trusted the Spirit would bring about in them. The laying on, or imposition, of hands and the prayer of ordination are the two essential elements of the ordination of bishops, priests and deacons. Through the laying on of hands God is asked to send down his grace on the ordinands. In the Church as we encounter it in the pastoral letters of the New Testament, ordination by the laying on of hands is a sacramental act, and the appropriate spiritual capacity is conferred as a gift of grace for the exercise of an office in the Church. The grace it conveys is a lasting gift.

In the course of the Church's history, these two basic rites were supplemented by various other rituals, primarily the anointing of hands, and the presentation of sacred vestments and of the liturgical instruments, the chalice and paten. Ordination ceremonies gradually became longer and more complex. In 1968, after the Second Vatican Council, the rite for the ordination of bishops, priests and deacons was revised, unified and reduced to the essential elements. I shall concentrate on the rite of priestly ordination, and then mention some aspects of the ordination of bishops and of that of deacons. I shall also touch on the services of profession of abbots and abbesses and ask whether such forms of ordination might not suggest suitable ways of celebrating induction into yet other services and offices.

a) Ordination of priests

Presentation of the candidates

Ordination is always conferred within the setting of a Eucharist, and takes place after the gospel reading. It should be celebrated on a day when as many people as possible are able to attend. The ordination service begins with the presentation of the candidates. One of the priests attending the service presents the ordinands to the bishop. He informs the bishop that the community has been asked whether these men are worthy candidates and that those responsible for their training have recommended them. The bishop confirms his readiness to appoint these men to the office and work of a priest. He then gives a brief address. The official ordination service prescribes the main lines of this address in model form, and the bishop is asked to include its salient points. The ordinands respond to this address by promising the bishop and the congregation to do all in their power to exercise their office as a service for the Church and in obedience to the bishop. Then the candidates place their hands in the bishop's hands.

Bishop Franz Kamphaus has commented on this particular part of the rite in an ordination sermon. He says that the ordinands do not put their hands in the bishop's hand to show that he can do what he wishes with them. The bishop is aware that it is not his hands that will bestow the blessing of Ordination. The future priests are placing their hands in the hand of God: 'Their freedom is not bought but won. God takes your hands not to hold them fast ... but so that they can be opened. If you entrust yourself to him and know that he supports you, then you can turn trustingly to other people, and especially to the poor, suffering and needy.'

Prostration

Now the bishop asks the faithful to pray for the ordinands, who lie stretched out on the ground in the gesture known as *prostratio*. They lie face down. This ancient custom symbolizes the priests' offering of themselves to God just as a husband offers himself to his wife. The priests' position is also a sign of complete surrender to God, an acknowledgement of their own powerlessness and of their own humanity. They are to be ordained not because they have deserved it, but because God has summoned them in all their weakness. While the ordinands lie stretched out on the ground, the congregation chants or sings the Litany of the Saints. The bishop closes the litany with his own prayer.

Silent laying on of hands

The most important part of the ordination rite takes place in silence. The bishop silently lays his hands on the head of each of the ordinands and silently prays that the Holy Spirit should flow through him, transform him and fit him for his work. After the bishop, all the priests who are present lay their hand on the candidates in silence. It is a simple but impressive sight when priests, old and young, impose their hands in total silence. It reminds each of them of his own ordination and of what he has made of it. He prays inwardly for the ordinands in his own words. Experience tells him what the exercise of this office calls for, what dangers will face these men, and what strength they will need to be good priests. The decisive action occurs in silence. This is no human act but one of confidence that the Holy Spirit works in peace and quiet. It is an impressive yet modest rite. No great feats of language are involved but all the priests who are there silently invoke the action of the Spirit. No human abilities but only the movement of the Holy Spirit is called for.

The ordination prayer

After this long silence, the bishop prays or chants the ordination prayer, which names the most important duties of a priest. In this prayer the bishop recalls the relation of the seventy elders to Moses. The priest is described primarily as the bishop's co-worker, a teacher of the faith, and a preacher of God's word. The bishop's most important petition is a request to God to: 'Give to these your servants the dignity of priests. Renew the Spirit of holiness in them. Grant, O God, that they may hold fast to the office which they receive from your hand; may their life offer encouragement and guidance to all. Bless, sanctify and ordain your servants, whom you have chosen.' The prayer breathes the spirit of Paul's first Letter to Timothy, which tells us how important it is for those holding office in the Church to produce the love which springs from a pure heart, a good conscience and a genuine faith, and to hold fast to God so that they can loyally pass on the great treasure which they have received in the message of Jesus Christ, our Redeemer. Even then the unknown author who incorporated the remains of Paul's correspondence with Timothy into his own work had to warn those who held any office in the early Church to live lives worthy of their commission. Those ordained to the priesthood must personally reflect some part of the sacred Truth which they minister to others.

Anointing of the hands

Now the ordinands are clothed in their priestly vestments. Then the bishop anoints their hands. Anointing always symbolizes the conferring of the Holy Spirit. When he anoints them the bishop tells the priests that they are to be strengthened by the Spirit in their work. Blessings are to flow from their hands. All the sacraments that priests administer are sacraments of touch, acts which touch the heart. Priests must use their hands to convey this. The anointing with chrism expresses the wish that these will always be tender and gentle hands to touch people, move them, and enable them to feel the closeness of God's love physically. The anointing is also a sign that it is the Holy Spirit who gives his gifts through these empty hands. These hands must be permeable if the Spirit is to work through them, so that Jesus himself can flow to people through the priest's hands.

Often enough a priest will find he has empty hands. He will feel that he has nothing to give because his hands are void of content. But precisely when they contain nothing, he can remind himself that they have been anointed with the Holy Spirit. What the priest bestows is never his property. He himself must first receive, over and over again, the words he preaches and the blessings he bestows. Blessings can flow through his hands only if he opens himself to the Source of blessing, and if through prayer he comes into contact with the inner Source of the Holy Spirit.

Presentation of bread and wine

After the anointing of hands, the bishop hands bread and wine to the priests. They will transform them into the Body and Blood of Jesus Christ whenever they say Mass. When he hands them these gifts, and asks them to receive the gifts of the people for the celebration of the Sacrifice, to consider very carefully what they are about, to execute it with care, and to place their lives in the mystery of the cross, the bishop speaks not so much of the *potestas*, or power, to transform these elements, but of the mystery of the Eucharist. A priest must direct his whole life to a personal emulation of Jesus's ultimate act of devotion on the cross.

If any priest feels that celebrating the Eucharist has become no more than a matter of routine, he should recall this rite. He should think of what he is doing as symbolic of his whole life. A priest must make his entire existence bread to give others nourishment. Modelling myself on what happens in the Eucharist means offering myself with Christ, being ready to risk my existence for people and for the service which Christ has called me to perform. A priest is continually reminded of the mystery of the cross when successful moments in his pastoral work seem few and far between, and he has to face up to his own darkness and loneliness. Being a priest is a constant challenge. I am not simply a priest. I must trust ever more deeply in the ultimate devotion of Jesus Christ, whom I celebrate every day in the Eucharist.

Sign of peace

The bishop now bestows the sign of peace on the newly ordained priests by embracing them warmly. The sign of peace expresses the fact that they have been received into the community of priests and that they should also feel emotionally at home in that fellowship. The newly ordained priests go from one priest to another to receive the sign of peace from each of them. Now a very personal note enters the prescribed rite. The sign of peace is filled with kindness and joy and each attending priest includes his own wishes for the former ordinands in his embrace. When I look back at my own ordination, I remember this as a moment when I experienced great tenderness, love and affirmation from everyone there.

Concelebration of the Eucharist

The newly ordained priests concelebrate the Eucharist with the bishop. They carry out together what they have received through the rite of ordination. They elevate bread and wine, symbols of this world's fragility and longing, into the divine realm. They extend their ordained hands over the gifts of bread and wine so that the Holy Spirit will descend on them and turn them into the Body and Blood of Christ. They realize the degree of risk involved in stretching their hands over the eucharistic offerings, for that draws them into the mystery of Jesus's death and resurrection. As they do so, they place their lives in the mystery of the cross, as they were told they must do when the bishop presented them with the gifts. During communion the newly ordained ministers distribute Christ's Body and Blood to the faithful.

First blessing

After the bishop's blessing the newly ordained priests give their first blessing to the whole congregation. There are many legends in this connection. At one time it was said that you had to be prepared to wear out a pair of shoes and get new ones to receive this blessing. This probably expressed the feeling that the power of the Holy Spirit flowed more strongly through the newly ordained than through the hands of worn-out, routine-laden priests. The myth symbolizes the new power and state that we wish the Holy Spirit to bring about in us too.

b) Consecration of a bishop

In the course of the Church's history theologians have argued about the relation between the ordination of a bishop and that of a priest.

Those theologians who saw priestly ordination as primarily conferring the right to celebrate the Eucharist denied that the ordination of a bishop was a sacrament in its own right. The Second Vatican Council clarified this ancient point of contention. The Council defines the fullness of the sacrament of ordination as conveyed to the bishop alone. The priest only shares in the bishop's priestly office. The priest is no longer the model for the bishop, but the bishop for the priest. Only a bishop can administer the sacrament of Ordination. He is also the proper minister of the sacrament of Confirmation. Priests are the bishop's 'co-workers', and participate in his priestly office.

The ordination, or consecration, of a bishop has the same structure as that of a priest. During the presentation of the candidates the papal brief appointing this man a bishop is read out. The bishop presides over the local church but he is connected with the whole Church. The laying on of hands is carried out only by those bishops who are present. This makes clear that this bishop is now included in the college (*collegium*) of bishops. During the prayer of ordination the book containing the gospels is laid on the bishop's head. The bishop is bound to hand on the word of Holy Scripture and the message of the apostles. The prayer of ordination concentrates on his duties of leadership, and on his pastoral office.

The rite of anointing is somewhat different, too. Since his hands have been anointed already during his ordination as a priest, the bishop's head is anointed now. This expresses the fact that not the bishop but Christ is the Head of the Church. The bishop can guide the Church only through the power of the Holy Spirit. Then the Gospel is presented to the bishop. The prophetic duty of the bishop is part of his pastoral role. He must interpret the word of Scripture so that it speaks to our own times, and so that it becomes a source of inspiration and guidance not only for individuals but for society. Finally the bishop is presented with the ring, the mitre is placed on his head, and he is given his bishop's crozier, or pastoral staff. The consecrating bishop asks him to receive this as a sign of his office as a pastor, so that he can watch over the whole of Christ's flock, for the

Holy Spirit has appointed him a bishop to guide God's Church. The bishop must follow the example of Jesus, the Good Shepherd. As an exemplary Shepherd, Jesus knows his sheep and gives his life for them. To be a shepherd does not mean primarily ruling, but serving. The service accepted by the bishop is one of guidance. After the ordination rite proper, the newly consecrated bishop is led to his throne, on which he then sits. The throne is a symbol of the rule the bishop now undertakes. But the preceding rites have warned him that he must not rule like earthly monarchs. Jesus's words apply to him: 'Among the heathen it is their kings who lord it over them, and their rulers are given the title of "benefactors". But it must not be so with you! Your greatest man must become like a junior and your leader must be a servant' (Luke 22.25f.).

c) Ordination of a deacon

The diaconate was an office in its own right in the early Church. In the Acts of the Apostles, Luke tells us that the apostles chose seven men to serve at meals so that the apostles could devote more effort to the ministries of prayer and to the word of God. In the course of the history of the Church, the diaconate became a mere intermediate stage on the way to priestly ordination. Priests had to be ordained as deacons before the priesthood was conferred on them. But it had little significance in itself. The Second Vatican Council revalued the work of a deacon and restored it to the status of an office in its own right. We now also have permanent deacons, who make a conscious decision not to become priests. Of course there is still a certain tension in the rite of ordination, since the ordinands either become permanent deacons or think of this office as just a step towards their ordination as priests.

The ordination of deacons has a similar structure to that of priests. The rite is even identical until the laying on of hands. But in the conferring of the diaconate, only the bishop lays hands on the prospective deacon. Priests are not involved. The ordination prayer stresses aspects different to those brought out when the priesthood is conferred. The service to which the deacon is called is repeatedly emphasized when the bishop prays that the ordinands should be guided on earth in the way of Jesus Christ who came to serve and not to be served.

After the ordination prayer the deacons are vested in the appropriate liturgical garments, the stole and dalmatic. Then the bishop gives each newly ordained deacon the gospels, asking them to receive the Gospel of Christ which they are appointed to proclaim, and enjoining them to believe what they read, proclaim what they believe, and breathe life into what they proclaim. The vesting with liturgical robes and the giving of the gospels emphasize the functions performed by deacons in the liturgy. They are to assist priests in the celebration of the Eucharist and to preach the word of God. Like priests, they must also take care constantly to meditate on the words of Holy Scripture so that it may move and transform their hearts. Only if the Word enters their hearts can they interpret it proficiently, so that it heals, liberates and straightens the people they serve.

d) Other forms of ordination

Ordination of virgins

Instances of other forms of ordination, especially the 'veiling' or profession of virgins and the induction of abbots and abbesses, are known to ecclesiastical tradition. There is evidence of the consecration of virgins as early as the fourth century AD, when it was not restricted to women in religious communities. But then a gradual trend led eventually to its exclusive use for professed nuns. Not until the renewed rite of 1970 was it applied to women who did not join a community of religious but wished to lead a dedicated celibate life in the world. This rite pays tribute to the position of women in the Church and to the varied forms of service which they perform for the benefit of others. The prayers of profession indicate the spiritual capabilities of women who could have such an inspiring effect on a Church led by males. The Church can't permanently refuse women's spiritual experience without suffering from spiritual dryness.

Women today criticize the rite of profession for single women because they see it as partly typifying the Church's devaluation of sexuality. But of course this is not the only rite for women. The sacrament of marriage pays tribute to women's sexuality and to motherhood. Nowadays, when there are so many single men and women, the profession of celibate women could be of special value. This rite can enable such women to experience their lives as the result not of a predicament – not finding a partner – but of a conscious choice to live alone as a form of existence with its own special value. Being a virgin doesn't mean that you are asexual but that you are free, and fruitful not in reliance on a male human being but on a divine basis; that you are defined both by God and by human relationships.

Ordination of abbots and abbesses

The induction of abbots and abbesses is an example that shows that men and women are equally entitled to receive an office. Abbots and abbesses are 'ordained' in special ceremonies to preside over their monastic communities. They receive a ring and a staff as signs of their office. They are shepherds and shepherdesses. Both men and women can lead their communities in the same way and thus share in Jesus's office as a Shepherd. The rings show that they are both bound to Christ and must work spiritually at the task of conforming themselves increasingly to Christ and allowing him to transform them.

Ordination for other offices in the Church?

The profession and induction of people to the religious life as nuns, abbesses and so on might serve as a model for other ordinations and rites in which men and women are appointed to their posts. Why shouldn't we have a special rite of induction for pastoral workers and carers, parish managers, and similar posts? This introduction to an office should not be confined to the outward commission. Rites of consecration and ordination are effective in part because of their visual and symbolic enactment of an inward disposition. Signs and symbols are needed to show how these changes affect the heart too. Appropriate rites should be designed for many other offices in the Church, such as those of readers, ministers of communion, and so on, that would bring out the special character of the service performed. The psychologist and thinker Carl Jung maintains that rites and ceremonies at a time of psychic transition can usefully release deeper emotional forces, canalizing and transferring energy. But he also reminds us that participants in rites of initiation symbolically experience the truth that their office implies more than a burden. In the rite they are immersed in the source of divine energy, which they can always draw on because it is inexhaustible. In the ancient world, a priest was thought of as someone with a special power, or 'mana', which was conferred on him or her in the rite of consecration or initiation. At the same time, the rite acted as a form of self-immersion in the priest's task or work, an initial exercise in carrying out the service to which he or she was appointed.

Ordination for 'secular' professions

The possible number of special ordinations could easily be extended. Why not ordain a mayor, a new headmistress or a new managing director? The Church with all its rich experience of rites of commissioning and consecration could help people to sense how every mission comes from God, and that ultimately every profession or job is a vocation. God issues a call to all of us. It has been said that people are called to do things that they couldn't do entirely by their own power. Everyone has a vocation to place his or her abilities at the service of humanity. An appointment to a position in the world evokes something in people that they hadn't quite discovered in themselves before. A rite can put people in contact with their innermost calling and capabilities and become a source of energy, imagination and creativity. There is certainly room for the development of special rites that would enable people in secular professions to appreciate the mystery of their vocation and mission in life.

III. LIVING AS A PRIEST

a) The priesthood of all believers

All Christians are anointed as priests, kings and prophets in baptism. Being a priest is an essential part of our lives as Christians. The Second Vatican Council explained the priesthood of the baptized as meaning they were consecrated so that through all their works 'they may offer spiritual sacrifices and proclaim the perfection of him who has called them out of darkness into his marvellous light, (cf. 1 Pet. 2.4–10). Therefore all the disciples of Christ, persevering in prayer and praising God (cf. Acts 2.42–7), should present themselves as a sacrifice, living, holy, and pleasing to God (cf. Rom. 12.1). They should everywhere on earth bear witness to Christ and give an answer to everyone who asks a reason for the hope of an eternal life which is theirs. (cf. 1 Pet. 3.15) ... The faithful ... exercise their priesthood ... by the reception of the sacraments, prayer and thanksgiving, the witness of a holy life, abnegation and active charity' (Constitution on the Church, I.10, *Vatican Council II*, ed. A. Flannery (1975), p. 361).

What do these somewhat abstract pronouncements have to say about my personal life as a priest? In answer, I shall offer some thoughts about how I understand myself as a priest against the background of these statements and against that of the archetypal images of priesthood. First, I shall look at the universal priesthood of all Christians, but in terms of what it means for me to have been anointed a priest in baptism. Then I shall try to describe how I see myself as an ordained priest, and say what I think distinguishes me as such from a priest in the general sense.

Transforming the earthly into the divine

The first conciliar statement refers to the priest as offering spiritual sacrifices. How does that apply to me? 'Sacrificing' means holding something out in the realm of the divine in order to acknowledge that it belongs to God. Sacrificing also means transforming something earthly into something divine. Being a priest in this sense means that all my everyday work visibly shows that I belong to God, that I am in God's service, not my own, and that the way in which I work and live has to make sure that people can see God and experience him. Ultimately, it is a matter of fulfilling the Benedictine precept that God should be glorified in everything (cf. *Rule of St Benedict*, 57.9). For me, the way to change the earthly into the divine is through prayer, in which I hold out to God everything that is of this earth: my work, my body, my soul and its abysses and wounds; and ask him to permeate it all with his light and love. God wants to illuminate not only my strengths but my weaknesses in this world.

The transformation of the earthly into the divine also occurs when praising God, which the Council sees as a priestly task. By praising God, the Creator of the whole world, I see the creation in a different light. I am no longer taken up exclusively with the problems of this world. God's beauty flows through the whole creation, and its radiance is especially apparent when he is praised. When Christians assemble to praise God together, they perform a priestly service. Organists, choirmasters and choristers in particular share in the office of a priest when they make sure that the praise of God resounds with beauty and dignity.

Bearing testimony

The Council sees the second task of a priest as proclaiming the wonderful things God has done and as bearing witness to Christ everywhere on earth. Here the Council has the universal mission of all Christians in mind. The proclamation of the word of God is the concern not only of officially appointed priests but of all Christians, and primarily of theologians, writers and poets. Some people interpret this duty of proclamation as having to preach Jesus's message at every street-corner. That can be appropriate. Often, however, this kind of enthusiasm is misplaced and oppressive. The Council is thinking of another type of proclamation. Christians should 'give an answer to everyone who asks for the reason for the hope of an eternal life which is theirs'. I should stand up for my faith in the middle of the world of work. If I am asked on what I base my life, I should name the basis of my hope. My testimony is credible only if my life makes people around me curious, when in the way I actually work, treat people and talk to them, they see convincing evidence that points to something they do not know themselves. Only if my life reflects some part of Christ can I bear faithful witness to him. Otherwise my testimonies will be no more than empty words. And of course there is always the danger that my compulsion to relate the wonders and truth of God everywhere and at all times will betray traces of a need to be special in some way and to stand out from the crowd.

Celebrating rites

The findings and statements of the Second Vatican Council are not the only important points of reference for my understanding of what it means to be a priest. The archetypal images I have already referred to are also essential. An archetype can be demanding but also immensely inspiring. Nevertheless, it can be dangerous to identify myself with an archetypal figure or concept, because it can blind me to my own needs. But if I see these fundamental images as instances of a power that can move and challenge me vitally, they can help me to discover my potential. In the following pages I shall offer brief descriptions of a few images that help me to define the nature of my priestly life.

A priest is a 'specialist' in rites. Nowadays we have begun to recognize the healing effect of rites and rituals once again. If I start and close my day with an effective and inspiring rite or ritual practice, I experience myself as a priest. Rites open up the heavens over my life. They bring God's healing and loving immediacy into my daily existence: into morning's greyness and evening's weariness. They enliven starting and ending work, meals in common, and my various discussions and consultations. I can rely on rituals. If I pick up a stone, light a candle, move or shape my hands in a gesture, and speak a certain word or phrase on the exhalation and inhalation of the air I breathe, I experience God himself promising me that my life will succeed. Jacob used a stone as a pillow and, as he rested his head on it, dreamed of a ladder extending right up and into heaven. It 'rested on the ground with its top reaching to heaven, and angels of God were going up and down on it'. Jacob made the stone 'a sacred pillar', as a reminder of God's saving closeness (cf. Gen. 28.10f.). As I carry out a ritual I remind myself that God is with me and in me, and focus my thoughts of God, seemingly so far away, on my innermost self, where he does indeed reside. Jacob anointed the hard stone with oil and treated it with tenderness. Rituals can turn the harsh and recalcitrant aspects of my everyday life into symbols of God's tender love.

Protecting the sacred aspects of the world

A priest is the guardian of the sacred place or sanctuary. He extends his hand protectively over all that is holy. This is another appropriate image for us as priests and priestesses. Each of us contains a sacred space which is demarcated from this world. The world has no power over it and no means of access to it. It is the holy place where peace and quiet reign in our innermost depths, where God dwells. As priestly people we watch over this space within our inner selves, to ensure that something healing radiates from the sacred to illuminate us and other people.

Priests and priestesses are also particularly sensitive to the sacred in their neighbours. They can discern the sacred area which every single person possesses. They are guardians of the sacred in this world, and make sure that it is not narrow and meanly restricted, let alone closed, but remains open to everything that resists the world's power. They know this is necessary if our world is to be sound, stable and wholesome. They also have the practical task of protecting the observance of sacred occasions (on Sunday, for instance) and sacred spots (churches and places of pilgrimage).

Watching over the fire of love

A priest is a guardian of the sacred fire. Fire is a symbol of passion and love. Fire burns away everything unclean. Many peoples treat the fire in the hearth as sacred. It is a guarantee that family life will continue. The fire burning in a hearth is an assurance that a family always has nourishment and warmth. Whoever watches as a priest or priestess over the sacred fire of love in himself or herself, and never allows that inner blaze to be extinguished, will help to ensure that this world remains a warmer and more vital place, that love never goes out in human hearts, and that people always have true nourishment. Henri Nouwen says that spiritual life means guarding the inner fire and mentions people who are burnt out because they always keep their stove door open. Quiet and prayer are needed to keep the blaze in our inner stove alight. Only if we watch over that fire within will people be able to warm themselves and find rest at our fireside.

Opening eyes to God's will

One of a priest's tasks is to discover the marks of God in people and to offer a practical interpretation of God's will for those people as expressed in dreams or oracles. Consequently, a priest needs a certain insight into God's intentions for humankind. He will have learnt to decipher and understand the traces of God in the events and occasions of our lives, and in the all-but-silent yearning of the heart. When I anoint a small child as a priest or priestess in baptism, I hope that God will open his or her eyes to see and interpret the traces of God in his or her own heart and in other human hearts. All pastors, pastoral workers and spiritual counsellors who discern God's gentle impulses in their clients' souls exercise a priestly office and open eyes to see and ears to hear God's will. The will of God is our sanctification (cf. 1 Thess. 4.3). God wants us to become whole and sound. Whoever opens the eyes of people to perceive the will of God contributes to their health and to their discovery of their true nature.

234

Induction into the way of self-development

Priests and priestesses introduce people to the mysteries of God and of humanity. They are our assistants on the way to true self-development. They are not only ordained themselves, but ordain other people into the mystery of life, and into the mystery of God who wishes to transform human life and to make his glory illuminate each human being in a unique way. In the world of antiquity, induction into the mysteries usually took place in a form of cultic worship, in celebrations of the mysteries. For me induction or 'ordination' into the way of self-development happens nowadays in the form of individual efforts, when people discover their own vocation or receive spiritual counselling, on courses when the participants pursue a joint quest for their very own way, or in rituals by means of which we find how to become our own true selves.

Comforting humanity

The final archetypal image that says something about the mystery of my priestly existence is that of the priest or priestess as someone who gives a blessing. The act of blessing has two meanings for me.

The first is to sign or seal, as in making the sign of the cross. In some countries, many mothers and fathers bless their children by making the sign of the cross on their forehead when they say goodbye to them. They do this to express the fact that they are blessed by God, that they are entirely loved, and that everything in them is good. They are, so to speak, inscribing on and in them the love with which Christ loved us to the point of ultimate devotion on the cross. They write that love on their children's bodies so that they can feel this love physically. The sign of the cross also says: 'You belong to God. You are free. No monarchs, emperors or empresses, or rulers, no people on earth, have power over you.'

Blessing also means 'saying something good', as in the Latin word *benedicere* (to speak well, say what is good). For me, being a priest means addressing what is good in people, saying good things about them and over them, and assuring them of God's healing and loving presence. I think of blessing as assuring people of the fullness of life offered to them by God, and saying to them: 'You are blessed. You are filled with God's love. God has given you many gifts. You are a blessing for us with your gifts but also with your whole existence. It is good that you exist. A part of God's fullness of life is here with us through you.'

b) Living on the basis of ordination

Everything I have said about the universal priesthood of all believers also applies to ordained priests. Yet we still have to ask what distinguishes the ordained priesthood from the general priesthood of Christians. What is special about an ordained priest? When I contemplate my own priesthood, I find the archetypal images of the priest important. I experience myself as a priest in a special way when I celebrate the Eucharist, when I preach, and when I absolve a penitent from his or her sins after a discussion in the sacrament of reconciliation. But is the special character of a priest only a matter of dispensing the sacraments?

I feel that the question about the specific difference between an ordained priest and a priest by virtue of the universal priesthood doesn't get us anywhere. I like to define myself in terms not of differences but of positive statements. If I said 'I am what you are not', that would demarcate me too much from others and set me above them. And so I would like to meditate on a few symbols from the rite of ordination to express my positive view of myself as a priest. I don't want to understand my being a priest at the cost of others but as a specific way in which I exist as a Christian. Some of the points I make were inspired by sermons given by Bishop Franz Kamphaus and by my memory of the rites of my own ordination, which have helped me to understand the mystery of my priestly life and to keep it before me even during the everyday round of my existence.

Hands – the priestly instruments

The most important rite in the ordination of a priest is the laying on of hands. God himself laid his hand on me. As far as I am concerned, this means that I can't simply live as I like. God laid his hand on me to bless me and to fill me with the Holy Spirit. That is a constant challenge for me. It is not primarily a matter of my abilities but of my receptivity to the Holy Spirit. I mustn't proclaim myself or my ability to put things over, but God. God wants to move people through me. But that will succeed only if I am constantly in touch with the inner Source through prayer and meditation. I shall soon be exhausted as a priest if all I have to draw on is my learning and my own strength.

When God lays his hand on me, it is not only a blessing but sometimes a burden. The Prophet Jeremiah complains to God: 'I sat alone, because your hand was upon me' (Jer. 15.17). When God takes me by the hand, I am forced to be solitary. I can't tell everyone what is happening to me. I am cradled in God's hand, but sometimes I am also shaken about by it. God's hand rests on me as it rested on Jesus and sent him out to announce the good news to humankind. But God's hand can also hold me fast at the very moment when I would like to flee from myself and the truth about my life. I have to ask myself continually whether I am really letting God take hold of me or just functioning and doing whatever is expected of me. Only if I allow myself to be gripped and moved by God can I grip people and move them sufficiently to pass on what God has to say.

My hands were anointed when I was ordained. The oil of anointing is a symbol not only of the Holy Spirit but of God's tender love. Therefore my hands always remind me to extend his love. It is not a matter of having everything under control, or of a thoroughly organized presbytery and parish, but of touching people tenderly and showing them that they are held in God's kind and loving hand. God has inscribed his name in my hand and my name in his hands.

Too often I find my hands are empty. I have nothing to give. I do not understand the mystery of God. I am not all that sure of myself. Yet these hands are there to give. They can only give what they continually receive. On the one hand, I find it comforting that I can still give with empty hands. Only empty hands can receive what God constantly puts in them. But sometimes it hurts to have nothing available. The words that I have composed for a sermon no longer seem to signify quite what they did. What I learned seems to have run away, between my fingers. And I can't be sure that my work will have a successful outcome. Many priests have the painful experience of, so it seems, working their hands to the bone, yet seeing fewer and fewer people coming to church. For me, being a priest means continually having to admit my powerlessness and holding my empty hands out to God. But I also think of anointed hands as signs of hope, and remember that they can pass on God's blessing, even if they do not feel it because the blessing has passed through this hand in the twinkling of an eye.

Bread and wine for humanity

I find the gifts of bread and wine a marvellous symbol of my work as a priest. I raise the parish's offering into the realm of the Divine. I understand my service to people as one of bearing their concerns before God. Of course all Christians are priestly individuals. They have direct access to God and do not need my mediation. But I constantly experience how people ask me to pray for them, and to include their cares and needs in the celebration of the Eucharist. I am not a priest for myself alone. Bread and wine refer me to people, to their work and efforts, to their longing for life and for a form of love that is not so fragile as the one they experience with their partners. As a priest I have been ordained for this world, so that some part of the world round me can become closer to wholeness. I not only celebrate the Eucharist on behalf of and out of service to humanity but have a life which is there wholly for people, and precisely for the poor and marginalized, for those whose prayer is stifled and those whose hope has been quenched.

The garment of resurrection

When I was ordained I was vested in a chasuble. Through this garment Jesus took possession of me. I put on the robe of his glory (cf. Gal. 3.27). When I celebrate the Eucharist, I am summoned to put on Christ and to grow together with him. Paul says that we should clothe ourselves by being merciful in action, kindly in heart, humble in mind, most patient and tolerant with one another, always ready to forgive, and truly loving (Col. 3.12). It is not a matter of putting on a beautiful robe in order to make myself stand out from the crowd, but of growing into the robe of Christ so that I reflect Christ's love and glory in my whole existence.

Putting on a new garment means that God has taken possession of me. When washing feet, Jesus removed his outer garment, the robe of glory, in order to put on the dress of a slave (John 13.4). In his resurrection God clothed him in the garment of glory and immortality. When I go to say Mass, I put on the radiant garment of resurrection. But I remove it after Mass in order to experience physically that, like Jesus, I must serve people and wash their feet.

Being ordained

When the anniversary of my priesthood comes round, I can't precisely remember the specific rites of my ordination, which took place more than thirty years ago. Nevertheless, the day of my ordination means a lot to me, for it constantly reminds me that I am an ordained priest. I have been ordained to serve people. For me, this means that I am not only commissioned but given the capability to carry out certain duties, because God has given me the necessary power, and continually renews it in me. Being ordained signifies consecration in the mystery of Jesus Christ, the true Priest. Because I am ordained I must allow myself to be drawn ever deeper into the priesthood of Jesus Christ. Jesus is the true High Priest. He devoted himself utterly to us, so that we might have life.

Therefore being a priest also means devotion in the sense of sacrifice. I must devote myself to the people whom I care for and advise, to whom I devote my time; and for whom I devote myself to the service of reconciliation. I must be devoted to the liturgy and be wholly taken up by the significance of what I am celebrating. Jesus is not only the Priest but the Shepherd who knows his own and leads them out onto the meadow. It is my responsibility to guide people, as Jesus did, to the place of true nourishment. Jesus follows the lost sheep in order to put it on his shoulder and take it where it really belongs. Jesus is the Pastor who addresses the human soul and opens it up for God. He straightens up those who are bent double and heals the sick. For me, being ordained is to be consecrated in Jesus's healing care. I can't copy Jesus. But I may trust that Jesus is at work in me too, if I am constantly with him in meditation, and allow myself to be drawn into his mystery in prayer and contemplation.

c) Living as a priest in the Church and world today

For more than ten years now I have been helping priests and religious on retreats or refresher courses. Many conversations and discussions have shown me how much priests suffer nowadays from the realities of their everyday life. There are those who have to 'run' three or four parishes and feel overburdened. They are torn between the different interests of individual parishes. Others feel lonely. They lead a solitary life in the presbytery. When they get back in the evening after so many services or meetings they miss the presence of someone to discuss the day's events with. Others can't deal with the high expectations of the parish. They realize they don't measure up to the image of the ideal priest the parish seems to entertain. They do everything they can, but they just aren't gifted preachers. They find they can't inspire and move people. Others are simply fed up with daily quarrels and infighting in the parish. So they fall back on their basic duties, which they carry out more or less inadequately. Work is constantly to the fore, whereas spiritual life gradually retreats very much into the background. Some priests only pray when they're conducting a service. Their spirituality dries up. They are dissatisfied, only too clearly, but they can't find any way out of the impasse.

Everyday routines for priests

It would exceed the scope of this book if I tried to examine all the problems that assail priests in the present-day world. I shall offer

---

only a few suggestions that might help a priest to maintain his interest in his daily routine.

It is essential to make sure that your day is balanced. When priests are on retreat or attending a refresher course, I ask them to draw up a weekly agenda with exact details of the time they get up, how the morning proceeds, what appointments they keep, and how the day ends. One important question is whether there is time for prayer, for peace and quiet, for a walk, for reading, for visits to concerts or theatres, and for conversations with friends. Or is everything over-planned? Many priests find it enriching to live a packed life. One of the pleasurable aspects of a priest's life is undoubtedly the constant variety of its demands. But taking an interest in too many things involves the danger of dissipation, of losing sight of the main thing. In spite of all the expectations people have of him, a priest must feel that he is living his life and that others and events are not living it for him. Healthy routines can help here. They enable him to sense that he is living his own life and enjoying it. Many priests tell me that they manage very well in the mornings. They have their usual quiet time or pray from their breviaries. But in the evenings they feel empty. If they come back frustrated after meetings, they find they haven't the strength to read or pray. Then they suppress their irritation by eating, drinking and television, and eventually fall into bed totally exhausted. That's an unhealthy way to spend the evening. They will wake up the next day with a diffuse, dissatisfied feeling. A worthwhile routine will help a celibate priest to feel at home, especially in the evening. If I consciously plan my evening and carry out my personal routine, I feel at home. Then I sense that I am really living myself, and celebrating my life as a feast, not carting it around with me as an oppressive burden.

Relationships

The second area that is important for a successful priestly life is that of relationships. The unmarried priest needs good relationships, friendships in which he can be entirely himself, and in which he plays no specific role but is welcome as a human being. Many priests have other priests as their friends because they can exchange similar experiences. They feel they can relax by showing each other how weak they are from time to time. Others relate to families where they find an emotional home. Priests can also have successful friendships with women. Nevertheless, they have to be alive to the possibility of friendship with a woman affecting their service to the community. Since the Church still associates ordination with the unmarried state (even though this won't necessarily be the case in the future), it's no help if a priest just puts up with celibacy. He has to see and accept his unmarried life positively as an opportunity to follow his spiritual path.

A priest is constantly in contact with people. Therefore he needs friendly relationships in which he feels at home. But the decisive question is whether he feels at home with God. If a priest who is not really in touch with himself makes strenuous efforts to find a male or female friend, he will expect too much from any friendship and overtax it. I have to be close to myself, be in contact with myself, and realize who I am, before I can thankfully accept the support or affection of people who will necessarily always fall short of my needs. Only God can fulfil my deepest need for security. Only if I am at home with God can I be secure in myself and not have to seek refuge with other people.

My own image of a priest's life

For me the third step towards a fulfilled life as a priest consists in meditation on biblical images. When I meditate on the accounts of healing and encounter in the Bible, I discover the possibilities within me and in my priestly life. I don't force myself to try to act exactly as Jesus would have done. Instead of putting myself under any kind of pressure, I contemplate Jesus. Then an image of his behaviour forms in me and brings me into contact with my own potential. For me, the most beautiful image in relation to my activity as a priest is the healing in Luke 13.10–17 of the woman who had been ill for eighteen years from some psychological cause, and was bent double and quite unable to straighten herself up. When I sense after a discussion that someone is going home straightened up, I feel the joy that a priest's help can bring. I realize how it fulfils me too when a weight is taken from someone's heart and he or she goes away upright. The story in Luke is also a fine image in regard to the celebration of the Eucharist. I am celebrating Mass in Jesus's sense if it straightens people up, comforts them, and they can go home feeling liberated.

Every priest has personal images that open his eyes to the mystery of his priestly activity. One might find it in the healing of the leper, and understand his service to others as enabling them to see that they are good as the people they are, that they are welcome, and that it is good that they exist. Another might see his agenda as a priest enacted in the healing of the blind man. This encourages him to open people's eyes so that they look fearlessly at their own reality, look through and behind things, and see God's healing and loving presence everywhere.

I often give priests I'm advising the task of writing a letter to their best friend. They have to imagine that they're facing death very soon, and must answer the following questions: 'What did I want my life to mean to people? What is the most profound message that I tried to give people in everything I did? What would I still like to leave people as a legacy? Why did I get up every day? What impelled me to be there for people? What is my deepest motivation, the impetus for my service as a priest? What did I want to radiate from me in this world? What mark do I want to leave behind me?'

I tell these priests not to be afraid of using lofty phrases. We all know that we always fall short of our ideals in this life. But sometimes we have to be clear about what the defining idea of our life is, the basic message that we want to proclaim with all our being. When priests read me their letters, I'm always deeply moved. I realize that, in spite of all his frustration, each of them has a sense of the splendour of his calling, and of the mystery of the priestly life through which in his own particular way he enables people in this world to experience Jesus Christ as the Priest who straightens them up, heals them, frees them from guilt, and helps them to find true access to God.

CONCLUSION

Before writing this section on ordination, I read the articles on the priest and the priesthood in all the major encyclopaedias and reference books. None of them seemed to have any personal relevance. They were all far too abstract. But when I began to deal with the subject of ordination I was deeply moved. Then I sensed that I was engaging once again with the mystery of my own priestly life. I would like to close this section with a few words about how I see myself as a priest.

First, I would like to say that I like being a priest. I realize how marvellous a priest's work is: celebrating the Eucharist, celebrating the feast of life in baptism, consoling those who mourn, freeing and reassuring those who are burdened with guilt, accompanying people on their spiritual way, preaching the word of God and interpreting its relevance to life as it actually is. But being a priest means more to me than carrying out these tasks. On the one hand, I am a priest in my capacity as a human being. God has touched and moved me, chosen me and spoken to me, and sent me out to people. I have a vocation for other people, a mission that God has given me to fulfil for the well-being of humanity. On the other hand, I am an ordained priest. I have been blessed by God, and taken by him from the ante-room of this world to be held in God's sacred space, so that it can make me whole and I can help other people to share in the holy truth that will heal their souls.

Although it has sometimes caused me pain and I have found it hard to be unmarried, I can say that I am happy to lead the life of a celibate priest. Every day this state challenges me to advance along my spiritual path, to focus entirely on God, and to experience my true home in God. It also makes me available for other people. Even though I can imagine a future in which not only married men but women will be priests, I can thankfully accept not being married as an opportunity to continue my own spiritual quest.

When people ask me what is special about a priest ordained by the Church compared with the general priesthood of all believers, I realize that this question really doesn't interest me. I don't want to define myself in comparison with other people, but in terms of the mystery of being a priest as I experience it in meeting Jesus Christ, the true Priest. For me, being a priest means becoming more and more like Jesus Christ, who offered his life for us with total devotion, and who healed, supported, comforted and challenged us, and opened our eyes. Jesus Christ is the Priest who leads us to God. For me, the fascinating and wholly fulfilling mission of a priest is to share in this work of opening people's eyes so that they can see God, helping their hearts to be touched by God, and enabling them to be open to God's healing and loving presence.

7

Anointing of the Sick: comfort and tenderness

INTRODUCTION

The sacrament of anointing the sick is an essential part of the Church's concern for the sick. The Church sees its service to sick people as pastoral care and attendance. Whoever suffers from an illness is in a state of physical but also mental and psychological, or 'psychic', crisis. The sick need the help of someone who listens to them and supports them.

The sacramental anointing of the sick is the most profound expression of the Church's service to humanity. Since the Second Vatican Council, the anointing of the sick has been restored to its former position of importance. It is no longer thought of as the Last Anointing, or Extreme Unction, but as giving strength to sick people in the physically and spiritually endangered state they have entered through illness.

Many parishes and church communities now offer special services for the sick that include an anointing. Once again, the Church has recognized its responsibility to sick people. How a community treats those who are ill is very indicative of its communal ethos and spirit of reciprocity. Society nowadays tries to suppress our awareness of sickness and death and to relegate them to hospitals, nursing homes and hospices. The general attitude is that there are specialists and trained nurses who know how to look after the sick and dying. Society isn't interested. The Church must not adopt this attitude to the sick. It offers the sacrament of anointing the sick precisely as a sign of its nature as a community that is concerned about and for ill people: one that wants not only to show them God's love but to approach them humanely and care for them.

My main purpose in this section is to describe the Christian attitude to sickness. We must no longer see the sacraments of the Church as an isolated set of phenomena administered solely by priests and pastoral workers by virtue of their office or recognized vocation. The sacraments are signs of how the Church actually treats such major themes as birth and death, health and sickness, growing up, love, responsibility, mission and guilt, and acts with regard to them. These are central topics addressed by all the sacraments.

The sacrament of anointing the sick asks us to face the challenges posed by the issues and reality of sickness and death, and to tackle them on the basis of faith. The sacrament also assures us that no aspect of our lives is excluded from God's loving concern. The essence of a sacrament is that we encounter the realm of the invisible in the midst of the visible world. The sacrament of anointing of the sick should make us more aware that in our sickness we meet God, and that it can open us to the God and Father of Jesus Christ, so that he can heal and transform our life.

I. THE SACRAMENT OF ANOINTING THE SICK

'Heal the sick and awaken the dead!': Jesus's commission to us

The sacrament of anointing the sick is derived from Jesus's commission to his disciples: 'Heal the sick, raise the dead, cure the lepers, drive out devils!' (Matt. 10.8). Jesus asked his disciples to do the same things he had done. Matthew laid great stress on the disciples doing what the Lord had done. When they do so now, Jesus is sending his disciples out to heal the sick by his own authority and power.

This particular commission from Jesus has not always been taken seriously in the history of the Church. Taking it seriously means that we also have to see ourselves as Jesus's disciples who are despatched into this world to heal the sick. Jesus's message has a therapeutic dimension. Through Jesus's power we are to approach the sick, those

247

who are infirm in body and soul, in order to heal them. Jesus trusts us to encourage those who are discouraged, to straighten the physically maimed and mentally downcast, to inspire the dumb to recover their voices and speak out, and to call on the crippled to stand up and walk as people in their own right. We are to take those marginalized by and expelled from human society into our own community. Our task is to show those who can't accept themselves that they are worthy of affection and love and are welcome. We should awaken to life those who are dead, who are only just functioning and have become inwardly void. We should try to drive out the demons that prevent people from being themselves. These devils or demons may be our inner compulsions, but also 'unclean spirits' that distort our thinking, as well as poisonous and bitter feelings, or illusions and delusions that lead us into a make-believe world that we substitute for reality.

Mark's gospel tells us how the disciples healed the sick: 'They expelled many evil spirits and anointed many sick people with oil and healed them' (Mark 6.13). The Fathers of the Church (followed by the Council of Trent) referred to this passage as a basis for the sacrament of anointing the sick. Oil was a recognized medicine in the ancient world. Olive oil especially was seen as a symbol of spiritual power, for it came from the fruit of the olive tree, which grew on unrelenting ground yet proved fruitful. Olive oil is not only a medicine but a symbol of light and of cleanness or purity. When the disciples anoint the sick with oil, they are acting not as physicians in the normal sense, but as witnesses to Jesus Christ. One commentator, Walter Grundmann, says that oil 'in the disciples' hands has a sacramental significance because, like the laying on of hands, it symbolizes the reality of God's helping hands'. By anointing the sick with oil, the disciples call down God's power of blessing on the infirm. They ask that just as oil heals wounds God will focus his healing power on the sick person in the name of Jesus Christ.

The early Church based the practice of anointing the sick primarily on a passage from the Letter of James: 'Is any among you sick? Let him call for the elders of the church, and let them pray over him, anointing him with oil in the name of the Lord; and the prayer of faith will save the sick man, and the Lord will raise him up; and if he has committed sins, he will be forgiven' (Jas. 5.14f.). The sick here obviously means those who are confined to their beds and therefore can't fetch the elders themselves, but have to send someone to do so on their behalf. But these sick people haven't lapsed into insensibility and aren't close to death. They can still call for the elders. The elders may be bishops; they are certainly those who govern the church and teach and preach in it. They are office-holders and not charismatic healers. They are to pray over the sick and anoint them with oil. The anointing accompanies and strengthens prayer.

Oil was a popular medicine in Israel as elsewhere in the ancient world. Oil was used to relieve the sick and, for example, the aged Adam as he lay dying. It was used to drive out demons. It protected people from death, and it maintained and reinforced life.

When they carry out the anointing, the elders call on the name of the Lord. They are not only acting on Jesus's commission to them but by his authority and power. As they anoint the sick with oil and pray for them, Jesus, the Lord himself, is present. As the elders call on the name of the Lord, they are filled with the power of Jesus, who heals the sick. This was Peter's experience when he healed the man who had been lame from birth at 'that gate of the temple which is called Beautiful': 'And his name, by faith in his name, has made this man strong whom you see and know; and the faith which is through Jesus has given the man this perfect health in the presence of you all' (Acts 3.16).

The anointing of the sick is not some kind of magic. The healing action should be ascribed to prayer empowered by faith and to the knowledge through faith that the Lord can help us, as well as to the firm conviction that he will actually do so. Ultimately, it is always Jesus Christ himself who heals the sick if the elders, out of faith, ask him to do so.

Commentators on the Bible have tried to explain the meaning of the three verbs 'save', 'raise up', and 'forgive' in James 5.14f., debating whether they refer to the physical and mental cure of the sick man or to his ultimate salvation, and to the resurrection of the dead. It is more probable that all three terms refer to the transformation of sickness now. If the elders pray out of strong conviction, then their prayer will heal and raise up the sick. 'Raising up' means spiritual encouragement and reinforcement, for the Lord gives the sick power and strength to master their illness spiritually.

The passage from James also encourages us to pray for a physical cure. But we shouldn't become fixated on the notion that prayer can dissolve physical disease like a magic amulet or formula. Prayer releases a process of trust and devout surrender to God which calms and reinforces the mind and soul, and then affects the body too. In any case, not every healing of mind and soul is also a physical cure. The decisive outcome is the state of trust produced in the sick person by prayer and anointing with oil. Jesus himself touches and raises this man or woman up. Then he or she has a new attitude to illness.

The phrasing of the reference to the forgiveness of sins shows that sickness and sin are not necessarily associated: '... and if he has committed sins, he will be forgiven' (Jas. 5.15). Sickness is not always accompanied by sin. The recipient of the anointing is a sick person and not always a sinner. But if he or she has sinned, it is right to trust that the prayer and anointing with oil will also bring down Jesus's power of forgiveness. Jesus himself holds his hand over the sick and accepts them unconditionally. If they have sinned and are suffering from guilt feelings, they can rest assured that their sins will be forgiven and that God will accept them absolutely.

The history of the anointing of the sick

As early as 200 AD bishops consecrated oil to endow it with the power of bestowing strength and health. During this consecration, the Holy Spirit is called down on the oil. Then the oil, already possessed of a healing virtue, becomes a symbol of the curative power of God's Spirit. In the earlier Church it was the oil itself, and not the anointing of the sick, that was a sacrament. The bishop consecrated this oil during the Eucharist and the faithful took it home as a medicine for body and soul. They either drank it, expecting it to strengthen them physically and spiritually, or anointed their wounds with it. A letter from Pope Innocent I in 416 AD shows that anointing was not reserved to priests but could be carried out by any believer. The Pope explained the passage from James's letter thus: 'This undoubtedly applies to sick believers who can be anointed with the holy oil of chrism. This oil is consecrated by the bishop and may be used for anointing not only by priests but by all Christians if they or their families are in need of it.' The Pope calls the oil a sacrament. Accordingly, its use was forbidden to penitents, who were excluded from the Church during the prescribed penitential period.

The early Church contrasted the sacrament of consecrated oil with superstitious and heathen practices. To ensure that Christians no longer frequented soothsayers and magicians, the Church took its ministry of healing seriously and consecrated the oil. Christians were to receive Christ's Body and Blood in the Eucharist and thus experience healing. They were also to take the consecrated oil home to anoint themselves or to be anointed with it by their relatives. This practice was a response to the fundamental human need for healing of physical and spiritual afflictions. At first believers brought the oil to church for it to be blessed after the consecration. From the fifth century AD the bishop blessed the oil only on Holy Thursday. Christians could obtain it only from the bishop if they wished to anoint the sick. Surviving liturgical texts name all the illnesses for which anointing was permitted. With the anointing of the sick, the Church responded to actual human needs, and by consecrating the oil which anyone was permitted to take with them, offered ill people a symbol of hope that their sickness would be cured.

In the early centuries of the Christian era, care for the sick was associated with every celebration of the Eucharist. In the Eucharist Christians not only celebrated the transformation of the lives of those present, but also drew from the memorial of Jesus's death and resurrection an assurance that Jesus's healing power would console the sick they had left at home. In later years, the administration of the anointing of the sick was associated more particularly with the bishop. He was the immediate source of the healing oil. But every Christian had the task of administering this sacrament, and the right to do so. The association with the bishop consisted merely in having to ask him for the oil. We should reconsider this practice nowadays when we debate possible contemporary forms of anointing the sick and discuss the administration of the sacrament by pastoral workers.

In the eighth century AD the bishops began to emphasize the anointing of the sick in a new way. They decided to make priests the ministers of the sacrament. They instructed priests to care for the sick and to support them while they were dying. But still the bishops thought of the anointing of the sick primarily as a preparation for death. In 769, therefore, a decree of Charlemagne insisted that 'the dying were not to die without an anointing with consecrated oil, and without reconciliation and viaticum.' At that time, under the influence of the Eastern Church, the anointing of the sick was associated with repentance. Because repentance carried weighty conditions with it, people left it to the last moment. Therefore the anointing of the sick became 'extreme unction'. When a separate sacramental theology developed in the eleventh and twelfth centuries, and it was finally decided that there should be seven sacraments, Thomas Aquinas defined the anointing of the sick as the 'ultimate and, as it were, all-embracing sacrament of our entire spiritual journey to salvation.' The anointing of the sick prepared people to share in divine glory. Accordingly, it became the sacrament of our last passage, from life through death into Life.

The Second Vatican Council discarded this one-sided view of the sacrament as extreme unction. Now it was no longer to be administered only in extreme danger of death, but even at the first sign that a Christian's life was threatened on account of sickness or the infirmities of age. In his Apostolic Constitution on the sacrament, Pope Paul VI no longer mentioned an actual danger of dying as a condition for the anointing of the sick, but spoke of people whose state of health was under serious threat. After this, a dispute arose among theologians. Some maintained that the anointing of the sick might now be seen too restrictively as consolation for illness of any kind, and that society's virtual suppression of the fact of death had possibly had some effect on the ways in which pastoral care was conceived and practised in the Church.

The theologian Gisbert Greshake, for instance, thinks that both considerations should be preserved. The sacrament should appear both as anointing of the sick and as extreme unction; as help for sick people and as a preparation for dying. Sickness always makes us think of dying. In some way it always presages death. Therefore prayer for the sick is prayer for healing, but also a request that the sick should accept their illness, and remember that they are mortal and have no guarantee that they will recover.

If we think of illness as a condition that upsets our assurance and well-being, the anointing of the sick promises us that in this fragile state we are open to the mystery of Jesus Christ, and that through this meeting with him we can enter the mystery of his own unsettled life. The anointing of the sick always enables us to experience our own finiteness. But when my own mortality is brought home to me, I can also be sure that I am in God's loving hand. His loving kindness can heal my sickness. It will be with me even if God decides to leave me in this state and asks me to pass through the doors of death.

In recent years, the question of the appropriate minister of the anointing of the sick has also been raised. Should this ministry be reserved for priests, or can anyone who cares for the sick exercise it? Many pastoral workers in hospitals and nursing homes think that they should be allowed to anoint the sick, since they are in continual contact with them. Then the sacrament would be the high point of pastoral care. Greshake argues that since James refers to 'elders', that is, representatives of the parish or church community, or office-bearers, anointing should be carried out only by priests and deacons. It is (he says) a matter not only of personal care, but of an action of the Church intended to convey the loving touch of Jesus Christ. But Pope Innocent I's letter of 416 AD would seem to support the view that the anointing of the sick should be entrusted to those who care for the sick: in other words, their relatives and pastoral workers in hospitals and similar institutions. The link to the official Church would be the oil consecrated by the bishop. Whoever administered the sacrament would do it with the bishop's commission and with the oil he had blessed. Then it would not be a private act of piety, but an action of the Church carried out on the bishop's behalf and with his blessing.

Jesus, the true physician

The anointing of the sick is one of the so-called 'rites of passage'. It is intended to help us through the transition from health to sickness and through that from life to death. All changeovers are frightening. In the history of religion, rites of passage have always signified both the vanquishing of any fear of what is new and the awakening of new powers in people so that they can comprehend and somehow negotiate this stage. Every threshold also seems threatening. In antiquity, crossing a threshold always evoked fear. A large number of 'threshold rites' came into being as a result. In the Middle Ages St Christopher was the patron saint of those using a ferry or making a crossing. Over-life-size images of him were painted on the side walls of church entrances so that those who saw them could pass the threshold safely, without any loss of strength. But how exactly is the anointing of the sick a rite of passage?

The passage from health to sickness is not a matter of course. The normal human state of health is unsettled by illness. Sick people's lives are like buildings that unexpectedly disclose a fissure and even crack open. Sick people suddenly find that their usual course of existence and what they took to be the certainties of work and social life have been disturbed. The experience of dwindling efficiency, of isolation and fear, and of physical and mental pain, can give rise to profound despondency, hopelessness, crises and even despair. People feel helpless. In any illness they also sense that their lives are endangered. They have no guarantee that good food and a healthy way of life will enable them to grow to the graceful old age they once dreamed of. And death can appear out of the blue in an apparently minor illness. Sickness means enforced idleness. All the appointments they once thought were so important and essential for life to function properly have to be cancelled. All plans for themselves, and at work or in the family, have to be postponed. No one can say if they will ever be realized.

In this situation of existential confusion, Jesus Christ who suffered meets such people in the sacrament of the anointing of the sick. We are not told that Jesus fell ill. But in his Passion we are confronted with archetypal images of the various stages of sickness. In illness we experience expulsion from the 'club' of strong and healthy people. We feel that no one understands us. We are lonely, rejected and forgotten. Like Jesus in his Passion, we suffer pains that we can scarcely stand. And we go through the experience of facing death. But in the anointing of the sick we encounter not only the suffering Jesus, but Jesus the physician who healed the sick. Jesus treated the sick in a special way. We are often told that he was filled with compassion when he saw a sick person. The Greek word for compassion (*splanchnizomai*) means that Jesus was affected by their illness 'in his very bowels', so that he did not treat ill people as objects but with fellow feeling. He came close to them and empathized with them. The Fathers of the Church saw the sacrament as one in which the hand of the historical Jesus touched us. In the anointing of the sick, Jesus looks at us as he looked at the paralyzed man at the pool of Bethesda. He understands us. He senses how we feel. He feels pity for us. He feels with us, and he touches us so that we come into contact with the inner sources of divine power that can cure us. But he not only treats us tenderly and sympathetically, as he did lepers or those born deaf and dumb. He also makes us turn round and face our own will, and asks us: 'Do you want to get well again?' (John 5.6). Do I really want to make an effort to get well again? Or have I given in to my illness? It could even be rather advantageous, offering me a chance simply to let go, to shun responsibility and allow myself to be looked after. But then Jesus suddenly says: 'Get up, pick up your bed and walk!' (John 5.8). He wants to rouse the power concealed within me.

Jesus meets me as the Physician who can really heal me. But I have no guarantee that he will also cure my body. I can't compel a cure by my faith. And the priest can't automatically work a miracle by administering the sacrament. If a cure happens, it is always a miracle. I can hope for one. But at the same time I should entrust myself to Jesus, the true Physician for body and soul. I should let him ask me: 'What do you want me to do for you?' (Mark 10.51). What is my deepest wish? Is it a cure for my sickness? Is it the disappearance of its symptoms? Or is it the healing of my soul, inner harmony, being one with God? What would take me a step further into my inward truth? What could bring about my inner peace, so that I am reconciled with myself? The sacrament of anointing the sick is a real meeting with Jesus Christ. He looks at me, talks to me, touches me gently, anoints me with oil as a sign of his healing love, and makes the sign of the cross on my forehead and hands. Then he offers me his love which has the power to vanquish death, so that I can feel it physically. This actual meeting with Jesus the Healer can transform my illness. A process of transformation and recovery begins in the depths of my heart. I can rest assured that this process will also have physical effects.

God's maternal love

Even when, as in the past, the anointing of the sick is thought of restrictively as extreme unction, its aspect as a preparation for death should not be forgotten. This anointing is not intended to suppress all thoughts of death. It must not have the limited effect of allowing sick people to hope that their illness will be cured and that they still have a long life ahead of them. In a certain sense illness is also 'sickness unto death'. In the anointing of the sick we enter the mystery of the passage from life to death. Christ, who overcame death and rose again, assures us that he will accompany us through the gateway of death. He will send us his angel to lead us safely over the final threshold. Christ takes away our fear of dying.

The tender anointing with oil removes the harsh and cruel aspects of death. This anointing has something loving, feminine and motherly about it. It was no accident that a woman anointed Jesus.

Jesus defended her when one of his disciples objected: ' "Why wasn't this perfume sold?" Jesus replied: "Let her alone, let her keep it for the day of my burial" ' (John 12.7). When Martha anointed Jesus's feet, she showed him her love, which extended beyond death. When his feet took him over the threshold of death he was to remember her love, which went with him. From time immemorial the Church has associated death with the maternal aspect of God. For centuries Mary, who held her dead Son in her bosom, has been the image of hope for Christians. As we die, we shall not fall into cold and darkness but into the warmth of God's motherly embrace. Dying is connected with motherhood, for to die is to be reborn.

The tender rite of anointing the sick is intended to give us hope that our illness will be healed, but also to remove our fear of death. It does not suppress the reality of dying. It makes us face it as a possibility. The decisive point is that we are surrounded by God's loving kindness in sickness, in health, and in death. Sickness as the undermining of our existence makes us sensitive enough to hope for this. To make sure that we do not suppress illness and the possibility of dying, we need the experience of Jesus's loving touch and of an encounter with Jesus the Physician, who walked through his death to resurrection.

St Anselm of Canterbury wrote of Jesus as our Mother. In the anointing of the sick we meet Jesus as the fatherly and motherly person who fills us with his masculine power and at the same time takes us into his arms like a mother. The meeting with Jesus strengthens us so that we can make the transition from health to sickness, and from life to death, fearlessly and trustingly. Our encounter with Christ assures us that we shall be enclosed in God's maternal love when we pass from this world into the next.

II. THE RITE OF ANOINTING THE SICK

The most important elements of the rite of anointing the sick are: the silent Laying on (or Imposition) of Hands and the Anointing with consecrated olive oil. This rite, however, should be centred in a brief spoken service or act of devotion and commitment. The actual anointing can be carried out in a small circle round the sick person, or as a joint service for the sick during which all those who require it have an opportunity to be anointed. The general service, of course, should be a celebration of the Eucharist.

Blessing with holy water

The official rite calls for the priest to greet the sick people and other members of the congregation. After this greeting, if appropriate, he can sprinkle the sick person and the room with holy water. Suitable words to accompany this would be: 'May this holy water remind us of our reception of baptism and of Christ who redeemed us by his Passion and Resurrection.' This brief rite tells us that baptism and the anointing of the sick are associated. Greshake says that the anointing of the sick is 'the renewal of baptism in a situation that brings people up against existential limits which they cannot overcome by themselves'. The holy water reminds the sick that in baptism they were received into communion with Christ, and that they have, as it were, grown up with Christ. Just so, they will endure their illness in Christ's company. In baptism we have already crossed the threshold of death. Now death has no power over us. In baptism we were buried with Christ and rose again with him (cf. Rom. 6). The holy water which the priest sprinkles over the sick person and the whole room is intended to show the sick person symbolically that he or she is lying in a sacred area filled by the Holy Spirit. True healing comes only from the very Source of holiness. The blessed water is intended to put the sick in contact with that inner Source within them: with the wellspring of the Holy Spirit, who will flow through them with his healing power.

The priest explains the meaning of the sacrament

The priest gives a brief address in which he explains the significance of the sacrament. He reminds everyone that in Jesus's time people brought the sick to him so that he could lay his hands on them and heal them. Jesus Christ is among us now. All those here will pray for the sick person in his name and through his power. James told the Christian community to make sure that the elders visited the sick to pray for them and anoint them with oil in the Lord's name. It is essential for the priest administering the sacrament to use words that reflect something of the healing atmosphere that radiated from Jesus himself. He can't just read it out. What he says must be spoken from the heart and touch the heart of the sick person. We are told that Jesus noticed the woman who for eighteen years had been ill from some psychological cause, was bent double, and couldn't straighten herself up (Luke 13.12). He spoke to her in such a way that she was released from her isolation, and came over to him. Only then did he say: 'You are set free from your illness!' Healing words have to be uttered in a healing atmosphere, not in a cold and uninspiring climate of formal language.

The confession

The rite then prescribes an act of confession, to be spoken not only by the sick person but by everyone present. Instead of a general confession, the priest can ask the sick person and his or her relatives to be silent for a while, and to hold their guilt before God trusting that he forgives all guilt and accepts us unconditionally. Since many sick people are plagued by feelings of guilt, thinking that they might be responsible for their illness or that it could be a punishment from God, it is advisable to stress God's forgiveness. It is pointless to start interrogating ourselves about the exact details of our guilt. Accusations or excuses won't help us. We should just hold out our guilt in God's presence without analyzing and assessing it ourselves. We should simply trust that we are accepted by God with all our indiscretions and errors, and that God's love is stronger than everything that might try to separate us from him.

The good news

Then the priest reads the gospel. The rite recommends various texts, especially the New Testament accounts of healing but also the

Beatitudes or the episode of the storm at sea or Jesus's invitation: 'Come to me, all who labour and are heavy laden, and I will give you rest' (Matt. 11.28). The gospel can be replaced by the consoling reading from Isaiah 35.1–10, or by texts from the Acts of the Apostles (Acts 3.1–10; 4.8–12), from the Letter to the Romans (Rom. 8.14–7; 8.18–27; 8.31–9), or from other letters to the young Christian churches. You have to choose these texts very carefully and with real sensitivity, and to interpret them in exactly the right way, so that sick people can feel their relevance to them personally and are encouraged by the messages they hear. The content and style of the short address must not be hortatory or admonitory in any way. It must speak to the hearts of the sick people and their relatives, and be couched so as to comfort and support them.

The bidding prayers, or petitions

Then come the bidding prayers, or petitions. The priest can ask everyone there to express their concerns, wishes and request in their own words. This will prompt an atmosphere of authentic prayer and hope for the sick. A sick person has an opportunity to sense that prayer encloses his or her relatives and friends like a protective shield or dome, within which he or she becomes the focus of an intense flow of warmth and love. The sick person and his or her condition are at the centre of all this intensity. The extempore petitions allow people to express feelings that might never be enunciated otherwise. This relieves any pressure on the others there and helps the sick people themselves. They feel that the people round them care for them, love them and hope for what is best for them. If no one is willing to pray in his or her own words, then friends and relatives should be asked to pray in silence. Silent prayer can also evoke an atmosphere of hope and love in which sick people can feel supported.

The Laying on of Hands

These petitions are followed by the sacramental celebration proper. The priest says nothing as he lays his hands on the sick persons' heads, thereby summarizing, as it were, the prayers of all the faithful. Sick people actually feel the prayer in the imposed hands. They sense the warmth emitted by the hands, and can imagine Christ himself laying his loving hands on their heads and calling on the Holy Spirit to descend on them. This silent prayer during the imposition is entirely appropriate to the anointing of the sick. Words often seem ambiguous. They can even hurt the sick if they do not fit a specific personal situation and too easily glide over actual infirmities. The Laying on of Hands can create an intense atmosphere and also transmit something of God's tender love. It is a protective gesture that opens up a space where sick people know they are defended by God's healing and loving closeness. Sick people can confront the truth of their own selves within this area of protective prayer. They realize that God is guarding them, even in the midst of their illness, and that they are safe in the loving kindness of his all-protective hands. Then I invite the others standing there to lay their hands on the sick person together with me, either on the head, so that he or she feels enclosed in loving hands, or on the shoulder or hands. Then the power of silent prayer ensures that God's love and human love and goodwill can flow into the sick individual's body.

The tender anointing with oil

After the Laying on of Hands, the priest says a prayer of thanksgiving over the oil. He praises God for his saving work in his Son Jesus Christ and through the Holy Spirit. At this point I like to describe the symbolism of oil. The olive oil used for anointing the sick has a cleansing power. Its purpose is to wash the sick people's hearts clean of everything that stains and obscures them. It is an image of fruitfulness and vitality. The olive tree is very resistant and can reach several hundred years of age. And so I wish the sick people the gift of resistance to illness through this anointing with holy oil. Oil is also a sign of victory, peace and reconciliation. Ill people want to vanquish their illness and experience inner peace. They want to be reconciled with themselves and their lives, and especially with their afflictions, against which they rebel inwardly. Only those who are reconciled can become healthy and whole. The prayer prescribed by the rite retains something of this symbolism: 'Lord, grant your servant who is anointed with this holy oil in the power of faith alleviation of his (her) pains and strengthen him (her) in his (her) weakness.'

After the prayer I anoint the sick person on the forehead and on the hands. When anointing the forehead I say: 'May the Lord of his great mercy help you through this holy anointing and accompany you with the power of the Holy Spirit. Amen.' When I anoint the hands I say: 'May the Lord who frees you from sin save you and raise you up through his grace. Amen.' In the Middle Ages, and before the Second Vatican Council, the priest anointed all five senses. Nowadays the anointing is limited to the forehead and the palms of the hands. Some bishops' conferences interpret this anointing as including the entire individual as a thinking and acting person. St John Chrysostom says that the forehead is a person's noblest part. He sees it as symbolic of the intellect by means of which one opens up to God and directs one's drives and emotions. The hands symbolize human action. We address our everyday problems with our hands. We work with them but we also touch each other with them. We shake another's hand. We stroke him or her tenderly. The hands stand for our relationships and for everything that goes to make up our daily existence. When sick people open their hands for the priest's blessing, this signifies that they are not clinging rigidly to their health but surrender themselves to God and are ready to accept his gift of healing in their empty hands.

Anointing is a gentle action. I anoint the sick person's forehead and hands attentively and lovingly. Some priests merely make the sign of the cross with the oil on the forehead and on the hands. It is more effective to anoint the hands entirely. If the illness has a precise location, it may be appropriate for the priest to anoint this area too while praying for healing in his own words. Some priests add a few drops of attar of roses to the oil for anointing, so that it is more fragrant. Anointing is a sensual action. Therefore the sense of smell should be affected in a pleasing and respectful way. The loving concern of the faithful standing round the bed is concentrated in this attentive anointing by the priest. The sick persons know then that they are supported by the prayers of friends and that Christ himself is caring for them. In the anointing they can picture Christ himself touching them with his healing and loving hands. When Christ anoints their foreheads, they may hope that they will now think clearly and their minds will be freed from any confusion. When their hands are anointed, they feel assured that they may be able to handle things again and take their own lives into their hands, and that those hands will become sources of blessing for others.

The prayer for the sick person

Then the priest says a prayer for the sick person. Various prayers are possible, depending on the specific situation of the sick individual: whether he or she is suffering from the symptoms of extreme old age, is in a critical state, or is actually in the throes of a final struggle with death. I can keep to the prescribed prayers or pray in my own words for the sick person, asking that the anointing with oil will strengthen, comfort and fill him or her with God's love. Then I ask everyone to say the Lord's Prayer. I suggest holding hands so that we form a circle of prayer round the sick person. Then we can feel the force of the prayer flowing through us and enclosing the ill man or woman in a protective circle. If I think it more appropriate, I invite relatives to open their hands to form an empty bowl, and to express our entire longing for God's kingdom and salvation in a joint Our Father. If the sick individual wants to receive communion, the best point would be after the Lord's Prayer. The early Church saw communion as a medicine for body and soul alike. In communion the sick person can physically experience the presence of Christ the Physician. Just as Jesus let his healing power flow to and through the sick, so his healing love enters the sick man or woman's body in communion.

The blessing: words of comfort

The priest closes this part of the service with a blessing. I prefer the form of blessing some versions of the rite offer as an alternative: 'May Jesus Christ, our Lord, be with you to protect you. May he go before you to guide you; may he stand behind you to guard you. May he look graciously on you, preserve you, and bless you. May almighty God, the Father, the Son and Holy Spirit, bless you (and all who are now present with you).' During the blessing I also lay my hands on the sick person again so that he or she can experience it with all the senses. A blessing (the Latin *benedicere* signifies saying something good) means wishing that the sick person may receive all conceivable good things from God's bounty. Blessing also includes actually touching a person to impart God's love to his or her body. As I say the blessing I lay my hands on the sick person's head, and with the final words I make the sign of the cross with my thumb on his or her forehead, mouth and chest. This enables the sick to experience physically God's healing love touching them, and the goodness I wish them in God's name to be inscribed in their thoughts, words and feelings.

Joint services for the sick

The anointing of the sick can be offered only to individuals, but it can also be celebrated in a communal setting. There are two different forms of administration: anointing within a service of the word, or within a eucharistic celebration. The rite provides for anointing of several people primarily during large-scale services such as a pilgrimage or assemblies of organizations for sick people, but also during parish services. In recent years, many parishes have made a service for the sick an annual event. This is a good way of showing the Church's concern for the sick. Some bishops' conferences, however, do not recommend 'indiscriminate' administration of anointing to everyone at a service, but ask for everyone requiring it to inform the priest and to be duly prepared by him. At the very least, this preparation for a joint service should explain what the sacrament means. The celebration should make it clear that Christ himself lays his hands on the sick in the sacrament and fills them with his healing power. If the anointing takes place during the Eucharist, it is advisable to focus all the texts and hymns on the theme of sickness and being whole and healed, dealing with sickness and experiencing God in that condition. Then it will appeal not only to those who are sick but to the parish in general. Sick people remind the healthy that they, too, can fall ill.

Some parishes hold not only a joint service of anointing the sick but services of blessing for ill people. All such efforts show that at least once a year parishes focus on the sick. They should not be kept out of sight and mind, and left to the care of a few select professionals. Care of the sick is a duty of the whole parish. Whatever form the service for the sick takes, a blessing of individuals, one with an additional anointing, or the sacrament of anointing the sick as the full rite, it is essential for the sick people to experience the loving attention of the community and to receive comfort and reinforcement through its prayers. The sacrament should make plain that Christ himself is the true Physician. Jesus healed the afflicted two thousand years ago, and does the same today. If they accept his concern and attention in faith, they may confidently hope to experience healing in their souls and bodies.

III. LIVING ON THE BASIS OF THE ANOINTING OF THE SICK

The sacrament of anointing the sick shows us that illness can become an opportunity to experience God. When Jesus healed sick people, he saw this as an expression of the coming of God's kingdom. God is the Healer. Vanquishing sickness is a sign of God as the Lord and Giver of life. God wants people to be sound and whole, to be saved. This is not just a matter of eternal salvation but has to do with the healing of sickness and infirmity. When John the Baptist's disciples ask Jesus if he is the Messiah, he replies: 'Go and tell John what you see and hear: the blind are recovering their sight, cripples are walking, lepers being healed, the deaf hearing, the dead being brought to life and the good news is being given to those in need' (Matt. 11.4f.). Jesus's disciples are to do what he did. Accordingly, he sends them out to heal the sick. The anointing of the sick is a fulfilment of his commission of healing.

I see two tasks as necessary elements for integration of the sacrament of anointing the sick into our lives. One is the summons we are all called on to answer: to heal one another. The other is the challenge to experience our sickness spiritually, to see it as a spiritual task.

A Christian's mission of healing

In recent years, Christian caring in hospitals and nursing homes has been given a new emphasis in pastoral thought and work. Hospital chaplains receive special training nowadays. They realize that it isn't sufficient simply to visit the sick and talk to them. They have to be especially sympathetic and understanding to carry on a conversation with someone who is ill. On the one hand, a sick person's situation makes him or her more inclined to consider the meaning of this individual life and God as the ultimate goal of our earthly journey. On the other hand, a sick person is sensitive and can be hurt if the visitor feeds him or her with inappropriate hopes, or jumps the gun with an enthusiastic exposition of the meaning of illness. Patients can tell whether carers are really addressing a particular illness, or using pious language as a means of keeping their distance. Sickness is always a crisis of faith too. Many sick people ask: 'Why has God allowed this to happen? How can God be so cruel? What kind of a God have I been so devoted to all these years? Have I been fooling myself all along?' Sickness is also a challenge for priests and other pastoral workers caring for sick people. It questions their belief and their image of God. I can't go on talking naively about God at the bedside of a mother with cancer. I have to abandon that kind of inarticulacy and ask myself searching questions about my own faith.

But we shouldn't leave care of the sick to professionals. It's a task for all of us. First and foremost it's a matter for relatives. Chaplains meet with a variety of attitudes in this respect. There are family members who visit their relatives in hospital and make time to talk to them. They don't chat about superficial things but listen attentively to what the sick people have to say to them. Others make regular visits but avoid the topic of illness. They relate what has been happening at home. They satisfy the patients' curiosity but not their longing for a real encounter. Yet others are frightened to visit the seriously sick. They don't want to have to deal with the theme of illness in any way. The sacrament of anointing the sick is a challenge to treat them as laid down in the rite: to lay hands on them and pray for them; to provide an opportunity for them to feel protected and speak openly about their infirmities; to touch them tenderly, as in the anointing itself; and to help them to hope and trust that God sees them in their condition, and that Jesus's healing power can transform their sickness.

But, as Christians, we are not only commissioned to care for the sick and to pray for them. Jesus sends his disciples out to heal the sick. Many Christians think they should leave healing to doctors and other specialists. But if we take Jesus's words seriously, we are all sent into the world to heal the sick. And if this is our mission, then we must be able to do it. But what exactly does this mean? It certainly doesn't mean becoming amateur healers. I think of Jesus's commission to heal as trusting in the healing power of prayer, and as striving with all our might to radiate a healing presence. We mustn't limit our faith to the illness itself. Concentrated prayer can heal people. On the other hand, prayer shouldn't be thought of as magical. We must avoid conveying any feeling of guilt to someone who isn't cured by prayer. It has nothing to do with his or her lack of faith. We must never forget the possibility of the miracle of healing, but we have to leave it to God to decide how to react to this particular illness. Prayer is not a magic formula. We can't be certain that God will answer our prayers as we would like them to be answered. He always listens to them. But his will remains a mystery.

How can we become healing individuals? We find some people

pleasant to be with. It does us good to be with them. We feel that we can live more healthily in their presence. Others make us ill. They infect us with their dissatisfaction, their constant nit-picking and complaints, criticism and abuse. We can't change the particular atmosphere we radiate overnight, but we can work on ourselves to ensure that we have a healing effect on others. Our first task is to become reconciled with ourselves and to live harmonious lives. Whoever is at peace with himself or herself is a peaceful person for others. Our second task is to listen sympathetically to the needs of the sick. What is their deepest wish? What do they need? What would be good for them? But we should be sensitive to everyone we know and meet. We should be healing people somehow even with healthy individuals. We have all received the gift of healing in some way. One person heals through humour, another through being under-standing, yet another by being gentle. One can say things that move others' hearts, whereas another makes others feel alive when he or she plays the piano or paints a picture.

The sacrament of anointing the sick challenges us to recognize our abilities and to have faith in their curative effect. We must put what God has given us to effective use. We can all create a healing atmosphere around us. But first we ourselves must be open to healing. We have to face up to our wounds and inadequacies and place ourselves in God's healing love. Then our injuries can become a source of healing power. The ancient Greeks believed that only a wounded physician could heal others. Only those who are aware of their own deficiencies and have experienced the transformation and cure of their injuries are capable of healing others. A curative force radiates only from wounded physicians of that calibre. They alone can enable sick people to hope that they will be healed.

During a course at Pentecost I asked the participants to draw cards, each of which bore the title of a gift of the Holy Spirit. One man drew the gift of healing. He flinched a little and asked what it meant. He said he couldn't heal anyone. The others encouraged him. He had a healing personality. Other people would feel that too. Everyone enjoyed his sense of humour and friendly attitude.

Nevertheless, he knew how ineffectual he was when he tried to face up to his wife's depression. But he came round to thinking that he had drawn the 'gift of healing' for some purpose. He went home with new trust and decided to make sure that he radiated a healing atmosphere. He wasn't trying to cure his wife, because he knew how hazardous it can be to assume the role of a healer as generally understood. He would just seem false or even pompous. All he did was to trust that if he prayed and remained always open to God's healing Spirit, he would be a more curative person.

Sickness as a spiritual challenge

None of us is immune to sickness. Even if we pride ourselves on a really healthy lifestyle, eat carefully selected foods and take sufficient exercise there is no guarantee that we shall be protected from illness. When we fall ill, we not only have to visit the doctor and make use of all possible medical resources available to us. We have to face sickness as a challenge. We have to see it as a task that can help us to grow as individuals. We also have to see it as a spiritual task. But what does that mean?

Sickness calls me in question and poses a whole range of questions. The first has to do with the right way to live. Does my sickness show me that I have overlooked something important, and ignored the truth in my life? Have I overreached myself? Have I worked too hard? Have I suppressed things? Have I refused to heed important warning signs in my body and soul? What is my illness telling me? What should I change? Should I emphasize quite different aspects of life? What do I really prize in life? Ought I to go slower and live more carefully and cautiously? What do my friends and my family mean to me? How have I neglected them? What do I need to do about them if I have only a short time left to do anything in? Sickness is an opportunity to look at my life, think it over, and stress quite different aspects of it.

The second question concerns the spiritual dimension of sickness. What does life amount to when it is restricted and damaged? What does my life mean? What is God trying to say to me through this sickness? What am I hoping for? Illness compels me to surrender certain illusions. I have to face up to my mortality and transience. Everything I have done to date has been made relative now. I can overcome this illness only if I am at peace in myself and consider who I really am. What is my innermost self? What is my true self? Everything superficial is banished. My body isn't working properly any longer. I look insignificant. So I have to look inside myself and try to find my real self there. In spite of all the external danger and visible weakness of my body, there is a space inside me in which I am sound and whole. It is the realm of inner quiet where God himself dwells within me. I have to withdraw into this space and concentrate on what is fundamental to and in me. Everything else is irrelevant.

Other questions occur to us during sickness. Why have I spent so many years without acknowledging who I am and the truth in my life? What will be left when I die? What is the essential meaning of my life? What mark have I made on life? Illness asks me to become aware of myself all over again, to ask what I want my life to say, what my mission in life really is, and what I want it to say to the people I love when I am gone. I shall have to let go of everything to which I have clung. I must let go of my health. I must leave my work and profession, and the people I like and love. Sickness isolates me and throws me back on my own resources. I shall have to pass through the checkpoint of death on my own, even if people who are dear to me are there with me to say goodbye. Sickness is an exercise in learning how to die.

Illness reveals the extent to which my spirituality has truly affected me. I know people who have spent a lot of time in meditation and impressed me as spiritual individuals. But the full extent of their susceptibility became clear when they fell ill and turned into egocentric creatures focused only on themselves. They became impossible to please, difficult and unbearable for their carers. I can't be sure what I shall be like as a patient. I don't know how I shall react if the pain is excessive. Sickness will bare my soul. At the same time it will force me to abandon all my former high opinions of myself. I have to abandon the illusion that I am self-controlled and imperturbable in all possible situations, and that even when I am sick I am all of one piece. Then all I can do is to recognize that I am powerless, put myself in God's hand, and ask him to guide me in and through my illness. Sickness unmasks people. I can only pray that a travesty of a human being is not revealed when the mask is finally off.

The final question posed by illness concerns my image of God. What is God to me? How did I see him when I was in good health? How do I think of him now that I am ill? Was my image of God far too dependent on unconscious projections of my own feelings? Who is God really? What am I to think of him if he lets me suffer like this? Can I still believe in a loving God when I am sick like this? Am I prepared to trust myself to a God like this? Do I believe that he holds me in his loving hand even when I am sick, and that in spite of all this pain I am still enclosed in his loving and healing presence?

Writers and sickness

Many writers have matured through sickness. But they have approached it very differently. The German historian and devotional writer Reinhold Schneider (1903–58) inherited his depression from his father, but accepted his illness. It became an inspiration for him as an author and influenced his image of God, the image of the suffering Christ. His illness led him to recognize that: 'A paradoxical aspect of the good news is that in a certain sense we have to be sick, because He can't get close to us otherwise. We have to be both infirm and healed. Physical illness is the ordeal of grace.' Schneider was deeply interested in the Frenchman Blaise Pascal (1623–62) and the German Novalis (the pseudonym of Friedrich von Hardenberg, 1772–1801), two profoundly spiritual writers and great thinkers who had a similar understanding of illness. Pascal was a most passionate and aspiring soul who experienced sickness as the power that 'frees me from the bonds of this world and bears me to God'. Novalis, a sufferer from lung disease at twenty-nine, celebrated his illness as a sign of divine election: 'Illnesses distinguish human beings from animals and plants. Humans are born to suffer. The more helpless we are, the more receptive we become to morality and religion. The more difficult life is, the higher we can climb.'

Other writers, such as Heinrich Heine (a leading German poet of the nineteenth century, 1797–1856), Maxim Gorky (the great Russian novelist and playwright, 1868–1936) and Leo Weismantel (a German teacher and novelist, 1888–1964), defied or protested against their sickness. Heine found it quite impossible to reconcile himself to illness. On the contrary, his pain made him oversensitive, and induced a mood of self-hatred and dislike of others. Gorky despised sickness. He simply refused to acknowledge it, derided it and fought it throughout his life. Yet it wore him down in the end. Leo Weismantel took no notice of his illness. 'I acted as if I were in good health.' He simply ignored it and devoted himself to his work. He decided to live a shorter but more intense life. This new-found dedication to his writing proved deeply rewarding. The resulting 'level-headed and intensified state of mind had a beneficial effect on my physical condition'.

The psychiatrist and philosopher Karl Jaspers (1883–1969) tried to 'live cheerfully and optimistically' in spite of his illness. Christian Morgenstern (a much-loved German writer of verse both poignant and amusing, 1871–1914) refused to allow his consumption to dictate the way in which he lived. He accepted his sickness, but treated it as something wholly external. He refused to let it affect his inner self. But he also saw illness as an opportunity: 'Every sickness has a particular meaning, for every affliction is also a process of cleansing from something. It is up to us to discover what that something is.' He tried to distance himself inwardly from his sickness. His wife Margarete tells us that Morgenstern smiled even though his suffering became unspeakable: 'He was full of the kind of light and pure good humour that gives one the power to surmount everything and turn it to good account – a power possessed only by those with an unshakeable awareness of the way to inner freedom.' Morgenstern himself said: 'I am sure that no truly free person can be ill. I want every line of my works to bear witness to this truth.' Because

Morgenstern felt inwardly healthy, he could withstand sickness without being ruled by it.

Just as writers and thinkers react variously to illness, so our attitudes to it can differ. We can see sickness as an opportunity to understand the mystery of being human and the mystery of God more profoundly. We can rebel against it and try to assert what is best in our lives to counter it. Or we can accept illness but distance ourselves from it inwardly, so that it can't determine us and our lives. How we deal with sickness always depends on our character and our life to date. But illness is always a major turning-point. It is decisive because it unmasks any pretensions. It forces us to confront the essential truth in and for us and to take our stand on that acknowledgement.

Love unto death

The sacrament of anointing the sick asks us to master illness spiritually. We have to act inwardly to ensure that the sacrament works for us. As far as I am concerned, this means subjecting my sickness to prayer, and making the illness itself a prayer. Of course my prayer will have to pass through a number of stages. Initially I ask God devoutly to free me from my sickness. I want to go on living and I ask God to let me carry out everything that I have dreamed of doing in my life. As I do so, I promise him to direct my life as he wishes, to love more attentively and consciously, and to focus on essentials. Then my prayer will also show that I want his will to be done, and that I am ready to accept what God decides. As I pray I create an inner distance from myself; which means from my egotistical self. I entrust myself to God.

The third stage of this approach is the sickness itself becoming a prayer. Many sick people tell me that they just can't pray any longer. They find it impossible to concentrate. The pain is too overwhelming, or their heads are simply empty. This is where making sickness a prayer comes in. By accepting my illness and holding myself out to God as a sick person who is no longer capable of composing my thoughts in the normal, considered way, I make my whole existence a prayer. I no longer pray against my illness but with it, in it, and through it. Then my illness becomes my way to God. It takes me ever deeper into his mystery, which is beyond the grasp of words.

Sickness as prayer

For me, the laying on of hands prescribed in the rite of anointing the sick symbolizes my holding myself and my sickness under the protection of God's loving hand, in the sure knowledge that in my condition I am under his protection. I can't understand my sickness. I just suffer from it. Nevertheless, I know that in this state I am in God's hands. When he was ill, Reinhold Schneider knew that God was holding him. Similarly, I realize that illness can be the place where I meet God. In this state I physically experience God holding me in order to open himself to me and embrace me.

The anointing with oil becomes a symbol of God's healing love pouring into me and into my hurt and agony. When the pain becomes too much to bear, I can imagine God's love flowing into it and soothing it. God's love can heal my sickness. But I mustn't become fixated on the idea of it freeing me from all my symptoms. Perhaps the healing will take place only in my soul. In any case, I shall experience my sickness differently if I keep submitting it to God's kindly love by thinking of Christ himself gently anointing me with the oil of his tenderness. If I experience pain only as something inimical and alien, I can be led astray: into bitterness and hardness of heart. Oil is soft and dissolves bitterness. It counteracts acidity and leaves a pleasant taste in the mouth. My illness will taste quite different if I allow it to be permeated by God's love acting like olive oil on and in me.

The oil used for anointing the sick is blessed by the bishop in Holy Week. The sacrament of anointing the sick enables us to share in the mystery of Jesus's death and resurrection. It helps us to comprehend Jesus's ultimate act of devotion on the cross. Jesus transformed his violent death on the cross into the culminating point of his love.

John's gospel tells us that Jesus on the cross loved us to the point of death and beyond. The anointing of the sick is also an invitation to see our suffering as an act of devotion, as sharing in Jesus's Passion. If I accept my sickness and endure it for the sake of my brothers and sisters, I transform it into a source of blessing. Then I do what Paul describes in his Letter to the Colossians: 'Indeed, I am glad, because it gives me a chance to complete in my own sufferings something of the untold pains which Christ suffers on behalf of his own body, the Church' (Col. 1.24). Elderly people often put it like this: 'I'll offer up my suffering for my children's and my family's sake.'

Nowadays we find it rather difficult to accept this idea of bearing our pain for other people. But I find that this attitude helps older people to accept their sickness, because it enables them still to see some kind of meaning in their suffering. They don't just experience it helplessly. Even in their sick state they can still do something for others: for their children and grandchildren. Even though they are not only suffering physical pain but have to cope with an impaired and handicapped life, they can still transform this harsh assault on them into a gesture of love.

I would express this 'offering up of sickness' somewhat differently. I would rather see it as wanting to be reconciled with my illness and to accept it in solidarity with the people around me. I don't want to suffer my illness passively but to change it into an act of devotion. If I succeed in this, it will be the greatest transformation I can experience in my life, for it will mean that Jesus's Spirit has transformed my heart.

I hope that God will heal my sickness. But if I sense that the end is near, and the doctor's diagnosis confirms this, it is pointless to cling stubbornly to life. For the anointing of the sick is also an exercise in learning how to die. Jesus's hand, which touches me in the sacrament, invites me to leave it all behind: my tasks, work, possessions, the people around me, and finally my own self. Then I know that even death cannot snatch me from Jesus's hand, but that he will be with me as I pass through the doors of death. I know that in death I shall fall into the motherly love of God's arms, and that they will clasp me and hold me to him. Then I shall be at home for ever. I shall have reached the culmination of all my dreams and wishes. My eyes will open and I shall see God as he is. Then I shall know what Paul describes thus: 'What no eye has seen, nor ear heard, nor the human heart has conceived, what God has prepared for those who love him' (1 Cor. 2.9).

CONCLUSION

The sacrament of anointing the sick is not merely a rite which priests administer to the sick. Christ meets us in the sacrament so that we can share in his life. He touches us as the Physician with power to heal our wounds. He stretches his loving hand over us so that, protected by his love, we can make our way into the mystery of life and death, and into the mystery of his death and resurrection.

The Church's concern for the sick reaches its high point in this sacrament. The growing number of old and sick people in our times strengthens the Church, the community of the faithful, for the task of caring for ill people during this period of disturbance and distress in their lives. The quality of a community is revealed in the way it treats its sick and aged members. Precisely in the sacrament of anointing of the sick, the Church undergoes its trial as a community of those who know that they are sent by Christ to proclaim the good news of the kingdom of God and to heal the sick.

This sacrament is an invitation to the sick to withstand their illness in communion with Christ and to see it as an opportunity to understand the mystery of humanity in God's presence. The anointing of the sick clearly shows that every sickness is a spiritual task, and that ultimately it demands not only medical or psychiatric care but spiritual fellowship, if it is to be accepted and transformed. The rite of anointing the sick shows us how to cope with sickness spiritually. In the end it is a matter of transforming illness into an act of devotion and love, and thereby making it the most intense of all possible forms of prayer. All our prayers must flow into the words with which Jesus himself entrusted his life to God's kind and loving hand: 'Lord, I commend my spirit into your hands' (Luke 23.46).